1 & 2 SAMUEL

J. Vernon McGee

THOMAS NELSON PUBLISHERS

Nashville • Atlanta • London • Vancouver

Published in Nashville, Tennessee, by Thomas Nelson, Inc.

Scripture quotations are from the KING JAMES VERSION of the Bible.

Library of Congress Cataloging-in-Publication Data

McGee, J. Vernon (John Vernon), 1904–1988
   [Thru the Bible with J. Vernon McGee]
   Thru the Bible commentary series / J. Vernon McGee.
     p.   cm.
   Reprint. Originally published: Thru the Bible with J. Vernon
McGee. 1975.
   Includes bibliographical references.
   ISBN 0-7852-1012-1 (TR)
   ISBN 0-7852-1079-2 (NRM)
   1. Bible—Commentaries. I. Title.
BS491.2.M37 1991
220.7'7—dc20
                                    90–41340
                                     CIP

Printed in the United States of America

2 3 4 5 6 7 8 9 — 99 98 97 96 95

CONTENTS

1 SAMUEL

2 SAMUEL

PREFACE

The radio broadcasts of the Thru the Bible Radio five-year program were transcribed, edited, and published first in single-volume paperbacks to accommodate the radio audience.

There has been a minimal amount of further editing for this publication. Therefore, these messages are not the word-for-word recording of the taped messages which went out over the air. The changes were necessary to accommodate a reading audience rather than a listening audience.

These are popular messages, prepared originally for a radio audience. They should not be considered a commentary on the entire Bible in any sense of that term. These messages are devoid of any attempt to present a theological or technical commentary on the Bible. Behind these messages is a great deal of research and study in order to interpret the Bible from a popular rather than from a scholarly (and too-often boring) viewpoint.

We have definitely and deliberately attempted "to put the cookies on the bottom shelf so that the kiddies could get them."

The fact that these messages have been translated into many languages for radio broadcasting and have been received with enthusiasm reveals the need for a simple teaching of the whole Bible for the masses of the world.

I am indebted to many people and to many sources for bringing this volume into existence. I should express my especial thanks to my secretary, Gertrude Cutler, who supervised the editorial work; to Dr. Elliott R. Cole, my associate, who handled all the detailed work with the publishers; and finally, to my wife Ruth for tenaciously encouraging me from the beginning to put my notes and messages into printed form.

Solomon wrote, ". . . of making many books there is no end; and much study is a weariness of the flesh" (Eccl. 12:12). On a sea of books that flood the marketplace, we launch this series of THRU THE BIBLE with the hope that it might draw many to the one Book, *The Bible.*

J. VERNON McGEE

The Book of
1 SAMUEL

INTRODUCTION

The two Books of Samuel are classified as one book in the Jewish canon and should be considered as such. In the Latin Vulgate they are the first of four Books of Kings. Our title identifies the name of Samuel with these first two historical books. This is not because he is the writer, although we do believe that he is the writer of a good portion of it. It is because his story occurs first, and he figures prominently as the one who poured the anointing oil on both Saul and David. Samuel, then, is considered the writer of 1 Samuel up to the twenty-fifth chapter, which records his death. Apparently, Nathan and Gad completed the writing of these books. We learn this from 1 Samuel 10:25 and 1 Chronicles 29:29.

The Books of Samuel contain many familiar features. We read of the rise of the kingdom of Israel. There is also the story of Hannah and her little boy Samuel. Recorded in these books is the story of David and Goliath and the unusual and touching friendship of David and Jonathan. We have the account of King Saul's visit to the witch of Endor, and 2 Samuel 7—one of the great chapters of the Word of God— gives us God's covenant with David. Finally, we have the record of David's great sin with Bathsheba and of the rebellion of his son Absalom.

In the Book of Judges we find that God used little people, many of whom had some serious fault or defect. Their stories are a great encouragement to those of us today who are little people. However, in 1 and 2 Samuel we meet some really outstanding folk: Hannah, Eli,

Samuel, Saul, Jonathan, and David. We will become acquainted with each of them as we go through these books.

There are three subjects that may be considered themes of the Books of 1 and 2 Samuel. Prayer is the first. First Samuel opens with prayer, and 2 Samuel closes with prayer. And there's a great deal of prayer in between. A second theme is the rise of the kingdom. We have recorded in these books the change in the government of Israel from a theocracy to a kingdom. Of great significance is God's covenant with David given to us in 2 Samuel 7. We will comment further on the kingdom in a moment. The third theme is the rise of the office of prophet. When Israel was a theocracy, God moved through the priesthood. However, when the priests failed and a king was anointed, God set the priests aside and raised up the prophets as His messengers. We will find that for the nation of Israel this resulted in deterioration rather than improvement.

The rise of the kingdom is of particular importance. First and Second Samuel record the origin of this kingdom, which continues as a very important subject throughout both the Old and New Testaments. The first message of the New Testament was the message of John the Baptist: ". . . Repent ye: for the kingdom of heaven is at hand" (Matt. 3:2). The kingdom of which he spoke is the kingdom of the Old Testament, the kingdom that begins in the Books of Samuel. This kingdom we find has a very historical basis, an earthly origin, and geographical borders. This kingdom has a king, and its subjects are real people.

God's chosen form of government is a kingdom ruled by a king. Yet to change the form of our government today would not solve our problems. It is not the *form* that is bad—it is the *people* connected with it. But a kingdom is God's ideal, and He intends to put His King on the throne of this earth someday. When Jesus Christ, the Prince of Peace, rules this world it will be very unlike the job men are doing today. There will be no need for a poverty program, an ecological program, or for moral reforms. Rather, there will be righteousness and peace covering this earth like the waters cover the sea.

In these books the coming millennial Kingdom is foreshadowed in several respects; and in the setting up of the kingdom of Israel we observe three things that our world needs: (1) a king with power who exercises that power in righteousness; (2) a king who will rule in full dependence upon God; and (3) a king who will rule in full obedience to God. The Lord Jesus Christ, the coming King of kings, is the very One the world so desperately needs today.

OUTLINE

I. Samuel, God's Prophet, Chapters 1—8
  A. Birth of Samuel, Chapters 1—2
    1. Hannah's Prayer and Answer, Chapter 1
    2. Hannah's Prophetic Prayer; Boy Samuel in Temple, Chapter 2
  B. Call of Samuel, Chapter 3
  C. Last Judge and First Prophet (Prophetic Office), Chapters 4—8
    1. Ark Captured by Philistines; Word of God to Samuel Fulfilled; Eli Dies and His Sons Slain, Chapter 4
    2. God Judged Philistines because of Ark; Ark Returned to Beth-shemesh, Chapters 5—6
    3. Samuel Leads in Revival (Put away Idols and Turn to Jehovah); Victory at Eben-ezer, Chapter 7
    4. Israel Rejects God and Demands a King; Samuel Warns Nation but Promises a King, Chapter 8

II. Saul, Satan's Man, Chapters 9—15
  A. Saul Received, Chapters 9—10
    1. Saul Chosen as King, Chapter 9
    2. Saul Anointed as King, Chapter 10
  B. Saul Reigning, Chapters 11—12
    1. Saul's Victory over Ammonites, Chapter 11
    2. Transfer of Authority from Samuel to Saul, Chapter 12
  C. Saul Rejected, Chapters 13—15
    1. Saul's Rebellion against God, Chapter 13
    2. Jonathan Responsible for Victory over Philistines; Saul Takes Credit, Chapter 14
    3. Saul's Glaring Rebellion and Disobedience Regarding Agag, Chapter 15

III. David, God's Man; Saul, Satan's Man, Chapters 16—31
  A. David Anointed, Chapter 16
  B. David Trained, Chapters 17—18

CHAPTER 1

THEME: Birth of Samuel; Samuel taken to Eli

This first Book of Samuel opens with the cry of a godly woman. While the people cry for a king, Hannah cries for a child. God builds the throne on a woman's cry. When a woman takes her exalted place, God builds her a throne.

Eli, the high priest, thinks Hannah is drunk as she prays before the tabernacle in Shiloh. When he discovers her true anxiety for a child, he blesses her. Samuel is born to Hannah and she brings him to Eli in fulfillment of her vow.

> **Now there was a certain man of Ramathaim-zophim, of mount Ephraim, and his name was Elkanah, the son of Jeroham, the son of Elihu, the son of Tohu, the son of Zuph, an Ephrathite:**
>
> **And he had two wives; the name of the one was Hannah, and the name of the other Peninnah: and Peninnah had children, but Hannah had no children [1 Sam. 1:1–2].**

Elkanah had two wives. Perhaps you are thinking that God approved of this. No, my friend, as you read this record you will find that God did not approve of his having two wives. The fact that certain things are recorded in Scripture does not mean that God sanctions them. He is merely giving you the facts concerning history, persons, and events. For example, you will find that the lie of Satan is recorded in Scripture, but that does not mean God approves it! God showed His disapproval when Abraham took the maid Hagar as his second wife. In fact, the fruits of his son are still in existence. Ishmael, Abraham's son by Hagar, became the head of the Arab nation, and the Jews and Arabs are still at odds today. Because Elkanah had two wives, there was trouble in the family. This is evidence that God is not blessing them at this particular time.

> And this man went up out of his city yearly to worship
> and to sacrifice unto the LORD of hosts in Shiloh. And the
> two sons of Eli, Hophni and Phinehas, the priests of the
> LORD, were there [1 Sam. 1:3].

This verse disturbed me for a long time. Why in the world did Samuel have to tell us that the sons of Eli were at the tabernacle? Later on we will find out. Going to worship God at the tabernacle was not all that you might suppose it to be. Actually it was a dangerous place to be, because these sons of Eli were "sons of Belial," or sons of the devil, if you please.

Some churches are the worst places you can be in and the most dangerous places for you. I have heard people say concerning the Upper Room, "How wonderful to have been there with Jesus!" Would it have been? Do you know who was in the Upper Room? Satan! He was not invited, but he was there. The record tells us that Satan entered into Judas. The Upper Room was the most dangerous place to be in Jerusalem that night. So, going to worship God had its difficulties in Samuel's day. Evil was present there in the persons of Eli's sons. It is interesting that this is mentioned at this juncture in 1 Samuel.

> And when the time was that Elkanah offered, he gave to
> Peninnah his wife, and to all her sons and her daugh-
> ters, portions:
>
> But unto Hannah he gave a worthy portion; for he loved
> Hannah: but the LORD had shut up her womb [1 Sam.
> 1:4–5].

Elkanah gave more to Hannah than he did to his other wife and all of their children. Why? He loved Hannah.

> And her adversary also provoked her sore, for to make
> her fret, because the LORD had shut up her womb
> [1 Sam. 1:6].

Who was Hannah's adversary? It was Peninnah, Elkanah's other wife. They were not on speaking terms, and it was not a very pleasant home. Who told you that God approves of a man having two wives? They were having family trouble, and they did not have a counselor to whom they could go for help. Hannah was probably one of the most miserable persons in the world at this time, but she went to God in prayer.

> And as he did so year by year, when she went up to the house of the LORD, so she provoked her; therefore she wept, and did not eat.

> Then said Elkanah her husband to her, Hannah, why weepest thou? and why eatest thou not? and why is thy heart grieved? am not I better to thee than ten sons?

> So Hannah rose up after they had eaten in Shiloh, and after they had drunk. Now Eli the priest sat upon a seat by a post of the temple of the LORD.

> And she was in bitterness of soul, and prayed unto the LORD, and wept sore.

> And she vowed a vow, and said, O LORD of hosts, if thou wilt indeed look on the affliction of thine handmaid, and remember me, and not forget thine handmaid, but wilt give unto thine handmaid a man child, then I will give him unto the LORD all the days of his life, and there shall no razor come upon his head [1 Sam. 1:7–11].

The expression "she was in bitterness of soul" describes her deep disappointment at not having a son. So she prayed for a son and promised God two things if her desire was granted: (1) He would be a priest in the Levitical service all the days of his life, and (2) she would make him a Nazarite unto God—that is, he would be separated unto the service of God.

And it came to pass, as she continued praying before the LORD, that Eli marked her mouth.

Now Hannah, she spake in her heart; only her lips moved, but her voice was not heard: therefore Eli thought she had been drunken [1 Sam. 1:12–13].

Eli was the high priest, and he saw this distraught woman come to the tabernacle and pray. He watched her mouth, saw her lips move, but could not hear any sound. Neither, apparently, could he read her lips. Notice his reaction, which is an insight into the conditions of that day. The sons of Eli drank and caroused there. Eli knew it but had shut his eyes to it—he was an indulgent father. When Hannah prayed with such zeal in her heart, Eli thought she was drunk. Do you know why? Others who were drunk had come to the house of the Lord. This place of worship wasn't really the best place to come in that day.

And Eli said unto her, How long wilt thou be drunken? put away thy wine from thee.

And Hannah answered and said, No, my lord, I am a woman of a sorrowful spirit: I have drunk neither wine nor strong drink, but have poured out my soul before the LORD [1 Sam. 1:14–15].

We don't see much praying like Hannah's today. Would people think you were drunk by the way you pray? Our prayers are very dignified. Hannah, not wanting Eli to have the wrong impression, said:

Count not thine handmaid for a daughter of Belial: for out of the abundance of my complaint and grief have I spoken hitherto.

Then Eli answered and said, Go in peace: and the God of Israel grant thee thy petition that thou hast asked of him.

> And she said, Let thine handmaid find grace in thy sight. So the woman went her way, and did eat, and her countenance was no more sad [1 Sam. 1:16–18].

Eli realized his mistake and gave a prophetic blessing. That Hannah's "countenance was no more sad" indicates her confidence that God had heard and would answer her prayer.

SAMUEL'S BIRTH

> Wherefore it came to pass, when the time was come about after Hannah had conceived, that she bare a son, and called his name Samuel, saying, Because I have asked him of the LORD [1 Sam. 1:20].

The name *Samuel* means "heard of God."

As I have said previously, this book of 1 Samuel opens with the cry of a godly woman. While the people are crying for a king, Hannah is crying out for a child. God builds the throne on a woman's cry. When a woman takes her exalted place, God builds her a throne.

What a contrast that is to our contemporary society. For the past few months we have heard nothing on the news but abortion, abortion, abortion. Here is Hannah who wants a child, and some women today do not want their children. Of course there are times when abortion is essential for the mother's life or even for the sake of the child, but that should be determined by expert, scientific consultation. However, the issue today is that people want to sin, but they do not want to pay the consequences for their sin. My position is that when people sin they should bear the fruit of their sin. If a child is conceived, that child should be born and should be the responsibility of those who brought him into the world. People are trying hard to get away from the fruit of sin. We need to understand this principle: "Be not deceived; God is not mocked: for whatsoever a man soweth, that shall he also reap" (Gal. 6:7). We are living in a day of abortion. Hannah lived in a day when she wanted a son, and she dedicated that son unto the Lord. On her cry, God built a kingdom. What a tremendous tribute and wonderful monument to this woman's cry!

SAMUEL TAKEN TO ELI

And when she had weaned him, she took him up with her, with three bullocks, and one ephah of flour, and a bottle of wine, and brought him unto the house of the Lord in Shiloh: and the child was young.

And they slew a bullock, and brought the child to Eli.

And she said, Oh my lord, as thy soul liveth, my lord, I am the woman that stood by thee here, praying unto the Lord.

For this child I prayed; and the Lord hath given me my petition which I asked of him:

Therefore also I have lent him to the Lord; as long as he liveth he shall be lent to the Lord. And he worshipped the Lord there [1 Sam. 1:24–28].

When Hannah took her offering to the Lord, she kept her vow to God. She said, "I have promised to bring this little one to the Lord, and here he is." Lent is definitely a poor word to describe Hannah's gift of Samuel to the Lord. Her decision to give him completely over to the service of the Lord is irrevocable.

CHAPTER 2

THEME: Hannah's prophetic prayer; Eli's evil sons; the boy Samuel in the tabernacle; Eli's sons judged

Hannah's prayer of thanksgiving is prophetic, as she mentions the Messiah for the first time.

Eli's sons are evil and unfit for the priest's office. An unnamed prophet warns Eli that his line will be cut off as high priest and God will raise up a faithful priest.

HANNAH'S PROPHETIC PRAYER

This is one of the great prayers of Scripture.

> **And Hannah prayed, and said, My heart rejoiceth in the LORD, mine horn is exalted in the LORD: my mouth is enlarged over mine enemies; because I rejoice in thy salvation [1 Sam. 2:1].**

A "horn" speaks of strength, something to hold on to. Hannah says "her strength," but she means her strength in the Lord. She is rejoicing over the fact that God has given her a son. She is victorious over those who ridiculed her for being barren, and she is rejoicing in her salvation. There has been a present deliverance.

Salvation comes in three tenses. (1) *We have been saved.* "Verily, verily, I say unto you, He that heareth my word, and believeth on him that sent me, hath [right now] everlasting life, and shall not come into condemnation; but is passed from death unto life" (John 5:24). That means that God has delivered us from the guilt of sin by the death of Christ. That is *justification*, and it is past tense. (2) God has also delivered us from what the old theologians called "the pollution of sin," which is present deliverance. *We are being saved.* It is a deliverance from the weaknesses of the flesh, the sins of the flesh, the faults of the

mind, and the actions of the will. This is the present deliverance that
Hannah is talking about. It is *sanctification* and is in the present
tense. (3) Finally there is the deliverance from death in the future—
not physical, but spiritual death. "Beloved, now are we the sons of
God, and it doth not yet appear what we shall be: but we know that,
when he shall appear, we shall be like him; for we shall see him as he
is" (1 John 3:2). This is a future deliverance. *We shall be saved*. That
will be *glorification*, which is future tense. We have been saved, we
are being saved, and we will be saved. Hannah was rejoicing in her
salvation.

You remember that Jonah said, "Salvation is of the LORD" (Jonah
2:9). The psalmist repeats again and again that salvation is of the
Lord. The great truth of salvation is that it is by the grace of God. That
is, we have been justified freely by His grace. The word *freely* means
"without a cause." God found nothing in us to merit salvation. He
found the explanation in Himself—He loves us.

> **There is none holy as the LORD: for there is none beside**
> **thee: neither is there any rock like our God [1 Sam. 2:2].**

The Lord is spoken of as a "rock" in the Old Testament. In the New
Testament the Lord Jesus Christ is called the "chief corner stone"
(1 Pet. 2:6). In Matthew 16:18 Christ spoke of Himself when He said,
". . . upon this rock I will build my church." That Rock upon which
Hannah rested is the same Rock upon which we rest today. There is no
Rock like our God.

> **Talk no more so exceeding proudly; let not arrogancy**
> **come out of your mouth: for the LORD is a God of knowl-**
> **edge, and by him actions are weighed [1 Sam. 2:3].**

When we come to God in prayer, we need to be very careful, friends,
that we do not let our pride cause us to stumble. We need to recognize
our weakness, our insufficiency, and our inability, and the fact that we
really have no claim on God. Sometimes we hear people ask, "Why
didn't God hear my prayer?" To be quite frank, why should He? What

claim do you have on Him? If you have accepted Jesus Christ as Savior, you have a wonderful claim on God, and you can come to Him in the name of Jesus Christ. As His children we have Jesus' right and claim. However, we must remember that our prayers must be in accordance with His will.

> **The bows of the mighty men are broken, and they that stumbled are girded with strength.**

> **They that were full have hired out themselves for bread; and they that were hungry ceased: so that the barren hath born seven; and she that hath many children is waxed feeble.**

> **The LORD killeth, and maketh alive: he bringeth down to the grave, and bringeth up [1 Sam. 2:4–6].**

The whole thought in this passage is that God gives life. As Job said, "the LORD gave, and the LORD hath taken away; blessed be the name of the LORD" (Job. 1:21). Only God has the power to give life, and only He has the right to take it away. Until you and I have the power to give life, we have no right to take life away. So far only God has that power. Believe me, God will take the blame (if that is what you want to call it) for the deaths of Ananias and Sapphira in Acts 5. He does not apologize for the fact that He intends to judge the wicked. They will go down into death and be separated from God. God does not apologize for what He does. Why? Because this is His universe; we are His creatures; He is running the universe His way.

Not long ago I talked to a young university student who had received Christ as Savior but who was still unwilling to accept many things. I said to him, "If you do not like the way God has worked out His plan of salvation, and you don't like the things He is doing, you can go off somewhere and make your own universe, set up your own rules, and run it your own way. But as long as you are in God's universe, you are going to have to do things His way." It is a most wonderful thing that you and I can bow to Him and come under His blessing if we are willing to do things His way.

> **The LORD maketh poor, and maketh rich: he bringeth low, and lifteth up [1 Sam. 2:7].**

This verse brings up a question that many of us have: "Why are some people rich and some people poor?" I cannot understand why God has permitted some folks to be wealthy and others to be needy. I think I could distribute the wealth a little bit better than He has done it, I will be frank with you. But, you know, He did not leave that to me. That is His business and He will be able to explain it some day. I am going to wait for the explanation, because I know He has the answer.

> **He raiseth up the poor out of the dust, and lifteth up the beggar from the dunghill, to set them among princes, and to make them inherit the throne of glory: for the pillars of the earth are the LORD's, and he hath set the world upon them.**

> **He will keep the feet of his saints, and the wicked shall be silent in darkness; for by strength shall no man prevail [1 Sam. 2:8–9].**

Man, by his own effort, power, and strength, can never accomplish anything for God. Christians today need to recognize that fact. It is only what you and I do by the power of the Holy Spirit that will count. We need to learn to be dependent upon Him and rest in Him.

> **The adversaries of the LORD shall be broken to pieces; out of heaven shall he thunder upon them: the LORD shall judge the ends of the earth; and he shall give strength unto his king, and exalt the horn of his anointed [1 Sam. 2:10].**

This is one of the great verses of Scripture and the first one to use the name *Messiah*—the word *anointed* is the Hebrew word *Messiah*. It is translated *Christos* in the Greek New Testament and comes to us as "Christ" in English. It is the title of the Lord Jesus. God is getting ready to set up a kingdom in Israel. Since Israel has rejected the theocracy, God is going to appoint them a king.

> **And Elkanah went to Ramah to his house. And the child did minister unto the LORD before Eli the priest [1 Sam. 2:11].**

It may sound as though Samuel was being left in a place of protection and shelter. The tabernacle should have been a place like that, but unfortunately it was not.

ELI'S EVIL SONS

> **Now the sons of Eli were sons of Belial; they knew not the LORD [1 Sam. 2:12].**

Eli's boys were "sons of Belial," meaning sons of the Devil. They were not saved. Here they were, sons of the high priest, hanging around the tabernacle and actually ministering there!

There are many folk who send a son to a Christian school and feel very comfortable about it. I don't want you to misunderstand what I am saying—I thank God for Christian schools. The problem is that since the boy is in a good place, they quit praying for him. That boy may be in the most dangerous place imaginable. Other parents feel secure in the fact that their son is in a fine church. My friend, that's where the Devil goes—to those wonderful places! Remember that the Devil was in the Upper Room where Christ celebrated the Last Supper with His disciples. That room was the most dangerous place in Jerusalem that night because the Devil was present. We need to remember that the boy who goes to a good church or a good school still needs prayer. He may be in a dangerous place.

This little fellow Samuel is in a dangerous place, and his mother is going to continue to pray for him, you may be sure of that.

> **And the priests' custom with the people was, that, when any man offered sacrifice, the priest's servant came,**

> while the flesh was in seething, with a fleshhook of three teeth in his hand;

> And he struck it into the pan, or kettle, or caldron, or pot; all that the fleshhook brought up the priest took for himself. So they did in Shiloh, unto all the Israelites that came thither.

> Also before they burnt the fat, the priest's servant came, and said to the man that sacrificed, Give flesh to roast for the priest; for he will not have sodden flesh of thee, but raw.

> And if any man said unto him, Let them not fail to burn the fat presently, and then take as much as thy soul desireth; then he would answer him, Nay; but thou shalt give it me now: and if not, I will take it by force [1 Sam. 2:13–16].

They were totally dishonest in the Lord's work. They were running one of the first religious rackets.

> Wherefore the sin of the young men was very great before the LORD: for men abhorred the offering of the LORD [1 Sam. 2:17].

Their dishonesty caused many people to turn from God. The Israelites saw what Eli's sons were doing at the tabernacle and, instead of being drawn closer to the Lord, they were driven away. Friends, we need to be careful about how we live our lives and how we run our churches. This idea of shutting our eyes to sin in the church and trying to cover it up just drives people away from God. That is one of the protests of our young people today. Recently I have had the privilege of seeing over one hundred of these young people turn to Christ. I have talked with them and have seen them in action. They are against the organized church because of the hypocrisy that is in it. That disturbs me because I know it is there—just as it was in the tabernacle in Eli's day.

THE BOY SAMUEL IN THE TABERNACLE

But Samuel ministered before the Lord, being a child, girded with a linen ephod.

Moreover his mother made him a little coat, and brought it to him year to year, when she came up with her husband to offer the yearly sacrifice [1 Sam. 2:18–19].

While Samuel is growing up under the influence of Eli's dishonest sons, his mother does not forget him. Hannah loves her little boy. She had promised to give him to the Lord, and she kept her word. And every year she makes a coat for him and gives it to him. There is nothing quite as tender and loving as this type of thing. I think one of the greatest joys that Mrs. McGee and I have is in selecting clothes, a little suit or something, for our grandson. Nothing is as satisfying as that. My heart goes out to Hannah as we see her here.

And Eli blessed Elkanah and his wife, and said, The Lord give thee seed of this woman for the loan which is lent to the Lord. And they went unto their own home.

And the Lord visited Hannah, so that she conceived, and bare three sons and two daughters. And the child Samuel grew before the Lord [1 Sam. 2:20–21].

God was good to Hannah. She had five other children, but she never forgot Samuel during all those years. Every year she made him a little coat. And, in spite of the bad environment of the tabernacle, Samuel grew before the Lord.

ELI'S SONS JUDGED

Now Eli was very old, and heard all that his sons did unto all Israel; and how they lay with the women that assembled at the door of the tabernacle of the congregation [1 Sam. 2:22].

Eli was an indulgent father who shut his eyes to the sins of his sons. Notice their awful, gross immorality "and how they lay with the women that assembled at the door of the tabernacle of the congregation"! There is a great deal of talk today about what is called the "new morality." I think Eli's sons beat the crowd today in the new morality. Actually, it was not even new in their day; it goes back to the time of the Flood.

> And he said unto them, Why do ye such things? for I hear of your evil dealings by all this people [1 Sam. 2:23].

The actions of Eli's sons were an open scandal in Israel, and all Eli did was give his boys a gentle slap on the wrist!

> Nay, my sons; for it is no good report that I hear: ye make the LORD's people to transgress [1 Sam. 2:24].

The people were doing what the priests were doing. Eli's sons were leading the Israelites into sin. Instead of taking positive steps to correct the situation, Eli gently rebukes them. He was an indulgent father.

> If one man sin against another, the judge shall judge him: but if a man sin against the LORD, who shall entreat for him? Notwithstanding they hearkened not unto the voice of their father, because the LORD would slay them.
>
> And the child Samuel grew on, and was in favour both with the LORD, and also with men [1 Sam. 2:25–26].

Even in this bad environment, Samuel is growing in favor with God and man. He is dedicated to God and backed by his mother's interest and prayer. God is going to use him.

> And there came a man of God unto Eli, and said unto him, Thus saith the LORD, Did I plainly appear unto the house of thy father, when they were in Egypt in Pharaoh's house?

> And did I choose him out of all the tribes of Israel to be my priest, to offer upon mine altar, to burn incense, to wear an ephod before me? and did I give unto the house of thy father all the offerings made by fire of the children of Israel?

> Wherefore kick ye at my sacrifice and at mine offering, which I have commanded in my habitation; and honourest thy sons above me, to make yourselves fat with the chiefest of all the offerings of Israel my people? [1 Sam. 2:27–29].

God sent a prophet to old Eli who told him that God was through with him as the high priest. No longer would God move through the priest. Instead, God was now raising up a priest-prophet. It was going to be Samuel. He would minister for the Lord, and his office would be that of a prophet.

> Wherefore the LORD God of Israel saith, I said indeed that thy house, and the house of thy father, should walk before me for ever: but now the LORD saith, Be it far from me; for them that honour me I will honour, and they that despise me shall be lightly esteemed [1 Sam. 2:30].

Let's be very careful in our lives to honor God. Psalm 107:1–2 says, "O give thanks unto the LORD, for he is good: for his mercy endureth for ever. Let the redeemed of the LORD say so, whom he hath redeemed from the hand of the enemy." The redeemed of the Lord need to say so today.

> Behold, the days come, that I will cut off thine arm, and the arm of thy father's house, that there shall not be an old man in thine house.

> And thou shalt see an enemy in my habitation, in all the
> wealth which God shall give Israel: and there shall not
> be an old man in thine house for ever.
>
> And the man of thine, whom I shall not cut off from
> mine altar, shall be to consume thine eyes, and to grieve
> thine heart: and all the increase of thine house shall die
> in the flower of their age.
>
> And this shall be a sign unto thee, that shall come upon
> thy two sons, on Hophni and Phinehas; in one day they
> shall die both of them [1 Sam. 2:31–34].

All of the prophecies mentioned in these verses came to pass. As we
move through the Word of God, we shall see these things happen.

> And I will raise me up a faithful priest, that shall do
> according to that which is in mine heart and in my
> mind: and I will build him a sure house; and he shall
> walk before mine anointed for ever [1 Sam. 2:35].

Who is this verse talking about? It is the Lord Jesus Christ. In Hannah's prayer, you remember, He is mentioned as the King, the Messiah, who is to come. He has been mentioned by Moses as a prophet
and now in 1 Samuel is mentioned as a priest. The Lord Jesus Christ is
Prophet, Priest, and King. He is the only One who ever fulfilled all of
these offices.

CHAPTER 3

THEME: Call of Samuel

The story of God's calling of Samuel is ordinarily reserved for children. Let's bring it out of the nursery into the adult department. Not only is it a beautiful story, but it marks one of the great transitional periods in Scripture: the change from theocracy to monarchy, from priest to king. There is a total of four calls to Samuel: the first and second calls were to salvation (v. 7); the last two calls were to service (v. 10). As *Alice in Wonderland,* ostensibly written by Carroll for Alice Liddell (a friend's child), was a philosophical indictment against the social order of his day, so the story of Samuel's call is much more than a delightful story for children. It initiates a drastic change in the form of government. The period of the judges is over, and no longer will God move through the priest. He is now raising up a priest-prophet. Samuel will minister for the Lord, but his office will be that of a prophet. It is he who will pour the anointing oil on both kings, Saul and David. God will never speak directly to a king but will speak only through a prophet.

> **And the child Samuel ministered unto the LORD before Eli. And the word of the LORD was precious in those days; there was no open vision [1 Sam. 3:1].**

I want to note the word *child.* Samuel was not a wee child. The historian Josephus says he was twelve years old. He probably was a teenager. Samuel was a young man, and he ministered unto the Lord before Eli. A four-year-old child would not be serving the Lord in the tabernacle.

This verse tells us that "the word of the Lord was precious." That means it was scarce. God was not revealing Himself at this particular time. He is just beginning to move when He calls Samuel to be a prophet. God is moving from the use of the judge and priest to the use of the prophet. The prophet becomes the spokesman to and for the king.

> **And it came to pass at that time, when Eli was laid down in his place, and his eyes began to wax dim, that he could not see;**
>
> **And ere the lamp of God went out in the temple of the LORD, where the ark of God was, and Samuel was laid down to sleep [1 Sam. 3:2–3].**

It was the duty of the priests to take care of the lamp in the tabernacle. They were to put oil in it and see that it was kept burning. Eli was old, his eyesight dim, and the lamp was about to go out.

> **That the LORD called Samuel: and he answered, Here am I.**
>
> **And he ran unto Eli, and said, Here am I; for thou calledst me. And he said, I called not; lie down again. And he went and lay down [1 Sam. 3:4–5].**

Eli thought that Samuel was dreaming and told him to go back to bed.

> **And the LORD called yet again, Samuel. And Samuel arose and went to Eli, and said, Here am I; for thou didst call me. And he answered, I called not, my son; lie down again [1 Sam. 3:6].**

We need to note here that God's first two calls to Samuel were calls to salvation.

> **Now Samuel did not yet know the LORD, neither was the word of the LORD yet revealed unto him [1 Sam. 3:7].**

Samuel did not know the Lord. God was calling him to salvation. What is the age of accountability? Whatever it is, Samuel had reached it, and God is now going to hold him responsible. In the Book of Numbers a man was not able to go to war until he was twenty. The Levites did not begin their service until they were twenty-five years old, and the priests began to serve at age thirty. When Israel turned back to wander in the wilderness because of unbelief, only those who were under twenty years of age were allowed to live and go into the Promised Land. I do not know exactly how old Samuel was, but we can be certain he was not a toddler. Is twenty the age of accountability? I do not know. I am merely suggesting that it is much older than many people think.

The question has always been, "Would God have called Samuel a fifth, sixth, seventh, or fiftieth time?" I do believe with all my heart that there is a *time* to be saved. It has been expressed like this:

> There is a time, I know not when;
> A place, I know not where;
> Which marks the destiny of men
> To heaven or despair.
>
> How long may men go on in sin?
> How long will God forbear?
> Where does hope end, and where begins
> The confines of despair?
>
> One answer from those skies is sent:
> "Ye who from God depart,
> While it is called today, repent,
> And harden not your heart."
>   —Author unknown

Apparently there will come a day when one is not able to turn to God.

When Hermann Goering was placed in prison at the time of his trial, and later when he was to be executed, the prison chaplain had a long interview with him. The chaplain emphasized the necessity of preparing himself to meet God. In the course of the conversation, Goering ridiculed certain Bible truths and refused to accept the fact that Christ died for sinners. His was a conscious denial of the power of the blood. "Death is death," was the substance of his last words. As the chaplain reminded him of the hope of his little daughter meeting him in heaven, he replied, "She believes in her manner, I in mine." The chaplain was very discouraged when he left. Less than an hour later he heard that Hermann Goering had committed suicide. God called this man, and he refused the call.

God may call many times, but there apparently comes a day when man's heart is hardened. Proverbs 29:1 says, "He, that being often reproved hardeneth his neck, shall suddenly be destroyed, and that without remedy." Now I do not believe you can commit an unpardonable sin—that is, that you can do something today which cannot be forgiven by God tomorrow. But, does God withdraw His grace? No, he will never do that. But men can resist and rebel and reject until their conscience becomes seared as with a hot iron. Men like Cain, Balaam, Samson, Korah, and Ahab all reached a day when they turned their backs against God. Acts 24:25 says of Felix, the Roman procurator before whom Paul was arraigned, "And as he reasoned of righteousness, temperance, and judgment to come, Felix trembled, and answered, Go thy way for this time; when I have a convenient season, I will call for thee." King Agrippa said to Paul, "Almost thou persuadest me to be a Christian" (Acts 26:28). Christ saved one thief that men need not despair, but He saved only one that men would not presume (Luke 23:39–43).

> **And the LORD called Samuel again the third time. And he arose and went to Eli, and said, Here am I; for thou didst call me. And Eli perceived that the LORD had called the child.**
>
> **Therefore Eli said unto Samuel, Go, lie down: and it shall be, if he call thee, that thou shalt say, Speak, LORD; for thy servant heareth. So Samuel went and lay down in his place.**
>
> **And the LORD came, and stood, and called as at other times, Samuel, Samuel. Then Samuel answered, Speak; for thy servant heareth [1 Sam. 3:8–10].**

These verses contain the third and fourth calls to Samuel, the calls to service.

> **And the LORD said to Samuel, Behold, I will do a thing in Israel, at which both the ears of every one that heareth it shall tingle.**
>
> **In that day I will perform against Eli all things which I have spoken concerning his house: when I begin, I will also make an end [1 Sam. 3:11–12].**

When God says something, it is the same as done. In the Old Testament we have what has been called "prophetic tense." It is a past tense, but it speaks of the future. God speaks of things that have not yet happened as if they had already taken place. When God says something is going to happen, it is going to happen. God speaks to Samuel in these verses and tells him that He is about to move against the house of Eli.

Now this boy Samuel is loyal to Eli to the very end. He did not attempt to undermine him. He went to Eli and told him everything God had said to him. I want to say that if you are in God's service today and serving under some other man, be loyal to him. Don't tell me that you can be loyal to Christ and be disloyal to God's man who is above you. Oh, how loyalty is needed today!

> **And the LORD appeared again in Shiloh: for the LORD revealed himself to Samuel in Shiloh by the word of the LORD [1 Sam. 3:21].**

How did God reveal Himself? By the Word. God today is also revealing Himself through His Word. He is illuminating by His Spirit the pages of Scripture. That is how you and I come to know Him, and to know Him is life eternal.

CHAPTER 4

THEME: God's judgment on Eli and his sons fulfilled

Israel, without consulting Samuel, went out to battle against the Philistines, which led to defeat. Then they brought the ark of the covenant into battle, thinking its presence would bring victory. This reveals the superstitious paganism of the people who thought there was some merit in an object. The ark was captured, the two sons of Eli were slain, and Eli died upon hearing the news.

THE ARK IS CAPTURED BY THE PHILISTINES

This chapter is a dark picture indeed. We see the spiritual condition of Israel at this particular time. God is going to bring to a conclusion the thing He said He would do to the house of Eli.

> And the word of Samuel came to all Israel. Now Israel went out against the Philistines to battle, and pitched beside Eben-ezer: and the Philistines pitched in Aphek.
>
> And the Philistines put themselves in array against Israel: and when they joined battle, Israel was smitten before the Philistines: and they slew of the army in the field about four thousand men.
>
> And when the people were come into the camp, the elders of Israel said, Wherefore hath the LORD smitten us to-day before the Philistines? Let us fetch the ark of the covenant of the LORD out of Shiloh unto us, that, when it cometh among us, it may save us out of the hand of our enemies [1 Sam. 4:1–3].

This section of Scripture gives us a revelation of Israel's superstition and just how far they are from God. It shows us how strong their self-sufficiency and selfishness are. With no thought of seeking God's direction, they go out to battle against the Philistines. What happens? They are defeated. What is lacking? They think perhaps they should have taken the ark with them into battle. Knowing the history of the ark—that as it had been carried down into the Jordan River, the water had been cut off so that Israel could cross over—they took the ark of the covenant into battle. The thought was that its presence would bring victory. My friend, this reveals the superstition and paganism of these people who thought there was some merit in the object. The merit was not in that box because God was not in that box. You cannot get God into a box! The merit was in the presence and person of God.

In church work today many people are equally as superstitious. They think that God, as it were, is in a box. They say, "Look at this method. It is a nice little package deal. It is success in a box. This method will solve our problem." So many people are moving in that direction today. My friend, that is not being spiritual. That is being superstitious. The merit is in Christ. Success is determined by whether or not we are with Him. That is all important.

> So the people sent to Shiloh, that they might bring from thence the ark of the covenant of the LORD of hosts, which dwelleth between the cherubims: and the two sons of Eli, Hophni and Phinehas, were there with the ark of the covenant of God.

> And when the ark of the covenant of the LORD came into the camp, all Israel shouted with a great shout, so that the earth rang again [1 Sam. 4:4–5].

Israel is going into battle. They send to Shiloh for the ark of the covenant. Because Hophni and Phinehas are "paid preachers," they are going to do what they are told to do. When the ark is brought into the camp, the Israelites have a great rally. They think they are getting somewhere spiritually, but this is nothing in the world but idolatry. They are worshiping a box—not God. Let us be careful in the ceremonies and rituals of our church. Are we worshiping a church? Are we worshiping a man? Are we worshiping a method? Are we worshiping a particular place? Or are we really worshiping the living and true God today?

> And when the Philistines heard the noise of the shout, they said, What meaneth the noise of this great shout in the camp of the Hebrews? And they understood that the ark of the LORD was come into the camp.

> And the Philistines were afraid, for they said, God is come into the camp. And they said, Woe unto us! for there hath not been such a thing heretofore.

> Woe unto us! who shall deliver us out of the hand of these mighty Gods? these are the Gods that smote the Egyptians with all the plagues in the wilderness [1 Sam. 4:6–8].

The Philistines understand that the ark of the covenant has come into the camp of the Israelites. They are afraid for they say, "God is come into the camp." To them the ark is an idol. This shows that the Philistines are both superstitious and ignorant. Although they have heard of His power, they are certainly ignorant of the living and true God.

ELI DIES AND THE GLORY OF GOD
DEPARTS FROM ISRAEL

The Philistines and the Israelites fight, and Israel loses the battle. There is a great slaughter of the Israelites, the ark of God is captured, and Eli's sons, Hophni and Phinehas, are slain.

> And there ran a man of Benjamin out of the army, and came to Shiloh the same day with his clothes rent, and with earth upon his head.

> And when he came, lo, Eli sat upon a seat by the wayside watching: for his heart trembled for the ark of God.

> **And when the man came into the city, and told it, all the city cried out [1 Sam. 4:12–13].**

Old Eli, with all his faults, was God's high priest, and he had a real concern for the things of God.

> **And when Eli heard the noise of the crying, he said, What meaneth the noise of this tumult? And the man came in hastily, and told Eli.**
>
> **Now Eli was ninety and eight years old; and his eyes were dim, that he could not see.**
>
> **And the man said unto Eli, I am he that came out of the army, and I fled to-day out of the army. And he said, What is there done, my son? [1 Sam. 4:14–16].**

When news of Israel's terrible defeat reached the city, a great wail arose. Eli, old and blind, asks the reason for it.

> **And the messenger answered and said, Israel is fled before the Philistines, and there hath been also a great slaughter among the people, and thy two sons also, Hophni and Phinehas, are dead, and the ark of God is taken.**
>
> **And it came to pass, when he made mention of the ark of God, that he fell from off the seat backward by the side of the gate, and his neck brake, and he died: for he was an old man, and heavy. And he had judged Israel forty years [1 Sam. 4:17–18].**

This man maintains his composure when he is told about the death of his sons, but when he learns that the ark of God has been captured, he falls backward and dies. He was a big fat fellow. Perhaps he suffered a heart attack. Although he was a weak, indulgent father, I believe he was God's man.

Eli's death brings Samuel into the position of being God's spokesman.

CHAPTERS 5 AND 6

THEME: Judgment of God upon Philistines

Chapters 5 and 6 describe the experience of the Philistines with the captured ark of the covenant in their possession. They learned there was no merit in the ark—it was by no means a good-luck charm. Because of it ". . . the hand of the LORD was heavy upon them" (1 Sam. 5:6). Their idol Dagon was toppled and broken; the men developed a strange illness and many died. Deadly destruction followed the ark wherever it was taken. The Philistines, fearing for their lives, returned the ark to Israel, carried on a cart to a field of Beth-shemesh.

> **And the Philistines took the ark of God, and brought it from Eben-ezer unto Ashdod.**
>
> **When the Philistines took the ark of God, they brought it into the house of Dagon, and set it by Dagon.**
>
> **And when they of Ashdod arose early on the morrow, behold, Dagon was fallen upon his face to the earth before the ark of the LORD. And they took Dagon, and set him in his place again.**
>
> **And when they arose early on the morrow morning, behold, Dagon was fallen upon his face to the ground before the ark of the LORD; and the head of Dagon and both the palms of his hands were cut off upon the threshold; only the stump of Dagon was left to him [1 Sam. 5:1–4].**

When the Philistines captured the ark, they thought they had something good in their hands; but, every time they set it up in the house of their god Dagon, the idol would fall over. Now I want to submit something to you that I don't think you will find in any commentary. When the presence of the ark of the Lord in the house of Dagon caused the idol to fall over and nothing was left but the stump, I believe this reveals God's sense of humor. God was revealing to the Philistines that their god was powerless in His presence. I think this shows that the Lord has a real sense of humor in doing this sort of thing, because it really annoyed the Philistines. They soon saw that there was no merit in their having the ark. In fact, it was a very real danger to them.

> But the hand of the LORD was heavy upon them of Ashdod, and he destroyed them, and smote them with emerods, even Ashdod and the coasts thereof.

> And when the men of Ashdod saw that it was so, they said, The ark of the God of Israel shall not abide with us: for his hand is sore upon us, and upon Dagon our god [1 Sam. 5:6–7].

Thinking these calamities might not be coincidental, they send the ark to another city of the Philistines.

> They sent therefore and gathered all the lords of the Philistines unto them, and said, What shall we do with the ark of the God of Israel? And they answered, Let the ark of the God of Israel be carried about unto Gath. And they carried the ark of the God of Israel about thither.

> And it was so, that, after they had carried it about, the hand of the LORD was against the city with a very great destruction: and he smote the men of the city, both small and great, and they had emerods in their secret parts.

> Therefore they sent the ark of God to Ekron. And it came to pass, as the ark of God came to Ekron, that the Ekronites cried out, saying, They have brought about the ark of the God of Israel to us, to slay us and our people [1 Sam. 5:8–10].

I do not mean to be irreverent but everyone was passing the buck. Finally there was a meeting of the lords of the Philistines and they decided to send the ark back to Israel. God had sent judgment upon the Philistines. The Philistines had one question, "What shall we do with Israel's ark?"

> **And the ark of the LORD was in the country of the Philistines seven months [1 Sam. 6:1].**

Again, I do not want to be irreverent, but having the ark was like having a hot potato. Whenever the ark was put near the idol of Dagon, it fell over. All that was left was a stump, and that is not a very satisfactory object to worship; an idol is bad enough! So the people of Gath had it and they didn't want it; so they sent it to Ekron and they, too, wanted to get rid of it.

> **And the Philistines called for the priests and the diviners, saying, What shall we do to the ark of the LORD? tell us wherewith we shall send it to his place.**
>
> **And they said, If ye send away the ark of the God of Israel, send it not empty; but in any wise return him a trespass offering: then ye shall be healed, and it shall be known to you why his hand is not removed from you.**
>
> **Then said they, What shall be the trespass offering which we shall return to him? They answered, Five golden emerods, and five golden mice, according to the number of the lords of the Philistines: for one plague was on you all, and on your lords [1 Sam. 6:2–4].**

The Philistines wanted to get rid of the ark, but they were not sure how to go about it. Therefore they consulted with the priests and diviners who told them not to send the ark of the God of Israel away empty. They were to send an offering, and that offering speaks of the vileness of the Philistine worship. Many people wonder why God put the Philistines out of His land. The Promised Land was right at the crossroads of the world, and those who occupied it would influence the people of the world. God put them out because of the vileness of their worship. They had turned completely from God. Here again God is giving them an opportunity to turn to Him.

The Philistine offering consisted of five golden emerods (hemorrhoids, possibly, tumors or boils) and five golden mice.

> **And they laid the ark of the LORD upon the cart, and the coffer with the mice of gold and the images of their emerods [1 Sam. 6:11].**

Notice that when the Philistines returned the ark to Israel, they put it on a cart. Nothing is going to happen to them for putting it on a cart. Do you know why? Very candidly, they did not know any better. God is not going to hold them responsible for this act. But Israel knew better, and we will see that God judged the Israelites because of the way they handled the ark. Why the difference? They knew better, friend.

> **And the kine took the straight way to the way of Beth-shemesh, and went along the highway, lowing as they went, and turned not aside to the right hand or to the left; and the lords of the Philistines went after them unto the border of Beth-shemesh [1 Sam. 6:12].**

The cows which were hitched to the cart were obviously going against their natural instinct by leaving their calves at home. This was convincing proof to the Philistines that their troubles had been caused by an act of God.

> **And they of Beth-shemesh were reaping their wheat harvest in the valley: and they lifted up their eyes, and saw the ark, and rejoiced to see it.**

> **And the cart came into the field of Joshua, a Beth-shemite, and stood there, where there was a great stone: and they clave the wood of the cart, and offered the kine a burnt offering unto the LORD.**

> And the Levites took down the ark of the LORD, and the
> coffer that was with it, wherein the jewels of gold were,
> and put them on the great stone: and the men of Beth-
> shemesh offered burnt offerings and sacrificed sacri-
> fices the same day unto the LORD [1 Sam. 6:13–15].

The Israelites will not accept anything, you see, for themselves from
the Philistines. They are, of course, to be commended for that.

> And when the five lords of the Philistines had seen it,
> they returned to Ekron the same day [1 Sam. 6:16].

The Philistines see that the ark is received back, and they are glad to
get it off their hands.
   Now we see that, when the ark was returned to the Israelites, they
immediately had problems with it.

> And he smote the men of Beth-shemesh, because they
> had looked into the ark of the LORD, even he smote of the
> people fifty thousand and threescore and ten men: and
> the people lamented, because the LORD had smitten
> many of the people with a great slaughter [1 Sam. 6:19].

The men of Beth-shemesh do that which God had strictly forbidden.
That ark belonged in the Holy of Holies in the tabernacle. It was to be
seen only by the high priest—even he was permitted to enter before it
only once a year. When the ark was transported, as it was on the
wilderness march, it was carefully and reverently covered. The Philistines did not known these things, but the Israelites did know.

> And the men of Beth-shemesh said, Who is able to stand
> before this holy LORD God? and to whom shall he go up
> from us? [1 Sam. 6:20].

It is not that they looked in the ark and saw something that they
should not have seen. That is not the point. The ark was a box. That is

all it ever was. The point is that it was at the ark in the Holy of Holies that God met with His people. He is not meeting with them now. They have turned from Him. Their rebellion and blasphemy are revealed in their disobedience. Because of this, God brings judgment upon them.

> **And they sent messengers to the inhabitants of Kirjath-jearim, saying, The Philistines have brought again the ark of the LORD; come ye down, and fetch it up to you [1 Sam. 6:21].**

Now in a superstitious way they want to get rid of the ark. They send messengers to Kirjath-jearim saying, "You come and get it." In other words, Israel is not ready to receive the ark. God's people are not prepared to return to Him.

CHAPTER 7

THEME: Samuel leads in revival; victory at Eben-ezer

After twenty years, Israel is prepared to receive the ark. Israel turns from Baalim and Ashtaroth to serve the Lord.

SAMUEL LEADS IN REVIVAL

And the men of Kirjath-jearim came, and fetched up the ark of the LORD, and brought it into the house of Abinadab in the hill, and sanctified Eleazar his son to keep the ark of the LORD.

And it came to pass, while the ark abode in Kirjath-jearim, that the time was long; for it was twenty years: and all the house of Israel lamented after the LORD [1 Sam. 7:1–2].

After twenty years the Israelites began to turn to God and away from Baalim and Ashtaroth. They have come to the place where they want God.

In this day in which we are living there is a renewed interest in the Word of God. I rejoice in this, because it is my firm conviction that God's people must get back to the Bible. I believe that all sixty-six books—all the way from Genesis to Revelation—are the Word of God. I believe in the Bible's integrity and inerrancy and in the fact that we need to get back to its teachings. We have been a long time getting back to God's Word. Progress has been slow. How many more years will it take? Many people today are getting very tired of listening to politicians who make promises, promises, promises, and then don't fulfill them. I want to say in their behalf that they *cannot* fulfill them—yet they promise. We also have all kinds of new nostrums coming from college professors and leaders in every field. There is only one thing wrong: they won't work. Maybe in desperation America will turn to God. That is what happened to Israel after twenty years.

> **And Samuel spake unto all the house of Israel, saying, If ye do return unto the LORD with all your hearts, then put away the strange gods and Ashtaroth from among you, and prepare your hearts unto the LORD, and serve him only: and he will deliver you out of the hand of the Philistines.**
>
> **Then the children of Israel did put away Baalim and Ashtaroth, and served the LORD only [1 Sam. 7:3–4].**

This is actually the beginning of Samuel's great ministry. Israel was deep in idolatry. They had turned from the living and true God. They had been defeated in so many battles that it had become old hat to them, and they were extremely discouraged. They were beginning to lament after the Lord. We, too, need to get back to the Lord. There is a hunger in the hearts of many people who are saying, "We are tired of eating the husks that pigs eat in the far country. We want to get back to the Father's house." Well, they have to come through the door of the Word of God.

> **And Samuel said, Gather all Israel to Mizpeh, and I will pray for you unto the LORD.**
>
> **And they gathered together to Mizpeh, and drew water, poured it out before the LORD, and fasted on that day, and said there, We have sinned against the LORD. And Samuel judged the children of Israel in Mizpeh [1 Sam. 7:5–6].**

Samuel is not only the prophet of Israel, he is also the judge of the nation. Here we find Israel turning from false gods to the true God. This man Samuel is praying for them, and they confess their sins. This is the way back for God's people. I do not think there is another way back. I hear about all kinds of methods today that will be blessed by God. Let me put it right down in bold letters and tell it like it is. What God's people need to do is to go to God and *confess* their *sins*. They need to see themselves in the light of the Word of God. If we really see ourselves, we see that we have come short of the glory of God (Rom. 3:23); and then we can be assured that the blood of Jesus Christ, God's Son, will keep on cleansing us from all sin (1 John 1:9).

VICTORY AT EBEN-EZER

And the children of Israel said to Samuel, Cease not to cry unto the LORD our God for us, that he will save us out of the hand of the Philistines.

And Samuel took a sucking lamb, and offered it for a burnt offering wholly unto the LORD: and Samuel cried unto the LORD for Israel; and the LORD heard him.

And as Samuel was offering up the burnt offering, the Philistines drew near to battle against Israel: but the LORD thundered with a great thunder on that day upon the Philistines, and discomfited them; and they were smitten before Israel.

And the men of Israel went out of Mizpeh, and pursued the Philistines, and smote them, until they came under Beth-car [1 Sam. 7:8–11].

God gave Israel a great victory, and it was the first one they had had for a long time. These people had lapsed into idolatry; they had been in sullen rebellion. When they began to turn to God, Samuel exacted a confession of sin and a promise to return to God. As a result God gave them a signal victory over the Philistines.

Then Samuel took a stone, and set it between Mizpeh and Shen, and called the name of it Eben-ezer, saying, Hitherto hath the LORD helped us [1 Sam. 7:12].

The name Eben-ezer means "stone of help." "Hitherto hath the Lord helped us." It was also a stone of remembrance, looking back to the past. It was a stone of recognition, a stone for the present. It was a stone of revelation, a stone for the future. "Hitherto [up to this point, up to the present time] God has helped us."

It is customary for us to look back over the past. Remember what the Lord said through Paul to the Philippians: "Being confident of this very thing, that he which hath begun a good work in you will perform it until the day of Jesus Christ" (Phil. 1:6). Friend, has God brought you to this point? Is He leading you today? Is He guiding you? If He has, you can say, "Hitherto has the Lord helped me." Since He has helped you up to this moment, He will continue to do that.

God has given us memories so that we can have roses in December. As memory plays on the keyboard of the past, I am sure that all of us can say, "Hitherto hath the Lord helped us." Joshua could say, ". . . as for me and my house, we will serve the LORD" (Josh. 24:15). David could say, "O give thanks unto the LORD, for he is good: for his mercy endureth for ever. Let the redeemed of the LORD say so, whom he hath redeemed form the hand of the enemy" (Ps. 107:1–2). I personally want to say that oh, the Lord is good! He is the One who has helped us and will help us.

A businessman said sometime ago, "You know, the use of time might be likened to the terminology of banking. Yesterday is a canceled check, tomorrow is a promissory note, but today is cash. Spend it wisely." Do you recognize God in your life? That is what Samuel meant by that Eben-ezer stone. It was a stone of revelation. It not only meant "hitherto," it also meant "henceforth." "The LORD is my shepherd," said David; then looking into the future, "I shall not want" (Ps. 23:1). Someone once said, "I am very interested in the future because I expect to spend the rest of my life there, and I want to be reasonably sure of what kind of a future it is going to be." "And we know that all things work together for good to them that love God, to them who are the called according to his purpose" (Rom. 8:28). Dr. R. A. Torrey always said that Romans 8:28 was a soft pillow for a tired heart. We all need an Eben-ezer stone. I trust that you have one in your life.

> So the Philistines were subdued, and they came no more into the coast of Israel: and the hand of the LORD was against the Philistines all the days of Samuel [1 Sam. 7:13].

I think it can be said that from this time on the Philistines were never again as dominant and formidable a foe as they had been before the battle. This was a significant battle, and a stone now stands in memory of it. The stone was about three or four miles north by northwest of Jerusalem, in sight of the city.

> And Samuel judged Israel all the days of his life.

> And he went from year to year in circuit to Beth-el, and Gilgal, and Mizpeh, and judged Israel in all those places.

> And his return was to Ramah; for there was his house; and there he judged Israel; and there he built an altar unto the LORD [1 Sam. 7:15–17].

This is the story. Samuel is a prophet and a judge of Israel. He is a circuit judge. He goes from Bethel to Gilgal to Mizpeh and back to Ramah, all areas north of Jerusalem. He "judged Israel in all those places."

CHAPTER 8

THEME: Israel rejects God and demands a king

Hosea 13:11 can be written over the remainder of 1 and 2 Samuel: "I gave thee a king in mine anger, and took him away in my wrath."

Samuel was a great judge and a man of God. He was brought up in the tabernacle where he saw the wickedness of Eli's sons and how God judged them. Yet notice what Samuel does.

> **And it came to pass, when Samuel was old, that he made his sons judges over Israel [1 Sam. 8:1].**

Samuel made his own sons judges to succeed him, although they were unworthy and incompetent for the job. This act was a mistake. Samuel was a great judge, a wonderful prophet, and a great man of God—but he was a failure as a father just as Eli had been.

> **Now the name of his firstborn was Joel; and the name of his second, Abiah: they were judges in Beer-sheba.**
>
> **And his sons walked not in his ways, but turned aside after lucre, and took bribes, and perverted judgment [1 Sam. 8:2–3].**

These were Samuel's sons. They were totally dishonest. Strange, isn't it? Today we see so much of that. Many pastors have said to me, "Why is it that you can have a godly family in your church and the son or daughter can become a dissolute vagrant or go on drugs?" Many times there is no explanation for it. Well, Samuel was a great man, God's man, and look what his sons did.

> **Then all the elders of Israel gathered themselves together, and came to Samuel unto Ramah,**

And said unto him, Behold, thou art old, and thy sons walk not in thy ways: now make us a king to judge us like all the nations [1 Sam. 8:4–5].

The people of Israel ask for a king. They are influenced, of course, by the surrounding nations. They give as their reason Samuel's advanced age and the waywardness of his sons.

But the thing displeased Samuel, when they said, Give us a king to judge us. And Samuel prayed unto the LORD.

And the LORD said unto Samuel, Hearken unto the voice of the people in all that they say unto thee: for they have not rejected thee, but they have rejected me, that I should not reign over them [1 Sam. 8:6–7].

The fact that Samuel had made his sons judges gives these people an excuse to ask for a king. Undoubtedly this was a heartbreak to Samuel. God comforts him with the assurance that Israel's rejection is not of him but of God himself. Samuel's sons are the excuse, but rejection of God's sovereignty is the real reason.

Then Samuel warns Israel what it will be like to have a king. He tells them that a king will reign over them, take their sons for soldiers, their daughters for cooks and maidservants, and part of their fields, vineyards, oliveyards, and animals for himself. He warns them that eventually they will cry out in their distress and that in that day the Lord will not hear them.

Nevertheless the people refused to obey the voice of Samuel; and they said, Nay; but we will have a king over us;

That we also may be like all the nations; and that our king may judge us, and go out before us, and fight our battles.

And Samuel heard all the words of the people, and he rehearsed them in the ears of the LORD.

And the LORD said to Samuel, Hearken unto their voice, and make them a king. And Samuel said unto the men of Israel, Go ye every man unto his city [1 Sam. 8:19–22].

The children of Israel are gong to have their way. God is going to give them a king. What was true of Israel in the days of Moses is still true. "And he gave them their request; but sent leanness into their soul" (Ps. 106:15). God will grant Israel's desire for a king, but it will not be to their advantage. God's guidance of the nation will be indirectly through the prophet. As we shall see, God will not speak directly to the king, but still through the prophet who will convey God's word to the king. The king will accept it or reject it as he chooses.

CHAPTERS 9 AND 10

THEME: Saul is chosen as king; Saul is anointed as king

SAUL IS CHOSEN AS KING

Chapter 9 begins the second major section of the book of 1 Samuel. The first section dealt with Samuel; now the emphasis shifts to Saul. Saul is one of those strange individuals whom we encounter in the Word of God. Like Balaam, it is difficult to interpret him. Both in the Old and New Testaments there are several strange characters who move across the pages of Scripture in semidarkness. They come out, as it were, into the light but, like the groundhog, they see their shadow and move back into the darkness again.

Saul is not a king when we first meet him. In fact, I do not think he ever was a king in the true sense of the word.

> **Now there was a man of Benjamin, whose name was Kish, the son of Abiel, the son of Zeror, the son of Bechorath, the son of Aphiah, a Benjamite, a mighty man of power [1 Sam. 9:1].**

Kish was Saul's father, and he belonged to the tribe of Benjamin. Recalling the history of the twelve sons of Jacob in Genesis, the tribe originated with the youngest son, Benjamin, a favorite of his father. His mother had died at his birth and, as she was passing, she named him Benoni, "son of my sorrow." But when Jacob looked at the little fellow, he said, "No, he is going to be the son of my right hand," and he named him Benjamin. The boy was the favorite son and was protected by his brothers. Then in the Book of Judges, the tribe was decimated because of an episode of gross sin that took place in the tribe. It is from this tribe, Benjamin, that the first king comes.

> **And he had a son, whose name was Saul, a choice young man, and a goodly: and there was not among the**

**children of Israel a goodlier person than he: from his
shoulders and upward he was higher than any of the
people [1 Sam. 9:2].**

This boy Saul was handsome. Physically he looked like a king, but he
was an actor that played a part. He was not a king at heart. The people,
however, were choosing their king by his outward appearance and not
according to his character.

It is this emphasis on "outward appearance" that places our nation
in such a dangerous position today. The most dangerous enemy we
have is the television. The man that will ultimately control this country is the man who has a good television appearance. Why? Because
we choose men by the way they look and the way they talk rather than
by their character. If only we had an X-ray—instead of the television—
that would reveal the true character of a man!

The children of Israel wanted a king, and they liked Saul. He was
handsome. He was tall. He was fine looking. There wasn't a more
kingly-looking man in the nation. He could have been both a television and a movie star. He looked the part and could play the part;
the trouble was he was not a king at heart.

**And the asses of Kish Saul's father were lost. And Kish
said to Saul his son, Take now one of the servants with
thee, and arise, go seek the asses [1 Sam. 9:3].**

I know that the Lord has a sense of humor. You just cannot miss it
because it is in too many places in the Word of God. Saul is out looking for the asses of his father, and the asses of Israel are looking for a
king. They are bound to get together, friend, and they do. The Lord
must smile when a thing like this takes place. What a commentary on
the human race!

**And when they were come to the land of Zuph, Saul said
to his servant that was with him, Come, and let us return; lest my father leave caring for the asses, and take
thought for us [1 Sam. 9:5].**

Saul and his servant had looked all around for his father's animals and could not find them. Finally Saul said, "Let's go home because we are going to get lost too, and they will have to send out a search party for us."

> And he said unto him, Behold now, there is in this city a man of God, and he is an honourable man; all that he saith cometh surely to pass: now let us go thither; peradventure he can shew us our way that we should go.

> Then said Saul to his servant, But, behold, if we go, what shall we bring the man? for the bread is spent in our vessels, and there is not a present to bring to the man of God: what have we?

> And the servant answered Saul again, and said, Behold, I have here at hand the fourth part of a shekel of silver: that will I give to the man of God, to tell us our way [1 Sam. 9:6–8].

Here is a little explanation inserted by the Spirit of God which is helpful:

> (Beforetime in Israel, when a man went to inquire of God, thus he spake, Come, and let us go to the seer: for he that is now called a Prophet was beforetime called a Seer.) [1 Sam. 9:9].

There is a change of names. Men who dealt in necromancy and spiritism were called "seers." God wanted a different name for His man, and so he is called a "prophet." This actually makes Samuel the first of the order of prophets. Although Moses is called a prophet, Samuel is the first of the order of prophets. Samuel, of course, is the man Saul and his servant are talking about.

> And they went up into the city: and when they were come into the city, behold, Samuel came out against them, for to go up to the high place [1 Sam. 9:14].

This does not mean that Samuel opposed Saul and his servant; it simply means that he met them on the way.

Now the LORD had told Samuel in his ear a day before Saul came, saying [1 Sam. 9:15].

The question is often asked, "Just how did God communicate in the Old Testament when it says, 'The Lord spake'?" I think that when it says the Lord spake, He spoke. That is the way communication came. It came by words. It is the words of Scripture that are inspired, not the thoughts. We are given an inkling of how God communicated when it says, "Now the Lord had told Samuel in his ear. . . ." What I hear in my ears are *words*. That is the only thing that makes sense and that, of course, is what Samuel heard.

To-morrow about this time I will send thee a man out of the land of Benjamin, and thou shalt anoint him to be captain over my people Israel, that he may save my people out of the hand of the Philistines: for I have looked upon my people, because their cry is come unto me [1 Sam. 9:16].

Many times God answers our request when it is not the best thing for us. When we keep crying to the Lord for whatever it is we want, finally He does for us what He did for Israel—He grants our request. When the children of Israel were in the wilderness, they cried for meat. God gave them meat, but He sent "leanness unto their souls." That is why prayer should be made in the name of Christ, which means that it must be according to His will and for His glory. All requests should hinge on that very important matter.

And when Samuel saw Saul, the LORD said to him, Behold the man whom I spake to thee of! this same shall reign over my people [1 Sam. 9:17].

God granted their request and gave them a king. Saul was a man that impressed even Samuel. We find out that Samuel regarded him highly and regretted the fact that he did not make good.

> **Then Saul drew near to Samuel in the gate, and said, Tell me, I pray thee, where the seer's house is.**

> **And Samuel answered Saul, and said, I am the seer: go up before me unto the high place; for ye shall eat with me to-day, and to-morrow I will let thee go, and will tell thee all that is in thine heart.**

> **And as for thine asses that were lost three days ago, set not thy mind on them; for they are found. And on whom is all the desire of Israel? Is it not on thee, and on all thy father's house? [1 Sam. 9:18–20].**

Saul was actually not God's choice. That is, He gave Israel the sort of man He knew they wanted. As Saul moved among the people, they saw that he was tall, handsome, and looked like a king. When they asked for a king, God granted their request.

> **And Saul answered and said, Am not I a Benjamite, of the smallest of the tribes of Israel? and my family the least of all the families of the tribe of Benjamin? wherefore then speakest thou so to me? [1 Sam. 9:21].**

Saul sounds a great deal like Gideon in this verse. He sounds very humble. Gideon said, ". . . Oh my Lord, wherewith shall I save Israel? behold, my family is poor in Manasseh, and I am the least in my father's house" (Jud. 6:15). Gideon was saying, "You can't get any smaller than I am." Gideon was telling the truth. He was a coward and frightened to death. Israel was at war and badly outnumbered. Saul had no reason to be afraid. Israel was not at war. He had been out looking for his father's longeared donkeys that had already been found. His mission was accomplished. The point is that there was nothing to prompt a speech like he gave. I personally feel that his was a false humility. I think Saul felt very much like he was the one who could be king.

> **And Samuel took Saul and his servant, and brought them into the parlour, and made them sit in the chiefest place among them that were bidden, which were about thirty persons [1 Sam. 9:22].**

Apparently Samuel called a small group of leaders together.

> **And Samuel said unto the cook, Bring the portion which I gave thee, of which I said unto thee, Set it by thee.**
>
> **And the cook took up the shoulder, and that which was upon it, and set it before Saul. And Samuel said, Behold that which is left! set it before thee, and eat: for unto this time hath it been kept for thee since I said, I have invited the people. So Saul did eat with Samuel that day.**
>
> **And when they were come down from the high place into the city, Samuel communed with Saul upon the top of the house.**
>
> **And they arose early: and it came to pass about the spring of the day, that Samuel called Saul to the top of the house, saying, Up, that I may send thee away. And Saul arose, and they went out both of them, he and Samuel, abroad.**
>
> **And as they were going down to the end of the city, Samuel said to Saul, Bid the servant pass on before us, (and he passed on,) but stand thou still a while, that I may shew thee the word of God [1 Sam. 9:23–27].**

We have here the formality they went through. Saul ate with Samuel that day, and they had a conference.

SAUL IS ANOINTED AS KING

Then Samuel took a vial of oil, and poured it upon his head, and kissed him, and said, Is it not because the LORD hath anointed thee to be captain over his inheritance? [1 Sam. 10:1].

Samuel anoints Saul as king and then kisses him, which was probably an act demonstrating his personal affection for Saul.

When thou art departed from me to day, then thou shalt find two men by Rachel's sepulchre in the border of Benjamin at Zelzah; and they will say unto thee, The asses which thou wentest to seek are found: and, lo, thy father hath left the care of the asses, and sorroweth for you, saying, What shall I do for my son? [1 Sam. 10:2].

As far as Kish is concerned, his son Saul is lost. But Saul is engaged in serious business. Samuel has anointed him king near the tomb of Rachel, which is in the territory of Benjamin near Bethlehem.

After that thou shalt come to the hill of God, where is the garrison of the Philistines: and it shall come to pass, when thou art come thither to the city, that thou shalt meet a company of prophets coming down from the high place with a psaltery, and a tabret, and a pipe, and a harp, before them; and they shall prophesy [1 Sam. 10:5].

This is what Saul is to encounter on his way back home.

And the spirit of the LORD will come upon thee, and thou shalt prophesy with them, and shalt be turned into another man [1 Sam. 10:6].

Here again we have a question: Was Saul converted? Is this verse the proof of his conversion? Certainly it is not a final proof.

I do not believe that he was converted. If I sound like I am preju-diced against Saul, I will tell you why. It is not because of the material we have already covered concerning him but what is coming that makes me believe that Saul was not genuine, and certainly not genu-inely converted at all.

Someone is bound to say, "But the Spirit of God came upon Saul and he was a different man." Yes, but it does not say that he became a *new* man. After all, didn't the Spirit of God come upon Balaam? And we have no proof that he was converted. What about Judas? Christ sent out twelve disciples, and we are told that all of them performed miracles. Did Judas perform miracles? Certainly he did. Would you say that Judas was converted? So let us withhold making a final deci-sion about Saul—although I seem to have already made one.

> **And it was so, that when he had turned his back to go from Samuel, God gave him another heart: and all those signs came to pass that day [1 Sam. 10:9].**

When Saul left Samuel, I think Samuel watched him walk away and said, "My, he is a fine fellow." But even a prophet can be wrong. The prophet Nathan was wrong when he told David to build God a house. God had to intervene, and Nathan had to correct himself. Samuel was wrong about Saul. As he looked at this young man Saul, he saw a big, husky, fine-looking fellow. He would have been able to play in the line of any professional football team. But he was no king at all.

> **And when they came thither to the hill, behold, a com-pany of prophets met him; and the spirit of God came upon him, and he prophesied among them.**
>
> **And it came to pass, when all that knew him beforetime saw that, behold, he prophesied among the prophets, then the people said one to another, What is this that is come unto the son of Kish? Is Saul also among the prophets? [1 Sam. 10:10–11].**

The Spirit of God came upon Saul and he prophesied. Everyone who had known him before knew that something had happened to him. They asked, "Is Saul also among the prophets?" God was giving Saul an opportunity. God never withheld anything from him, and yet he failed.

> And Saul said unto his uncle, He told us plainly that the asses were found. But of the matter of the kingdom, whereof Samuel spake, he told him not [1 Sam. 10:16].

He kept quiet about that.

> And Samuel called the people together unto the LORD to Mizpeh;
>
> And said unto the children of Israel, Thus saith the LORD God of Israel, I brought up Israel out of Egypt, and delivered you out of the hand of the Egyptians, and out of the hand of all kingdoms, and of them that oppressed you:
>
> And ye have this day rejected your God, who himself saved you out of all your adversities and your tribulations; and ye have said unto him, Nay, but set a king over us. Now therefore present yourselves before the LORD by your tribes, and by your thousands [1 Sam. 10:17–19].

When the children of Israel asked for a king and took Saul, it meant they were turning their backs upon God. We need to note that their reception of Saul as king meant their rejection of God.

> When he had caused the tribe of Benjamin to come near by their families, the family of Matri was taken, and Saul the son of Kish was taken: and when they sought him, he could not be found.

> Therefore they inquired of the LORD further, if the man should yet come thither. And the LORD answered, Behold, he hath hid himself among the stuff [1 Sam. 10:21–22].

When the time came for Samuel to introduce Saul to the crowd as their king, he could not find him. This great big fellow, Saul, acted just like a little child. He ran and hid, and they had to find him and bring him out. Again, in my judgment, this is an evidence of false modesty. The anointing oil has been poured upon him, and if he is given an opportunity to be king and serve God, then let him step out in the open and act like a king.

> And Samuel said to all the people, See ye him whom the LORD hath chosen, that there is none like him among all the people? and all the people shouted, and said, God save the king [1 Sam. 10:24].

And God save the people also! This was the first time this cry "God save the king!" was uttered. As you know, it is still used in modern England.

> Then Samuel told the people the manner of the kingdom, and wrote it in a book, and laid it up before the LORD. And Samuel sent all the people away, every man to his house [1 Sam. 10:25].

"Then Samuel told" the children of Israel about "the manner of the kingdom, and wrote it in a book." On the basis of this we believe that Samuel wrote the first part of the book of 1 Samuel.

CHAPTERS 11 AND 12

THEME: Saul's victory over the Ammonites; transfer of authority from Samuel to Saul

SAUL'S VICTORY OVER THE AMMONITES

In the previous chapter I said some rather harsh things about King Saul, although I did not seem to have sufficient grounds at the time. I had only a strong suspicion that he was not genuine. I felt that he would have made a good actor but not a good king, even though he had a good beginning.

> **Then Nahash the Ammonite came up, and encamped against Jabesh-gilead: and all the men of Jabesh said unto Nahash, Make a covenant with us, and we will serve thee.**
>
> **And Nahash the Ammonite answered them, On this condition will I make a covenant with you, that I may thrust out all your right eyes, and lay it for a reproach upon all Israel.**
>
> **And the elders of Jabesh said unto him, Give us seven days' respite, that we may send messengers unto all the coasts of Israel: and then, if there be no man to save us, we will come out to thee [1 Sam. 11:1–3].**

This was a very strong, ugly demand made by Nahash on the men of Jabesh. They needed deliverance.

> **Then came the messengers to Gibeah of Saul, and told the tidings in the ears of the people: and all the people lifted up their voices, and wept.**

> And, behold, Saul came after the herd out of the field; and Saul said, What aileth the people that they weep? And they told him the tidings of the men of Jabesh.
>
> And the spirit of God came upon Saul when he heard those tidings, and his anger was kindled greatly.
>
> And he took a yoke of oxen, and hewed them in pieces, and sent them throughout all the coasts of Israel by the hands of messengers, saying, Whosoever cometh not forth after Saul and after Samuel, so shall it be done unto his oxen. And the fear of the LORD fell on the people, and they came out with one consent [1 Sam. 11:4–7].

Notice how Saul identifies himself with Samuel. I do not think at this particular time that Saul's name could have stood alone. When Saul asked the people to come and linked his name with Samuel's name, however, the people came. They also came because of two main fears. They were afraid of Saul and also fearful of what the Ammonites might do to them.

> And it was so on the morrow, that Saul put the people in three companies; and they came into the minds of the host in the morning watch, and slew the Ammonites until the heat of the day: and it came to pass, that they which remained were scattered, so that two of them were not left together [1 Sam. 11:11].

Saul divided his men into three companies. Then the Israelites went after the Ammonites and slew and scattered them so badly that not two of them were left together. Each Ammonite that survived fled by himself.

> And the people said unto Samuel, Who is he that said, Shall Saul reign over us? bring the men, that we may put them to death [1 Sam. 11:12].

Some of the Israelites opposed the idea of having Saul as their king. Samuel ignored that opposition until the nation was united in favor of Saul. Saul's leadership in dealing with the Ammonites took care of the resistance.

> **And Saul said, There shall not a man be put to death this day: for to-day the LORD hath wrought salvation in Israel.**

> **Then said Samuel to the people, Come, and let us go to Gilgal, and renew the kingdom there.**

> **And all the people went to Gilgal; and there they made Saul king before the LORD in Gilgal; and there they sacrificed sacrifices of peace offerings before the LORD; and there Saul and all the men of Israel rejoiced greatly [1 Sam. 11:13–15].**

Now all of Israel accepts Saul as king.

You may be saying, "Well, now, preacher, you see that you were wrong. You were prejudiced against King Saul, and look, he is making good!" Yes, he certainly started off like a great king, but let's keep reading. It is too bad that his story doesn't end here.

TRANSFER OF AUTHORITY
FROM SAMUEL TO SAUL

Chapter 12 begins with the swan song of Samuel.

> **And Samuel said unto all Israel, Behold, I have hearkened unto your voice in all that ye said unto me, and have made a king over you [1 Sam. 12:1].**

This is Samuel's swan song, his final speech. He was a remarkable man, and he was now succeeded by Saul. Although Israel's choice was a king rather than God, He would still bless the people if they would obey. That is evident. Saul was king, and God would give him every opportunity.

> And now, behold, the king walketh before you: and I am old and grayheaded; and, behold, my sons are with you: and I have walked before you from my childhood unto this day [1 Sam. 12:2].

Samuel was brought up in the tabernacle. His life was spent in a "fish bowl"—he was always in public view. Probably no man ever had quite the public life that Samuel had. Many times in our age a man moves into public life and the people accept him. Then suddenly someone finds out about his black past, and the hero comes falling to the ground. Such was not the case with Samuel. He was brought as a little boy, by his mother, to the tabernacle. He lived his entire life before the people. Then he put in this sad note of a fond father, "My sons are with you." In other words, "Why didn't you accept them?" Samuel tried to put them in position but God would not have them. They were boys who were not acceptable to Him.

> Behold, here I am: witness against me before the LORD, and before his anointed: whose ox have I taken? or whose ass have I taken? or whom have I defrauded? whom have I oppressed? or of whose hand have I received any bribe to blind mine eyes therewith? and I will restore it you [1 Sam. 12:3].

This is quite a statement for a man to make who had been before the public eye for so many years, and who had been a judge. He had had many opportunities to become rich but had not yielded to the temptation. Samuel is one of the outstanding men of the Word of God—yet he was a failure as a father. Many public men are like that. Many popular Christian leaders have had children who were failures. It is difficult to understand, but that is the way the human family has been moving down through the centuries and millenniums of the past.

Samuel said that if he had done any of the things he had mentioned to any of the people, he would restore it. It would have been easy for some men who had been miffed at one of Samuel's decisions to step out and say, "Well, you certainly were not fair with me." But nobody stepped out.

> And he said unto them, The LORD is witness against you, and his anointed is witness this day, that ye have not found aught in my hand. And they answered, He is witness [1 Sam. 12:5].

Samuel's life could stand public inspection. It could be put under the hot spotlight of public opinion. He was truly a man of God.

Samuel continues by rehearsing Israel's history. Many men whom God made great used this method. Moses used it, Joshua used it, Gideon used it, and now Samuel uses it. In the New Testament we see that Stephen, when he appeared before the Sanhedrin, also rehearsed the history of Israel. Samuel is reminding his people of God's faithfulness and mercy to them. When their apostasy led to servitude and they cried to the Lord in their distress, He graciously heard and sent a deliverer. He is saying, as he did at Mizpeh, "Hitherto hath the LORD helped us."

Then he moves to their present state and condition.

> Now therefore behold the king whom ye have chosen, and whom ye have desired! and, behold, the LORD hath set a king over you [1 Sam. 12:13].

Samuel makes it quite clear that Saul was the people's choice. Many people believe that the voice of the majority, the choice of the people, is the voice of God. The Bible contradicts this thinking. Generally the minority is closer to determining the will of God. The people wanted Saul. God was the One who chose David. What a difference when God makes the choice!

> If ye will fear the LORD, and serve him, and obey his voice, and not rebel against the commandment of the LORD, then shall both ye and also the king that reigneth over you continue following the LORD your God [1 Sam. 12:14].

Just because Saul is the people's choice, God will not reject him. God is going to give him an opportunity.

> But if ye will not obey the voice of the LORD, but rebel against the commandment of the LORD, then shall the hand of the LORD be against you, as it was against your fathers [1 Sam. 12:15].

Samuel is telling it like it is. If the people will serve God, He will bless them. If they do not serve Him, judgment will come.
Now God will respond to this in a dramatic and miraculous way.

> Now therefore stand and see this great thing, which the LORD will do before your eyes.

> Is it not wheat harvest to-day? I will call unto the LORD, and he shall send thunder and rain; that ye may perceive and see that your wickedness is great, which ye have done in the sight of the LORD, in asking you a king.

> So Samuel called unto the LORD; and the LORD sent thunder and rain that day: and all the people greatly feared the LORD and Samuel [1 Sam. 12:16–18].

Elijah was not the first man that could "preach up a storm"—he brought in a thunderstorm, but Samuel did it before Elijah did. And this is God's seal, I think, upon Samuel's life. The thunder and rain were God's great "amen" on Samuel's career as God's spokesman.

> And all the people said unto Samuel, Pray for thy servants unto the LORD thy God, that we die not; for we have

> **added unto all our sins this evil, to ask us a king**
> **[1 Sam. 12:19].**

It was sin for these people to ask for a king. They were rejecting God by wanting a king to rule over them like the other nations.

> **And Samuel said unto the people, Fear not: ye have**
> **done all this wickedness: yet turn not aside from follow-**
> **ing the LORD, but serve the LORD with all your heart**
> **[1 Sam. 12:20].**

Friend, don't let past sins and mistakes spoil your life. Regardless of who you are or what you have done, if you will turn to the Lord for salvation and forgiveness, God will accept and richly bless you. Don't let the past destroy the future and ruin the present for you. Move out for God today, my Christian friend.

> **And turn ye not aside: for then should ye go after vain**
> **things, which cannot profit nor deliver; for they are vain**
> **[1 Sam. 12:21].**

Hold to the Lord alone. Let the gimmicks alone. Today the church is experimenting with methods. The church does not seem to realize that only God can bless. We need to hold on to the Lord and His Word. I don't think the Bible needs defending. It needs explaining; it needs to be proclaimed. We need the exclamation point and the declaration mark more than we need a question mark.

> **For the LORD will not forsake his people for his great**
> **name's sake: because it hath pleased the LORD to make**
> **you his people [1 Sam. 12:22].**

This is a glorious verse. Have you taken the name of the Lord? Is He your Savior? Are you resting in Him? He will not forsake you. The Lord says through the writer of Hebrews, "Let your conversation be without covetousness; and be content with such things as ye have: for

he hath said, I will never leave thee, nor forsake thee" (Heb. 13:5).
How wonderful is our God! It has pleased Him to make us His people.

Why did God choose the nation Israel? When you are looking for
the answer, look to God and not to the people. God did it and that is
enough. Perhaps God chose you, and some of your friends are wondering why. The important thing is that God chose us and that is enough.
Thank God for that. He could have passed me by, but I rejoice in the
fact that He did not. This is a tremendous message Samuel is giving
the Israelites! Aren't you glad that you are on the Lord's side? Isn't it
wonderful that you and the Lord are friends? Isn't it great that He is
your Savior? He is for you and not against you. He wants to help you.
He is a mighty Helper, friend, as well as a Savior. And He saves to the
uttermost.

> Moreover as for me, God forbid that I should sin against
> the LORD in ceasing to pray for you: but I will teach you
> the good and the right way [1 Sam. 12:23].

I have found in my radio ministry that many people have a gift. It is a
gift of prayer, and I believe it is from God. There are some people in
Southern California on beds of sickness and pain—some who will
never leave their beds—who have a ministry of prayer. I wouldn't take
anything for their prayers. I need their prayers.

Now that I am retired I have more opportunity to move out across
the country. I am enjoying my greatest ministry today, and it is largely
because of the prayers of God's people. For example, in Chicago a man
shook hands with me and said, "You know, I have been praying for
you for years." When I hear something like this, I feel like weeping
and getting down on my knees before Him. It is a privilege to pray for
others.

Samuel said, "God forbid that I should sin against the LORD in
ceasing to pray for you." Each one of us has a prayer responsibility. I
feel the necessity to pray for a certain group of ministers in this country, most of whom are my friends. I have been in their churches, and I
know something about their problems. I pray for them regularly. I also
have a responsibility to pray for my family. If I don't pray for them,

who will? I have a responsibility to pray for my radio ministry. You too have a responsibility, Christian friend. We ought to pray for one another. There are many needy people. God forbid that we should sin against the Lord in ceasing to pray for one another.

> **Only fear the LORD, and serve him in truth with all your heart; for consider how great things he hath done for you.**

> **But if ye shall still do wickedly, ye shall be consumed, both ye and your king [1 Sam. 12:24–25].**

The last time I went to a football game it was at the Rose Bowl in Pasadena, California. It was a long time ago. I sat next to a man who was rooting for the other team, and I want to tell you he was a nut. His team would make an inch on the field and he would jump to his feet. You would think he was having a conniption fit of some kind. My, how he carried on. He irritated me because I was rooting for the other side. But as I looked at him, I could not help wishing that I had that kind of enthusiasm for the things of God. My friend, we need to serve Him with all of our hearts!

What a message there is for you and me in this swan song of Samuel the prophet.

CHAPTER 13

THEME: Saul rebels against God

The real nature of Saul begins to show. His son Jonathan got the victory at Michmash, but Saul blew the trumpet and took credit for it. In presumption, Saul intruded into the priest's office. Samuel rebuked and rejected Saul. The disarmament of Israel is revealed.

In this chapter I think I will be able to sustain the thesis that I presented in chapter 9 relative to King Saul. Saul's outward veneer made him look like a king, but underneath he was no king at all. He was nothing but a paper-doll king.

> **Saul reigned one year; and when he had reigned two years over Israel,**
>
> **Saul chose him three thousand men of Israel; whereof two thousand were with Saul in Michmash and in mount Beth-el, and a thousand were with Jonathan in Gibeah of Benjamin: and the rest of the people he sent every man to his tent.**
>
> **And Jonathan smote the garrison of the Philistines that was in Geba, and the Philistines heard of it. And Saul blew the trumpet throughout all the land, saying, Let the Hebrews hear.**
>
> **And all Israel heard say that Saul had smitten a garrison of the Philistines, and that Israel also was had in abomination with the Philistines. And the people were called together after Saul to Gilgal [1 Sam. 13:1–4].**

The true character of Saul is beginning to emerge. When we get a good view of him, we are going to see that he is a phony. We read in these verses that Jonathan "smote the garrison of the Philistines." Who got credit for the victory? It was Saul. Jonathan appears to be a capable military leader. Later on we will find that he gains another great victory by using very interesting strategy. But in this particular battle Jonathan did the fighting, and Saul blew the trumpet. Saul took the credit for winning. Saul believed in the motto: "He who tooteth not his own horn, said horn will go untooted." Saul blew his own horn. He did not give his son credit for winning the battle. He called all of Israel together and gave a phony report. The army knew Saul's report was not true and so did the followers of Jonathan. Folk are beginning to suspect that there is a weakness in Saul's army and that it is his Achilles' heel. Is he humble? I said at the beginning that Saul had a case of false humility, and this fact is coming to light now.

> **And the Philistines gathered themselves together to fight with Israel, thirty thousand chariots, and six thousand horsemen, and people as the sand which is on the sea shore in multitude: and they came up, and pitched in Michmash, eastward from Beth-aven.**

> **When the men of Israel saw that they were in a strait, (for the people were distressed,) then the people did hide themselves in caves, and in thickets, and in rocks, and in high places, and in pits [1 Sam. 13:5–6].**

Apparently the Philistines recovered from their losses and came with force against the Israelites.

> **And he tarried seven days, according to the set time that Samuel had appointed: but Samuel came not to Gilgal; and the people were scattered from him.**

> **And Saul said, Bring hither a burnt offering to me, and peace offerings. And he offered the burnt offering [1 Sam. 13:8–9].**

Here is another revelation concerning Saul. He presumed that because of his position as king he could offer a burnt offering. Later on we will find that another king by the name of Uzziah also presumed he could

perform a priestly duty. God judged him severely—he became a leper
(2 Chron. 26). Saul ignored God's explicit instructions that only a
priest from the tribe of Levi could offer a burnt offering.

> **And it came to pass, that as soon as he had made an end
> of offering the burnt offering, behold, Samuel came; and
> Saul went out to meet him, that he might salute him.**

> **And Samuel said, What hast thou done? And Saul said,
> Because I saw that the people were scattered from me,
> and that thou camest not within the days appointed,
> and that the Philistines gathered themselves together at
> Michmash [1 Sam. 13:10–11].**

Saul was not willing to wait for Samuel. He was impatient and pre-
sumptuous. He thought he had three good reasons for not waiting for
Samuel to appear: (1) The people were scattered; (2) the Philistines
were coming against him; and (3) Samuel was a little late in arriving.
Saul was rationalizing, of course. He was blaming everything and
everyone else.

> **Therefore said I, The Philistines will come down now
> upon me to Gilgal, and I have not made supplication
> unto the LORD: I forced myself therefore, and offered a
> burnt offering [1 Sam. 13:12].**

Saul "forced" himself to offer an offering and make supplication unto
the Lord. May I say that he was lying. He was being falsely pious. This
is the real Saul emerging.

> **And Samuel said to Saul, Thou hast done foolishly:
> thou hast not kept the commandment of the LORD thy
> God, which he commanded thee: for now would the
> Lord have established thy kingdom upon Israel for ever.**

> **But now thy kingdom shall not continue: the LORD hath
> sought him a man after his own heart, and the LORD**

> hath commanded him to be captain over his people, be-
> cause thou hast not kept that which the LORD com-
> manded thee [1 Sam. 13:13–14].

Saul was told in the beginning that if he obeyed God, he would be blessed, but if he disobeyed, there would be judgment. The ruler must obey the Lord. And what the world needs today is a ruler who is being ruled by the Lord. Our problems stem from the fact that we don't have that kind of ruler. Of course we will not get one until the Lord Jesus comes back to earth; that is God's ultimate goal for this earth. Saul has disobeyed, so God has another man to be king. He is going to bring him on the scene a little later. Even Samuel, at this time, does not know who he is.

> And Samuel arose, and gat him up from Gilgal unto
> Gibeah of Benjamin. And Saul numbered the people
> that were present with him, about six hundred men.
>
> And Saul, and Jonathan his son, and the people that
> were present with them, abode in Gibeah of Benjamin:
> but the Philistines encamped in Michmash.
>
> And the spoilers came out of the camp of the Philistines
> in three companies: one company turned unto the way
> that leadeth to Ophrah, unto the land of Shual [1 Sam.
> 13:15–17].

The battle is about to begin. We will see here the real danger of disarmament.

There are people today who are trying to disarm America. They think that if you destroy all of the ammunition somehow or other war will be eliminated. Others believe that if a gun law is passed and honest people are disarmed, this will stop the crooks. You cannot disarm the crooks, friend. All you do is lay honest people open to violation by the unlawful ones. This is idealistic, foolish thinking.

Now there was no smith found throughout all the land of Israel: for the Philistines said, Lest the Hebrews make them swords or spears:

But all the Israelites went down to the Philistines, to sharpen every man his share, and his coulter, and his axe, and his mattock.

Yet they had a file for the mattocks, and for the coulters, and for the forks, and for the axes, and to sharpen the goads [1 Sam. 13:19–21].

The Philistines had disarmed the Israelites. The Israelites were permitted, however, some farm implements. But in order to sharpen them, they had to go down to the Philistines. In this way the enemy was able to keep an accurate count of what the Israelites had in the way of weapons.

So it came to pass in the day of battle, that there was neither sword nor spear found in the hand of any of the people that were with Saul and Jonathan: but with Saul and with Jonathan his son was there found.

And the garrison of the Philistines went out to the passage of Michmash [1 Sam. 13:22–23].

Only two men, Saul and Jonathan, had swords. I suppose the other men in the army carried mattocks, axes, clubs, and similar instruments. This was the way Saul's army was equipped to fight!

CHAPTER 14

THEME: Jonathan's victory over the Philistines; Saul's hasty order is overridden

JONATHAN'S VICTORY OVER THE PHILISTINES

Once again Jonathan gains a great victory, but Saul takes the credit for it and reveals his jealousy. He actually would have destroyed his own son!

Chapter 14 gives us the strategy of battle that Jonathan used against the Philistines. It is said that this is the chapter which the British General Allenby read the night before he made his successful attack upon the Turks in World War I. To me this is an interesting sidelight. I am unable to give you the details of the strategy of this battle since I am not well acquainted with the geography of the region—on a trip to Palestine I wanted to go there, but our time was limited—neither am I a military man. I am sure that when General Allenby read this chapter, it was a thrilling revelation to him to see how Jonathan executed his military tactics. General Allenby was a Christian who knew his Bible.

Apparently Jonathan's strategy was to take his men through a narrow pass. Here, with the few weapons they had to fight with, Jonathan's army had a distinct advantage. A similar battle took place at Thermopylae, a mountain pass in eastern Greece, where the Greeks, although greatly outnumbered, were able to hold off the Persian army. In Israel's case, this strategy certainly worked to their advantage since Israel was hopelessly outnumbered and almost unarmed.

We will pass over the details of this battle and look instead at the great spiritual lesson that is here.

And Saul said unto Ahiah, Bring hither the ark of God. For the ark of God was at that time with the children of Israel [1 Sam. 14:18].

Saul should not have taken the ark to the battlefield. As we have seen before in the days of Samuel, the children of Israel used the ark in a superstitious manner, thinking it would help them win their battles. Apparently Saul has the same reason.

> **So the LORD saved Israel that day: and the battle passed over unto Beth-aven [1 Sam. 14:23].**

In spite of Saul's action in bringing out the ark, Jonathan's strategy won the battle on the human side. God is with this young man—it is too bad that he did not live long. God saved Israel that day.

SAUL'S HASTY ORDER IS OVERRIDDEN

> **And the men of Israel were distressed that day: for Saul had adjured the people, saying, Cursed be the man that eateth any food until evening, that I may be avenged on mine enemies. So none of the people tasted any food.**

> **And all they of the land came to a wood; and there was honey upon the ground.**

> **And when the people were come into the wood, behold, the honey dropped; but no man put his hand to his mouth: for the people feared the oath.**

> **But Jonathan heard not when his father charged the people with the oath: wherefore he put forth the end of the rod that was in his hand, and dipped it in an honey-comb, and put his hand to his mouth; and his eyes were enlightened [1 Sam. 14:24–27].**

It is interesting to note that Jonathan did not know about his father's strange order that no man was to eat until the battle was won. Actually Jonathan had already won the battle. Now we are beginning to see the real nature of Saul. Jonathan gained the victory, and Saul takes credit for it. He is not willing to give the credit to his son. His "modesty" is gone, and his jealousy is revealed.

> Then answered one of the people, and said, Thy father straitly charged the people with an oath, saying, Cursed be the man that eateth any food this day. And the people were faint.
>
> Then said Jonathan, My father hath troubled the land: see, I pray you, how mine eyes have been enlightened, because I tasted a little of this honey.
>
> How much more, if haply the people had eaten freely today of the spoil of their enemies which they found? for had there not been now a much greater slaughter among the Philistines? [1 Sam. 14:28–30].

It was a foolish command that Saul had given. The men were weary. They had fought a battle and won. They needed something to eat. Saul said, "I will not let anyone eat anything until I am avenged of my enemies." His modesty was absolutely gone.

> And Saul built an altar unto the LORD: the same was the first altar that he built unto the LORD [1 Sam. 14:35].

He actually built an altar to the Lord and offered sacrifices!

> And Saul said, Let us go down after the Philistines by night, and spoil them until the morning light, and let us not leave a man of them. And they said, Do whatsoever seemeth good unto thee. Then said the priest, Let us draw near hither unto God.
>
> And Saul asked counsel of God, Shall I go down after the Philistines? wilt thou deliver them into the hand of Israel? But he answered him not that day [1 Sam. 14:36–37].

God is not using this man at all.

> **And Saul said, Draw ye near hither, all the chief of the people: and know and see wherein this sin hath been this day.**

> **For, as the LORD liveth, which saveth Israel, though it be in Jonathan my son, he shall surely die. But there was not a man among all the people that answered him [1 Sam. 14:38–39].**

Saul, you see, is not willing to take the blame himself. He says that someone else has sinned. The army stood silently. They knew the victory was Jonathan's. And now Saul was saying, "The reason God did not answer me was because someone did not obey me and broke the oath." The army knew that Jonathan had tasted the honey, and they knew that Saul was putting up a tremendous front at this time. They stood in silence because he was the king.

> **Then said he unto all Israel, Be ye on one side, and I and Jonathan my son will be on the other side. And the people said unto Saul, Do what seemeth good unto thee [1 Sam. 14:40].**

The army is not saying much.

> **Therefore Saul said unto the LORD God of Israel, Give a perfect lot. And Saul and Jonathan were taken: but the people escaped [1 Sam. 14:41].**

Saul believed Jonathan was guilty.

> **And Saul said, Cast lots between me and Jonathan my son. And Jonathan was taken.**

> **Then Saul said to Jonathan, Tell me what thou hast done. And Jonathan told him, and said, I did but taste a**

little honey with the end of the rod that was in mine hand, and, lo, I must die [1 Sam. 14:42–43].

Jonathan was guilty—guilty of doing what Saul had not wanted him to do. Saul had said, "Cursed be the man that eateth any food this day." But was this something to die for?

> **And Saul answered, God do so and more also: for thou shalt surely die, Jonathan.**
>
> **And the people said unto Saul, Shall Jonathan die, who hath wrought this great salvation in Israel? God forbid: as the LORD liveth, there shall not one hair of his head fall to the ground; for he hath wrought with God this day. So the people rescued Jonathan, that he died not [1 Sam. 14:44–45].**

Saul would actually destroy his own son if he stood in his way. Why? Because Saul is jealous of Jonathan. He wants all of the glory for himself. The army had remained silent through all of Saul's rantings and ravings, but when Jonathan's life was at stake, they no longer kept quiet.

We are now seeing the true character of Saul. Later on we will see how he will act in direct disobedience to God. He is going to do something that will bring tragedy to the nation Israel. Had not God intervened, it would have meant the extermination of the nation. Saul is revealing that he is not God's man at all. He is actually Satan's man. We will see in the next chapter that Saul is not obeying God any longer—he is following his own devices. Finally the Spirit of God will no longer speak to him. God will no longer give him leading, and he will turn from God to the demonic world. Then we will study that remarkable incident when Saul actually consults the witch of En-dor. It is a section with a great lesson for us in these days in which we are seeing the manifestation of demonism, the occult, the worship of Satan, and astrology. God help America today because there are many Sauls abroad!

CHAPTER 15

THEME: Saul's rebellion concerning Agag; Samuel rebukes Saul

SAUL'S REBELLION CONCERNING AGAG

Saul's rebellion against the command of God is revealed in this chapter. Also we see his facade in wanting Samuel's help in covering up his sin before the people. Saul is rejected now as king, with no hope of recovery. We see Samuel's love for Saul as he mourns for him.

Why the extreme surgery in slaying the Amalekites and Agag? The answer is found in the Book of Esther. Haman, who almost succeeded in destroying the entire Jewish race, was an Amalekite. God knew the true character of this people, which was first revealed in their unprovoked and malicious attack upon Israel in the wilderness (Exod. 17:8–16).

As we continue our study in the life of Saul, we find that he is indeed Satan's man. I trust we have not done him an injustice by identifying him as such. Personally I do not believe that he was ever saved, and I believe there was something of the hypocrite in the man—he pretended to be God's man, but he never was. Also he tried to cover up his rebellion and disobedience regarding Agag.

> Samuel also said unto Saul, The LORD sent me to anoint thee to be king over his people, over Israel: now therefore hearken thou unto the voice of the words of the LORD.
>
> Thus saith the LORD of hosts, I remember that which Amalek did to Israel, how he laid wait for him in the way, when he came up from Egypt.
>
> Now go and smite Amalek, and utterly destroy all that they have, and spare them not; but slay both man and woman, infant and suckling, ox and sheep, and camel and ass [1 Sam. 15:1–3].

These instructions may seem extreme to you if you are not familiar with the history of Amalek. Moses, who was there when it happened, rehearsed the episode for the younger generation in Deuteronomy 25:17–19: "Remember what Amalek did unto thee by the way, when ye were come forth out of Egypt; How he met thee by the way, and smote the hindmost of thee, even all that were feeble behind thee, when thou wast faint and weary; and he feared not God. Therefore it shall be, when the LORD thy God hath given thee rest from all thine enemies round about, in the land which the LORD thy God giveth thee for an inheritance to possess it, that thou shalt blot out the remembrance of Amalek from under heaven; thou shalt not forget it."

If these people had been permitted to live, they would probably have caused more trouble in the future than is imaginable. Apparently Saul spared some of these people, and when we come to the Book of Esther, we will get acquainted with one of them, Haman. He tried to exterminate the Hebrew nation and would have succeeded had not God intervened. When we get God's perspective we understand His immediate action. Very candidly, since you and I are not God and are not obligated to make God's decisions, we cannot pass judgment upon Him.

> **And Saul gathered the people together, and numbered them in Telaim, two hundred thousand footmen, and ten thousand men of Judah.**
>
> **And Saul came to a city of Amalek, and laid wait in the valley.**
>
> **And Saul said unto the Kenites, Go, depart, get you down from among the Amalekites, lest I destroy you with them: for ye shewed kindness to all the children of Israel, when they came up out of Egypt. So the Kenites departed from the Amalekites [1 Sam. 15:4–6].**

We find here that Saul gathered the people together and numbered them. Then he came to a city of Amalek and warned the Kenites to leave the Amalekites before they were destroyed. The Kenites, you recall, were descendants of Moses' father-in-law. We saw references to them in Judges 1:16 and 4:11–17. This was an act of mercy that no pagan nation would have practiced in that day.

And Saul smote the Amalekites from Havilah until thou comest to Shur, that is over against Egypt [1 Sam. 15:7].

Now up to this point Saul is being obedient.

And he took Agag the king of the Amalekites alive, and utterly destroyed all the people with the edge of the sword.

But Saul and the people spared Agag, and the best of the sheep, and of the oxen, and of the fatlings, and the lambs, and all that was good, and would not utterly destroy them: but every thing that was vile and refuse, that they destroyed utterly [1 Sam. 15:8–9].

He thought, *what a shame to destroy everything!* So he saved Agag, who was the ruler of the Amalekites. Saul had no right to spare him any more than he had the right to spare the humblest peasant among these people. This nation was wholly given to evil, and the king, above all others, should have been destroyed and judged at this time. Neither had Saul the right to save from destruction the best of the cattle. It would appear that he made his attack for the purpose of obtaining booty and spoil, and God had forbidden that. The Israelites were bringing judgment upon the Amalekites for almighty God in this particular case.

Then came the word of the LORD unto Samuel, saying,

It repenteth me that I have set up Saul to be king: for he is turned back from following me, and hath not performed my commandments. And it grieved Samuel; and he cried unto the LORD all night [1 Sam. 15:10–11].

Not only did the people choose Saul, Samuel chose him also. Samuel loved Saul. He wanted him to make good as king. I think he wanted Saul, even more than David, to be successful. Now, however, God has rejected Saul, and Samuel, who is obedient to God, must execute God's orders. Saul has not been obedient and judgment is coming.

SAMUEL REBUKES SAUL

And when Samuel rose early to meet Saul in the morning, it was told Samuel, saying, Saul came to Carmel, and, behold, he set him up a place, and is gone about, and passed on, and gone down to Gilgal.

And Samuel came to Saul: and Saul said unto him, Blessed be thou of the LORD: I have performed the commandment of the LORD [1 Sam. 15:12–13].

Saul says that he had been obedient, but notice Samuel's retort to this.

And Samuel said, What meaneth then this bleating of the sheep in mine ears, and the lowing of the oxen which I hear?

And Saul said, They have brought them from the Amalekites: for the people spared the best of the sheep and of the oxen, to sacrifice unto the LORD thy God; and the rest we have utterly destroyed [1 Sam. 15:14–15].

Listen to Saul as he begins to use double-talk and subterfuge in an attempt to camouflage his conduct. He had a very pious reason for sparing some of the animals. He wanted to have excellent animals to sacrifice to the Lord! This was, of course, an attempt to cover up his disobedience with pious pretense.

You can find that same kind of hypocrisy in our contemporary culture. I become rather amused when it is reported that the liquor interests donate money for beautiful gardens and scenic spots for people to visit and enjoy. They always like to make it known—and the media is apparently delighted to report—how much the liquor interests pay in taxes each year. Of course, anyone knows that the alcoholics are costing our government more than any taxes the liquor interests pay. There is the tendency to cover our evil businesses with good works. Many of God's people try to turn their disobedience into some pious project. I am not sure but what we are all guilty of that sort of thing.

When I came out of seminary and entered the ministry, I drove an old, beat-up jalopy, an old Chevrolet. As a young preacher I was satisfied with it. I was not married, and I enjoyed driving it around, although my congregation was embarrassed by it. In fact, they felt it was sort of a joke. Then I met a young lady, and I began to pray that the Lord would give me a new car. I told Him I needed a new car so that I could be more efficient in my visitation. To be honest, "more efficient visitation" did not enter into it at all. I wanted a nice car to impress this young lady! It is so easy for human beings, believers and nonbelievers, to rationalize.

When Saul's disobedience was discovered, you will notice, he tried to blame the *people* for what happened. He said, "The people spared the best of the sheep and of the oxen." However, the record states that it was "Saul and the people." He was the king and the one who was responsible.

> **And Saul said unto Samuel, Yea, I have obeyed the voice of the LORD, and have gone the way which the LORD sent me, and have brought Agag the king of Amalek, and have utterly destroyed the Amalekites.**
>
> **But the people took of the spoil, sheep and oxen, the chief of the things which should have been utterly destroyed, to sacrifice unto the LORD thy God in Gilgal [1 Sam. 15:20–21].**

Saul says that he obeyed the voice of the Lord. Notice he does not say, "My God," or "*our* God," but "*thy* God." He does not take any responsibility at all for sparing the animals, yet he is the one to blame.

> And Samuel said, Hath the LORD as great delight in burnt offerings and sacrifices, as in obeying the voice of the LORD? Behold, to obey is better than sacrifice, and to hearken than the fat of rams.

> For rebellion is as the sin of witchcraft, and stubbornness is as iniquity and idolatry. Because thou hast rejected the word of the LORD, he hath also rejected thee from being king [1 Sam. 15:22–23].

This is one of those remarkable passages of Scripture. This is God's rejection of Saul as king on the basis of his rebellion and disobedience to God. This is an important message for all of us who claim to be children of God.

There is a great deal of this informal and friendly approach to the Lord Jesus Christ today. There are so many little songs that go something like this: "Jesus is a friend of mine." We need to be careful how we use an approach like this to Him. When you say that Jesus is a friend of yours, what do you mean? Actually, you are trying to bring Him down to your level. If I would say that the president of the United States is a friend of mine, I would be bringing him down to my level. But suppose that the president announced that Vernon McGee is his friend. That would bring me up to his level. When we begin to talk about Jesus as "a friend of mine," we are not being Scriptural. The Lord said, "Ye are my friends, if ye do whatsoever I command you" (John 15:14). Are you obedient unto Him? How dare any of us call Him friend if we are not obeying Him? To disobey Him is worse than witchcraft. It is rebellion against God. When you meet a person who is totally disobedient to the Lord, you almost have to conclude that he does not belong to the Lord at all. Now I am not saying that works enter into salvation. I *am* saying that if you are a child of God, if you come to the place where you know Him, you will obey Him. He also said, "If ye love me, keep my commandments" (John 14:15). I am of the opinion that if you would say to the Lord, "I don't love you," He would say, "Forget about My commandments." The important thing is to be rightly related to the Lord Jesus Christ. To be a child of God is to know Him personally. That is what makes Christianity different from any religion in the world. You can be a Buddhist without knowing Buddha. You can be a follower of Confucius without knowing him. You can be a member of any other religion without knowing the founder, but you cannot be a Christian, friend, without knowing the Lord Jesus Christ. And to know Him is life eternal.

> **And Saul said unto Samuel, I have sinned: for I have transgressed the commandment of the LORD, and thy words: because I feared the people, and obeyed their voice [1 Sam. 15:24].**

Notice the low motivation of this man. He said he was afraid of the people and so he obeyed their wishes. He wanted to please everyone. Many folks are like Saul. Lots of preachers try to please everybody. I heard about a prominent minister lately who has begun to compromise, and he says he is doing it because he wants to get along with everyone. That was Saul's approach. It is true that he confesses that he has transgressed, but his penitence is not genuine.

> **Now therefore, I pray thee, pardon my sin, and turn again with me, that I may worship the LORD.**
>
> **And Samuel said unto Saul, I will not return with thee: for thou hast rejected the word of the LORD, and the LORD hath rejected thee from being king over Israel.**
>
> **And as Samuel turned about to go away, he laid hold upon the skirt of his mantle, and it rent.**
>
> **And Samuel said unto him, The LORD hath rent the kingdom of Israel from thee this day, and hath given it to a neighbour of thine, that is better than thou.**
>
> **And also the Strength of Israel will not lie nor repent: for he is not a man, that he should repent [1 Sam. 15:25–29].**

God made Saul king, and now He is taking the kingdom away from him because of his sin. It looks as if God has changed His mind when in reality He has not at all. It is not God who has changed, but Saul. Saul has sinned and so God must deal with him accordingly.

> **Then he said, I have sinned: yet honour me now, I pray thee, before the elders of my people, and before Israel, and turn again with me, that I may worship the LORD thy God [1 Sam. 15:30].**

I do not believe Saul's repentance is genuine. Look how he is covering up his sin. He says to Samuel, "Let us go through the forms of worship together and not let the people know that I have been rejected." He wanted to repent, but not have to pay the penalty for his disobedience. He was a hypocrite right to the end.

> **Then said Samuel, Bring ye hither to me Agag the king of the Amalekites. And Agag came unto him delicately. And Agag said, Surely the bitterness of death is past.**

> **And Samuel said, As thy sword hath made women childless, so shall thy mother be childless among women. And Samuel hewed Agag in pieces before the LORD in Gilgal [1 Sam. 15:32–33].**

Agag came "delicately" unto Samuel because he knew he was in trouble. And Samuel killed Agag. Now that may be strong medicine for some folk today, but my friend, our God is a God of judgment and He is going to judge wrong and evil. I am glad that God is going to judge. I don't know about you, but I thank God that no one is getting away with evil today. There may be those, even in high places, who think they are getting away with their sin, and dishonesty, and murder, and adultery, but they are not. God is going to judge them. No one is going to get away with sin, and we need to make that very clear today. So Samuel executed the judgment of God upon this vile, wicked ruler, Agag.

> **Then Samuel went to Ramah; and Saul went up to his house to Gibeah of Saul.**

And Samuel came no more to see Saul until the day of his death: nevertheless Samuel mourned for Saul: and the LORD repented that he had made Saul king over Israel [1 Sam. 15:34–35].

When the Bible says that God repented, it means that His actions look as though He changed His mind. He has not. God said all along that if Saul did not make good, He would remove him. Saul sinned, and so God removed him from his position as king. God still hates sin and will judge it. Saul was the choice of the people, and he failed. Yet Samuel mourned for him. I think Samuel loved Saul a great deal more than he loved David. He hated to see this man fail and turn aside. That is why his words to Saul were so strong and harsh; they came from a person who loved him. The words of Samuel were also coming from the heart of God.

My friend, God's love will not deter Him from judging sinners. He can love them and still execute judgment. Our God is holy and righteous and just, as well as loving.

CHAPTER 16

THEME: David anointed

God chooses David as king to succeed Saul and sends Samuel to Bethlehem to anoint him as king. Because Saul is forsaken of God, David is brought into court to play upon his harp to soothe the evil spirit of Saul.

Chapter 16 brings us to a new subject. We will see David in contrast to Saul. David is God's man, and Saul is Satan's man. In chapter 15 we saw God's rejection of Saul. God gave Saul not just one opportunity but several opportunities to see if he would obey Him. Saul revealed that he was totally disobedient unto God. He should have made good, but he did not. The Lord did not need to wait to see the results of Saul's kingship. He already knew. But Saul needed to know. Samuel needed to know because he loved Saul. The people needed to know because they had chosen Saul.

Today you and I need to know if we are genuine children of God. For this reason we will be tested. We need the help of the Spirit of God because we are told in Hebrews 12:6, "For whom the Lord loveth he chasteneth, and scourgeth every son whom he receiveth." The Lord tests those whom He loves. This was God's method in Saul's day, and it is His method today. "Blessed is the man that endureth temptation: for when he is tried, he shall receive the crown of life, which the Lord hath promised to them that love him" (James 1:12).

Again, why extreme surgery in slaying the Amalekites and Agag? Amalek was a son of Esau. The Amalekites fought the children of Israel when they were trying to get into the Promised Land. God said He would have war with Amalek from generation to generation and would finally judge them. The Amalekites had five hundred years to change their ways. Because they had definitely turned their backs upon God, He judged them.

Now we come to the place where God chooses David to succeed Saul as king. God is sending Samuel to Bethlehem to anoint David king. David was God's choice. Although God had trouble with him, God has trouble with all of us, doesn't He?

> And the LORD said unto Samuel, How long wilt thou mourn for Saul, seeing I have rejected him from reigning over Israel? fill thine horn with oil, and go, I will send thee to Jesse the Beth-lehemite: for I have provided me a king among his sons [1 Sam. 16:1].

Believe me, Saul had Samuel on his side. Samuel loved him and hated to see God set him aside. It hurt Samuel to give Saul the ultimatum that he had been rejected and dismissed as king. Samuel's sorrow makes it all the more impressive.

> And Samuel said, How can I go? if Saul hear it, he will kill me. And the LORD said, Take an heifer with thee, and say, I am come to sacrifice to the LORD.
>
> And call Jesse to the sacrifice, and I will shew thee what thou shalt do: and thou shalt anoint unto me him whom I name unto thee [1 Sam. 16:2–3].

Samuel is afraid to go to Jesse because Saul is in no mood for opposition. He is desperate. As we move into this story, however, we find that it is God who makes the choice. He tells Samuel exactly what to do, but He does not give him any advance information. His lack of knowledge will protect him. So Samuel goes to Bethlehem and to the house of Jesse. He asks Jesse and his sons to come for a sacrifice.

> And it came to pass, when they were come, that he looked on Eliab, and said, Surely the LORD's anointed is before him.
>
> But the LORD said unto Samuel, Look not on his countenance, or on the height of his stature; because I have refused him: for the LORD seeth not as man seeth; for man looketh on the outward appearance, but the LORD looketh on the heart [1 Sam. 16:6–7].

All through this section we are given excellent spiritual principles. In chapter 15 Samuel said to Saul, "To obey is better than sacrifice, and to hearken than the fat of rams" (1 Sam. 15:22). You and I demonstrate whether or not we are children of the Lord Jesus Christ by our love for Him. It is not what we say in a testimony; it is whether or not we are obeying Him. The Christian life is one of reality. It is not a life of "put-on" and pretense.

When God looks at us, friend, He looks at us from the inside. He is an interior decorator. He always checks the interior. Samuel looks at this well-built, handsome young man and feels this must be God's choice for the next king of Israel. But God says to Samuel, "I don't want you to look at his outward appearance. Don't judge a man by his looks. Let me select the man this time. I will choose the king." God sees the heart, and thank God for that. We are so apt to judge folk, even in Christian circles, by their looks, by their pocketbook, by their status symbol—the Cadillac they drive, by the home they live in, or by the position they occupy. God never judges anyone on that basis. He is telling Samuel not to pay any attention to the outward appearance. God is going to look at the heart.

So Jesse had his sons pass before Samuel one by one. Samuel made it clear to Jesse why he had come, and Jesse had seven of his sons pass before Samuel.

> **Again, Jessee made seven of his sons to pass before Samuel. And Samuel said unto Jesse, The LORD hath not chosen these.**
>
> **And Samuel said unto Jesse, Are here all thy children? And he said, There remaineth yet the youngest, and, behold, he keepeth the sheep. And Samuel said unto Jesse, Send and fetch him: for we will not sit down till he come hither [1 Sam. 16:10–11].**

Surely even the father of David would never have chosen him above the other seven brothers. To begin with, David was only a boy. It is believed that he was about sixteen years old—possibly younger. He was a shepherd. He was out with the sheep. He didn't really know very much. Jesse certainly would not have chosen him above his brethren to be a king. In fact, he had ignored him entirely. He was so sure one of his other sons would be selected that he did not even invite David to the sacrifice. When Samuel found out that David was tending sheep, he said in substance, "This is important business, and I'm not about to sit down and eat until I have accomplished my mission."

> **And he sent, and brought him in. Now he was ruddy, and withal of a beautiful countenance, and goodly to look to. And the Lord said, Arise, anoint him: for this is he [1 Sam. 16:12].**

When this verse says that David was "ruddy," it means that he had red hair—and he had a temper to match his red hair, a hot temper. But in addition to the fact that he was red-headed, he was a fine-looking fellow. He had a "beautiful countenance." God does not despise that which is beautiful. God can use beauty. He is the Creator of beauty. No one who lives on this earth can ignore the beauty in the many scenic spots in every state and country. And a sunset in any place is a thing of glory. God majors in beauty.

I resent the fact that the non-Christian world gets everything that is worthwhile and beautiful. Why is not beauty and talent dedicated to God today?

Well, David was a handsome young man, but God did not choose him for that reason. God knew his heart. He was God's choice. God knows what you and I do not know about him. Although David failed, down underneath was a faith that never failed. David loved and trusted God. He wanted to walk with Him. God took him to the woodshed and punished him within an inch of his life, and David never whimpered or cried aloud. He wanted that fellowship with God, and God loved him. He was a man after God's own heart.

> **Then Samuel took the horn of oil, and anointed him in the midst of his brethren: and the spirit of the Lord**

> came upon David from that day forward. So Samuel
> rose up, and went to Ramah [1 Sam. 16:13].

Samuel anointed David king, and the Spirit of the Lord came upon
him. At this time the Spirit of the Lord departed from Saul.

> But the spirit of the LORD departed from Saul, and an
> evil spirit from the LORD troubled him.
>
> And Saul's servants said unto him, Behold now, an evil
> spirit from God troubleth thee.
>
> Let our lord now command thy servants, which are be-
> fore thee, to seek out a man, who is a cunning player on
> an harp: and it shall come to pass, when the evil spirit
> from God is upon thee, that he shall play with his hand,
> and thou shalt be well [1 Sam. 16:14–16].

I believe Saul was completely taken over by Satan. His servants noted
that he had this mental malady, this spiritual sickness. It is said that
music has power to tame the savage beast. Saul's servants suggested a
contest to find who was the best musician. David was a musician.

> And Saul said unto his servants, Provide me now a man
> that can play well, and bring him to me.
>
> Then answered one of the servants, and said, Behold, I
> have seen a son of Jesse the Beth-lehemite, that is cun-
> ning in playing, and a mighty valiant man, and a man
> of war, and prudent in matters, and a comely person,
> and the LORD is with him.
>
> Wherefore Saul sent messengers unto Jesse, and said,
> Send me David thy son, which is with the sheep.
>
> And Jesse took an ass laden with bread, and a bottle of
> wine, and a kid, and sent them by David his son unto
> Saul.

And David came to Saul, and stood before him: and he loved him greatly; and he became his armour-bearer.

And Saul sent to Jesse, saying, Let David, I pray thee, stand before me; for he hath found favour in my sight.

And it came to pass, when the evil spirit from God was upon Saul, that David took an harp, and played with his hand: so Saul was refreshed, and was well, and the evil spirit departed from him [1 Sam. 16:17–23].

David was an unusual person in many ways. David is brought into the palace. God looks at the inner man when He chooses someone for a particular office or task. Saul is now forsaken of God, and David is brought into court to play upon his harp. Although it is not yet known, Israel has a new king.

CHAPTERS 17 AND 18

THEME: God trains David

Chapter 17 is one of the most familiar in the Bible. This wonderful episode of David and Goliath reveals more than human bravery. It reveals that, even as a boy, David had a heart for God. He didn't volunteer to fight the giant because his people were being shamed, but because Goliath was defying the armies of the living God! As he faced his formidable foe, he testified to his faith in God: "Thou comest to me with a sword, and with a spear, and with a shield: but I come to thee in the name of the LORD of hosts, the God of the armies of Israel, whom thou hast defied" (1 Sam. 17:45).

DAVID SLAYS GOLIATH, GIANT OF GATH

Now the Philistines gathered together their armies to battle, and were gathered together at Shochoh, which belongeth to Judah, and pitched between Shochoh and Azekah, in Ephes-dammim.

And Saul and the men of Israel were gathered together and pitched by the valley of Elah, and set the battle in array against the Philistines [1 Sam. 17:1–2].

Israel is at war again with the Philistines, their perennial and perpetual enemy.

And the Philistines stood on a mountain on the one side, and Israel stood on a mountain on the other side: and there was a valley between them [1 Sam. 17:3].

These two armies were at a standstill. They were poised to enter the battle and did not want to fight. It was similar to Israel's present conflict. At the Suez Canal Israel is on one side and Egypt is on the other. Well, here are the Philistines on one mountain; Israel is on the other mountain, with a valley between. The Philistines are the aggressors.

> **And there went out a champion out of the camp of the Philistines, named Goliath, of Gath, whose height was six cubits and a span.**
>
> **And he had an helmet of brass upon his head, and he was armed with a coat of mail; and the weight of the coat was five thousand shekels of brass [1 Sam. 17:4–5].**

If a cubit is eighteen inches, Goliath was a pretty tall man. Since one span is about nine inches, Goliath was about nine feet, nine inches tall. He was a big boy. He could have played center or forward on any basketball team. Certainly these soldiers wanted to put the decision of the battle in the hands of Goliath and one Israelite.

> **And the staff of his spear was like a weaver's beam; and his spear's head weighed six hundred shekels of iron: and one bearing a shield went before him.**
>
> **And he stood and cried unto the armies of Israel, and said unto them, Why are ye come out to set your battle in array? am not I a Philistine, and ye servants to Saul? choose you a man for you, and let him come down to me [1 Sam. 17:7–8].**

Every day Goliath challenged the Israelites to send out a man to fight him, but after forty days, no one had accepted. David came on the scene because he had brought food to his brothers who were serving in the army. David was alarmed that no one would accept the challenge. His brothers tried to send him home, but David would not go. When Saul heard that David would go against Goliath, he tried to put his armor on him. David, however, was just a boy. He said, "I can't fight with these because I haven't tested them. I will just have to fight with the equipment I'm used to." What a lesson there is for us in this. Let's not try to be something we are not, or try to do something we are really not called to do. If God has called you to use a slingshot, friend, don't try to use a sword. If God has called you to speak, then speak. If God has called you to do something else, well, do that. If God has called you to sing, sing. But if He has not called you to sing, for goodness sake, don't do it. Too many people are trying to use a sword when the slingshot is really more their size.

> **And he took his staff in his hand, and chose him five smooth stones out of the brook, and put them in a shepherd's bag which he had, even in a scrip; and his sling was in his hand: and he drew near to the Philistine [1 Sam. 17:40].**

Some people believe that David chose five smooth stones so that if he missed his first shot, he could use one or all of the others. David did not intend to miss, friend. Then why did he select five stones? The answer is found in 2 Samuel 21:22: "These four were born to the giant in Gath, and fell by the hand of David, and by the hand of his servants." Goliath had four sons, and David was sure they would come out when he killed their father. This is why David picked up five stones. That was the number he needed.

> **Then said David to the Philistine, Thou comest to me with a sword, and with a spear, and with a shield: but I come to thee in the name of the LORD of hosts, the God of the armies of Israel, whom thou hast defied.**

> **This day will the LORD deliver thee into mine hand; and I will smite thee, and take thine head from thee; and I will give the carcases of the host of the Philistines this day unto the fowls of the air, and to the wild beasts of the earth; that all the earth may know that there is a God in Israel.**

> And all this assembly shall know that the LORD saveth
> not with sword and spear: for the battle is the LORD's,
> and he will give you into our hands [1 Sam. 17:45–47].

You know the rest of the story. It is so familiar. God gave David the victory, and he killed Goliath. The battle was the Lord's, and the giant was delivered into David's hands.

There are many great spiritual lessons in this chapter. For example, the giant represents the world; Saul, I think, represents Satan; and David represents the believer in the Lord Jesus Christ. We are admonished, "Love not the world, neither the things that are in the world. If any man love the world, the love of the Father is not in him" (1 John 2:15). We are in the world but not of it. What a difference there is between David and Samson. Samson treated the Philistines as friends—he even married one of them. David treated Goliath as an enemy. The world system, the *Kosmos*—which includes all governments, educational programs, and entertainments—is the enemy of the believer today. The interesting thing is that David's faith enabled him to go out to meet the giant and defeat him. "For whatsoever is born of God overcometh the world: and this is the victory that overcometh the world, even our faith" (1 John 5:4). It is the same lesson Joshua learned at Jericho: he found out that the battle is the Lord's. David also learned that he could not use the weapons of this world to fight the battle. He had to use his own weapons, his own methods—those in which God had schooled him. The believer today needs to recognize that the world can be overcome only by his faith and confidence in God.

JONATHAN AND DAVID MAKE A COVENANT

> And it came to pass, when he had made an end of speaking unto Saul, that the soul of Jonathan was knit with the soul of David, and Jonathan loved him as his own soul [1 Sam. 18:1].

David was speaking to Saul. Saul had called David after the battle because he wanted to give him recognition for his deed. (I think Saul felt that he gave him too much recognition in light of what happened later.) As Jonathan, Saul's son, stood there listening as David and his father talked, "the soul of Jonathan was knit with the soul of David." The relationship of these two men was quite wonderful. We often speak about the love of a man for a woman—and that is wonderful—but nothing is as fine and noble as the love of two men for each other. They see in each other a mirror of themselves and are drawn together. Two men can be real friends. They can enjoy athletics and recreation together. They can work together and have a social life together. Jonathan was an outstanding man, as we have seen, and he loved David for his courage and his confidence in God.

> **And Saul took him that day, and would let him go no more home to his father's house [1 Sam. 18:2].**

David now becomes a public figure, and he will occupy that position for the rest of his life.

> **Then Jonathan and David made a covenant, because he loved him as his own soul [1 Sam. 18:3].**

The covenant that these two men made was that they would stick together. It is difficult to find another friendship equal to what these men had. There is nothing quite like it.

> **And Jonathan stripped himself of the robe that was upon him, and gave it to David, and his garments, even to his sword, and to his bow, and to his girdle [1 Sam. 18:4].**

David was a peasant boy, and he did not have the clothes befitting his new public life. Jonathan shared his wardrobe with David. It was a very generous thing to do.

> And David went out whithersoever Saul sent him, and
> behaved himself wisely: and Saul set him over the men
> of war, and he was accepted over the men of war, and he
> was accepted in the sight of all the people, and also in
> the sight of Saul's servants [1 Sam. 18:5].

David had that charisma that we hear so much about, which made
him accepted by the public. David was actually a great man. God
looked on his heart, the people are looking at the outside, and David
looked good both on the inside and on the outside. Of course David
was not sinless, as we shall see, but he had a real heart for God, and
people loved him for it.

> And it came to pass as they came, when David was re-
> turned from the slaughter of the Philistine, that the
> women came out of all cities of Israel, singing and danc-
> ing, to meet king Saul, with tabrets, with joy, and with
> instruments of music.
>
> And the women answered one another as they played,
> and said, Saul hath slain his thousands, and David his
> ten thousands.
>
> And Saul was very wroth, and the saying displeased
> him; and he said, They have ascribed unto David ten
> thousands, and to me they have ascribed but thousands:
> and what can he have more but the kingdom?
>
> And Saul eyed David from that day and forward [1 Sam.
> 18:6–9].

Saul did not like the new song that the women were singing. Saul
became jealous of David because of the people's applause and accep-
tance of him. As the story progresses, Saul will attempt to remove him
from the limelight by actually destroying him. As David becomes the
favorite of the people, he begins to see that Saul is not as friendly as he
once was.

> And it came to pass on the morrow, that the evil spirit
> from God came upon Saul, and he prophesied in the
> midst of the house: and David played with his hand, as
> at other times: and there was a javelin in Saul's hand
> [1 Sam. 18:10].

This is quite a dramatic scene. As David is playing on a harp, and Saul
is sitting over there playing with a javelin, David may have guessed
what he had in mind. He may have hit a sour note or two, I don't
know, but suddenly Saul threw the javelin.

> And Saul cast the javelin; for he said, I will smite David
> even to the wall with it. And David avoided out of his
> presence twice [1 Sam. 18:11].

Saul wanted to get rid of David permanently. David dodged the javelin
and then departed. He took French leave—got out of the palace and
the area as quickly as he could.

> Wherefore when Saul saw that he behaved himself very
> wisely, he was afraid of him.

> But all Israel and Judah loved David, because he went
> out and came in before them [1 Sam. 18:15–16].

DAVID MARRIES MICHAL, SAUL'S DAUGHTER

David is now the one who is being accepted by the nation. Saul has
been wondering how he can trap him and finally decides upon a
clever method. He promises David his daughter Merab for his wife on
the condition that he continue to war with the Philistines, hoping he
will be killed in battle. Then he fails to keep faith with David and
gives Merab to another. Now we will see that he wants to give his
younger daughter to David. Why? That would put David in the family
where Saul could get to him any time he wanted to. I do not believe

David ever loved Michal. We blame David for having several marriages, but he certainly got off to a bad start with this girl.

And Michal Saul's daughter loved David: and they told Saul, and the thing pleased him [1 Sam. 18:20].

It says here that Michal loved David, but it was not that marital love that is needed to make a success of marriage. In the beginning it was that love of the hero and his popularity. The day will come when she will ridicule him and despise him for his enthusiasm for God.

CHAPTERS 19 AND 20

THEME: Saul attempts to kill David again; Jonathan helps David escape

This chapter begins a section which I have labeled "David Disciplined." Saul personally attempts to kill David, then he openly gives orders that David be slain. Although several times King Saul briefly repents of his murderous intent, David's life is in jeopardy until Saul's death. During these days of exile—possibly a period of ten years—David is hunted like a wild animal. He is a nomad, a vagabond. Living in caves in the wilderness, he endures many hardships and privations. However, he is being tested and trained in God's school. He takes the full course and graduates *magna cum laude*. He becomes Israel's greatest king—in fact, the world's greatest king—and a man after God's own heart. Many of the wonderful Psalms of David are written during this rough and rugged period.

SAUL ATTEMPTS TO KILL DAVID AGAIN

And Saul spake to Jonathan his son, and to all his servants, that they should kill David.

But Jonathan Saul's son delighted much in David: and Jonathan told David, saying, Saul my father seeketh to kill thee: now therefore, I pray thee, take heed to thyself until the morning, and abide in a secret place, and hide thyself [1 Sam. 19:1–2].

Jonathan told David to get out of the palace, because his life was in danger there, and hide himself. Saul was now openly trying to take David's life. His friend, Jonathan, wants to help him.

And I will go out and stand beside my father in the field where thou art, and I will commune with my father of thee; and what I see, that I will tell thee.

And Jonathan spake good of David unto Saul his father, and said unto him, Let not the king sin against his servant, against David; because he hath not sinned against thee, and because his works have been to thee-ward very good [1 Sam. 19:3–4].

Jonathan has a plan. He is going to try to talk to his father. Saul and Jonathan go out into the field and Jonathan says, "David has actually helped you. He is one of your followers. He is a wonderful citizen of your kingdom. You should not try to kill him."

For he did put his life in his hand, and slew the Philistine, and the LORD wrought a great salvation for all Israel: thou sawest it, and didst rejoice: wherefore then wilt thou sin against innocent blood, to slay David without a cause?

And Saul hearkened unto the voice of Jonathan: and Saul sware, As the LORD liveth, he shall not be slain.

And Jonathan called David, and Jonathan shewed him all those things. And Jonathan brought David to Saul, and he was in his presence, as in times past [1 Sam. 19:5–7].

Saul listened to his son, and David came back to the palace. David was wary, however, because he knew his life was in danger.

And there was war again: and David went out, and fought with the Philistines, and slew them with a great slaughter; and they fled from him [1 Sam. 19:8].

Notice Saul's reaction to David's success.

> **And the evil spirit from the LORD was upon Saul, as he sat in his house with his javelin in his hand: and David played with his hand.**
>
> **And Saul sought to smite David even to the wall with the javelin; but he slipped away out of Saul's presence, and he smote the javelin into the wall: and David fled, and escaped that night [1 Sam. 19:9–10].**

An evil spirit comes upon Saul again, and he wants to kill David. It is a very dramatic scene. David is playing his harp, and Saul is fingering his javelin. David senses his murderous mood. Saul throws that javelin with the intent of pinning him to the wall. David knows that he is no longer safe in the palace even though he is married to Saul's daughter.

> **Saul also sent messengers unto David's house, to watch him, and to slay him in the morning: and Michal David's wife told him, saying, If thou save not thy life tonight, to-morrow thou shalt be slain.**
>
> **So Michal let David down through a window: and he went, and fled, and escaped.**
>
> **And Michal took an image, and laid it in the bed, and put a pillow of goats' hair for his bolster, and covered it with a cloth [1 Sam. 19:11–13].**

Here in the beginning Michal was on David's side. She told David that if he did not escape that very night he would be slain the next day. She knew her father meant business. So David fled from the palace, and Michal fixed up the bed to make it look like he was still in it.

> **And when Saul sent messengers to take David, she said, He is sick.**

And Saul sent the messengers again to see David, saying, Bring him up to me in the bed, that I may slay him.

And when the messengers were come in, behold, there was an image in the bed, with a pillow of goats' hair for his bolster.

And Saul said unto Michal, Why hast thou deceived me so, and sent away mine enemy, that he is escaped? And Michal answered Saul, He said unto me, Let me go; why should I kill thee? [1 Sam. 19:14–17].

When Saul found out that he had been deceived, he demanded an explanation from his daughter. She placated him by saying that David would have killed her if she had failed to help him.

So David fled, and escaped, and came to Samuel to Ramah, and told him all that Saul had done to him. And he and Samuel went and dwelt in Naioth [1 Sam. 19:18].

Because Samuel had anointed David as king, his life, too, is in danger. Saul is now openly attempting to slay David. From now on David will live like a hunted animal. What will the future hold for David at this particular time? He will be on the run until the death of Saul.

JONATHAN HELPS DAVID ESCAPE

Saul knew his daughter Michal had deceived him concerning David. He knew Jonathan and David were good friends. Therefore Jonathan had to be wary, careful, and very secretive about communicating with David. That is why he used the method of shooting arrows.

And David fled from Naioth in Ramah, and came and said before Jonathan, What have I done? what is mine iniquity? and what is my sin before thy father, that he seeketh my life? [1 Sam. 20:1].

David asked the question, "What have I done?" He had never hurt Saul. In fact, he had actually helped him. But Saul was never a king. God knew he was not a king, and he was not God's choice. The people had wanted a king and they wanted Saul to be that king. God granted their request but, as it was during the time of Moses, He sent leanness to their souls. In the wilderness the children of Israel wanted meat, and He fattened them up with quail. He gave them what they wanted, but it was evident that they were not trusting God. If they had trusted the Lord, they would have been satisfied with manna and would not have cried out for meat, and they would have found joy and peace in their lives.

Many Christians today are way ahead of the Lord, begging Him for this, that, and the other thing. They are not willing to rest quietly and let God work things out in their lives. Many times when He grants our requests, we say, "Isn't it wonderful that He answered my prayer?" Not always. Sometimes we beg Him for something and, after He gives it to us, we realize it is the worst thing that could have happened to us. A wealthy man in Florida told me how he lost his son. He said, "The biggest mistake I ever made was to give him everything he wanted." Sometimes when we keep after God, He sends us what we are begging for, but the result is leanness to our souls. That was true of the children of Israel who wanted Saul as their king. He certainly is causing a problem for the nation.

David is puzzled. He cannot understand why Saul is after him.

> And he said unto him, God forbid; thou shalt not die: behold, my father will do nothing either great or small, but that he will shew it me: and why should my father hide this thing from me? it is not so [1 Sam. 20:2].

Jonathan tells David that if his father makes a move to slay him, he will know about it.

> And David sware moreover, and said, Thy father certainly knoweth that I have found grace in thine eyes; and he saith, Let not Jonathan know this, lest he be

grieved: but truly as the LORD liveth, and as thy soul liveth, there is but a step between me and death [1 Sam. 20:3].

What a statement!—"there is but a step between me and death." It was not only that way in David's day, it is also that way today. Whether we drive the freeways of the city or the highways of the country, you and I are within a step of death. Isaiah said that there is only a heartbeat between you and death. Death can come at any time. That is the reason we ought to be ready at any moment to move out into eternity and into the presence of God. How many folk have made every arrangement for this life but none for the next life! Are you a saved individual—that is, are you trusting Christ as Savior—so that if you should die at this moment you would go into the presence of God? Let me caution you not to put off accepting Christ as your Lord and Savior any longer.

Then said Jonathan unto David, Whatsoever thy soul desireth, I will even do it for thee [1 Sam. 20:4].

Jonathan was a *real* friend to David. It is wonderful to have a friend like that. Proverbs 18:24 says, "A man that hath friends must shew himself friendly: and there is a friend that sticketh closer than a brother." A brother may sometime let you down, but a real friend never will. A friend, we are told, is one who is born for adversity. A man proves he is your friend when you are in trouble. When David was in trouble, Jonathan proved to be his friend. He would do anything to protect David.

And David said unto Jonathan, Behold, to-morrow is the new moon, and I should not fail to sit with the king at meat: but let me go, that I may hide myself in the field unto the third day at even [1 Sam. 20:5].

David was expected to be at the palace at mealtime, but he was afraid to go. Instead he is asking Jonathan's permission to disappear for three days.

If thy father at all miss me, then say, David earnestly
asked leave of me that he might run to Beth-lehem his
city: for there is a yearly sacrifice there for all the family.

If he say thus, It is well; thy servant shall have peace:
but if he be very wroth, then be sure that evil is determined by him [1 Sam. 20:6–7].

This was the way that David was going to find out the true feelings of
Saul.

And Jonathan said, Far be it from thee: for if I knew certainly that evil were determined by my father to come
upon thee, then would not I tell it thee?

Then said David to Jonathan, Who shall tell me? or what
if thy father answer thee roughly?

And Jonathan said unto David, Come, and let us go out
into the field. And they went out both of them into the
field.

And Jonathan said unto David, O Lord God of Israel,
when I have sounded my father about to-morrow any
time, or the third day, and, behold, if there be good
toward David, and I then send not unto thee, and shew it
thee;

The Lord do so and much more to Jonathan: but if it
please my father to do thee evil, then I will shew it thee,
and send thee away, that thou mayest go in peace: and
the Lord be with thee, as he hath been with my father.

And thou shalt not only while yet I live shew me the
kindness of the Lord, that I die not:

But also thou shalt not cut off thy kindness from my
house for ever: no, not when the Lord hath cut off the
enemies of David every one from the face of the earth.

> So Jonathan made a covenant with the house of David,
> saying, Let the LORD even require it at the hand of
> David's enemies.
>
> And Jonathan caused David to swear again, because he
> loved him: for he loved him as he loved his own soul
> [1 Sam. 20:9–17].

Jonathan realized that David, his brother-in-law, would probably succeed Saul upon the throne. So he requested that when David came
into power his own relationship with David's house might not be forgotten.

Plans were made so that these two friends could communicate.
Jonathan would be watched to see if they made contact, so they had to
be extremely careful. The plan called for Jonathan to shoot with his
bow and arrows. No suspicion would be aroused if he went out often
for archery because he was a warrior. David would be hiding in the
field. Jonathan would go into the field with his armor-bearer and
shoot an arrow. If he shot the arrow way beyond David, it meant that
evil was determined against him and he should flee. If he shot the
arrow closer to David, in front of him instead of beyond him, he would
know it was safe to return.

On the third day Jonathan went out into the field with his bow.
There would be no way for Saul to know that his son was about to
deliver a message to David. The word about Saul was not favorable.
Saul had made it very clear that he wanted to slay David. The arrow
went flying through the air and landed way on the other side of him.
That meant he was to flee. Jonathan instructed his armor-bearer to
pick up the arrows he had shot and then take his artillery into the city.
When the boy is gone, David and Jonathan meet and talk.

> And Jonathan said to David, Go in peace, forasmuch as
> we have sworn both of us in the name of the LORD, say-
> ing, The LORD be between me and thee, and between my
> seed and thy seed for ever. And he arose and departed:
> and Jonathan went into the city [1 Sam. 20:42].

David is in danger from here on. He is going to flee, but the interesting thing is the covenant that David and Jonathan make. We will find that Jonathan kept his part of the covenant. He was faithful and true to David to the very end of his life. David was also faithful and true to Jonathan and his descendants.

Later on, both Saul and Jonathan are slain by the Philistines, and David comes to the throne. The safe thing for him to have done would have been to exterminate every member of the house of Saul. That means that if Jonathan had a son he should have been killed. The fact of the matter is that Jonathan did have a son. We are going to meet him a little later on in the story. His name was Mephibosheth, and he was crippled. When Saul and Jonathan were slain, a servant took the boy and hid him. But David is going to make good his covenant. David found the boy, took him to the palace, put him at his table, fed him, and cared for him. Why? He is making good his covenant with Jonathan because his friend showed him grace.

I will have occasion later on to go into more detail concerning this subject, but right now let me call your attention to the wonderful meaning of this story. David showed kindness to Mephibosheth for the sake of Jonathan. God has shown kindness to you and me for the sake of the Lord Jesus Christ. It is not because of who we are or what we have done that He saved us. Our salvation comes because of who Christ is and what He has done for us. "For God so loved the world, that he gave his only begotten Son, that whosoever believeth in him should not perish, but have everlasting life" (John 3:16). Because His Son died for us, God extends favor to us for Jesus' sake.

After David and Jonathan talked, Jonathan returned to the palace. I think he was a very sad man because he knew that his father was determined to slay his beloved friend.

CHAPTERS 21 AND 22

THEME: David involves the priests; David gathers his mighty men; Saul slays the priests of God

DAVID INVOLVES THE PRIESTS

Then came David to Nob to Ahimelech the priest: and Ahimelech was afraid at the meeting of David, and said unto him, Why art thou alone, and no man with thee? [1 Sam. 21:1].

David is very much alone as he flees from Saul. His young men are with him, of course, so he is not alone in that respect. He is alone in that no one in his party is wearing the livery of King Saul.

And David said unto Ahimelech the priest, The king hath commanded me a business, and hath said unto me, Let no man know any thing of the business whereabout I send thee, and what I have commanded thee: and I have appointed my servants to such and such a place.

Now therefore what is under thine hand? give me five loaves of bread in mine hand, or what there is present.

And the priest answered David, and said, There is no common bread under mine hand, but there is hallowed bread; if the young men have kept themselves at least from women [1 Sam. 21:2–4].

The thought in this portion of Scripture is simply that the only bread available was on the table of showbread, which was not to be eaten except by the priest and only at a certain time—which was at the changing of the bread each Sabbath day.

And David answered the priest, and said unto him, Of a truth women have been kept from us about these three days, since I came out, and the vessels of the young men are holy, and the bread is in a manner common, yea, though it were sanctified this day in the vessel.

So the priest gave him hallowed bread: for there was no bread there but the shewbread, that was taken from before the LORD, to put hot bread in the day when it was taken away [1 Sam. 21:5–6].

Although Israel had a God-given religion, and this bread was dedicated for religious purposes, there were some hungry men present who needed food. That bread would have become commonplace if it could not have been used to feed hungry mouths. That is what David was saying.

In giving David and his men the bread, the priest was breaking the letter of the Law but not the spirit of the Law. You will recall that the Pharisees challenged the Lord Jesus Christ about breaking the Law (which He did not do). The Lord refuted their accusations by referring to this incident in the life of David. Mark 2:23–28 tells us, "And it came to pass, that he went through the corn fields on the sabbath day; and his disciples began, as they went, to pluck the ears of corn. And the Pharisees said unto him, Behold, why do they on the sabbath day that which is not lawful? And he said unto them, Have ye never read what David did, when he had need, and was an hungered, he, and they that were with him? How he went into the house of God in the days of Abiathar the high priest, and did eat the shewbread, which is not lawful to eat but for the priests, and gave also to them which were with him? And he said unto them, The sabbath was made for man, and not man for the sabbath: therefore the Son of man is Lord also of the sabbath."

What the Lord was saying in His day was, "If David could do it, and it was all right, there is One here greater than David, and He can do it also." David ate the showbread because he had *need*. Christ is saying that human need supersedes all ritual and ceremonial laws.

> Now a certain man of the servants of Saul was there that
> day, detained before the LORD; and his name was Doeg,
> an Edomite, the chiefest of the herdmen that belonged to
> Saul [1 Sam. 21:7].

There is a "Judas Iscariot" in the crowd that day at the tabernacle. His
name is Doeg, and he is an Edomite. He is in Saul's service, and he is
going to betray David and the high priest. David has a great deal to say
about this man in Psalm 52.

> And David said unto Ahimelech, And is there not here
> under thine hand spear or sword? for I have neither
> brought my sword nor my weapons with me, because
> the king's business required haste [1 Sam. 21:8].

Now I would like to call your attention to the way that last clause is
misquoted. I have heard it said that certain things should be done for
the Lord and done quickly because "the King's business requires
haste." To begin with, let's understand what David is actually saying.
He does not have a sword or a spear because he had to leave in a hurry.
Also David is *not* on a mission for his king—he is misrepresenting
here.

I am here to say that the King's business does not require haste.
Have you ever noticed how patiently God works? He is going to work
that way in the life of David. David is going to be schooled and trained
in the caves of the earth. That is God's method. God is in no hurry.
Moses was in a hurry, and he wanted to deliver the children of Israel
forty years before God was ready. Moses was not ready either. God put
him out in the desert and trained him and schooled him for forty years
until he was ready. God brought His Son into the world thirty-three
years before He went to the Cross! The thing that marks the work of
God is not haste but the fact that He works slowly and patiently. Oh
my, how impatient we become! I am sure my wife would say, "Yes,
and you are not the one to talk to people about patience because you
are a very impatient man." That is true, I am impatient. I am trying,
now that I am retired, to learn the art of waiting before the Lord. That

is something we all need to learn. David needed to learn it too. God has had to train His men like that. God has had to teach patience to every man He has ever used. God moves and works slowly. If you want to see the way He moves, look how long it takes Him to make a diamond or a redwood tree. God's work does not require haste, friends. That is not God's method.

David is saying something in this chapter that is not true, as the context reveals. David was not on a mission for the king, and "the king's business requires haste" is in no way applicable to Christian work.

> **And the priest said, The sword of Goliath the Philistine, whom thou slewest in the valley of Elah, behold, it is here wrapped in a cloth behind the ephod: if thou wilt take that, take it: for there is no other save that here. And David said, There is none like that; give it me [1 Sam. 21:9].**

It is interesting that David could use the slingshot when he was a youngster, but he has been in the king's palace a long time. Perhaps he has lost his cunning with the slingshot. Now he needs a sword and he uses Goliath's sword because it is available.

> **And David arose, and fled that day for fear of Saul, and went to Achish the king of Gath [1 Sam. 21:10].**

David got as far away from Saul as he possibly could and went to Achish. When he arrived among these foreigners, he found he was in danger. They were enemies of Israel; so David had to pretend that he was a madman. He had to put on an act. Shakespeare's Hamlet had to do the same thing to keep from being slain.

> **Have I need of mad men, that ye have brought this fellow to play the mad man in my presence? shall this fellow come into my house? [1 Sam. 21:15].**

David's act was good and the king of Achish believed it. David would not be in danger there.

DAVID GATHERS HIS MIGHTY MEN

Chapter 22 begins that period in David's life when he hides in the caves and dens of the earth. He is learning that the King's business does not require haste. God is schooling and training him as He has His other men. During these years when he hides from the presence of Saul who seeks to kill him, he is hunted and hounded. He is driven from pillar to post. He is forced to hide in the forests and caves of the earth to escape the king's wrath. During this time David describes himself in the following ways: (1) I am hunted like a partridge (1 Sam. 26:20); (2) I am like a pelican of the wilderness (Ps. 102:6); (3) I am like an owl of the desert (Ps. 102:6); (4) My soul is among lions (Ps. 57:4); and (5) They have prepared a net for my steps (Ps. 57:6).

David becomes weary during these years of running away from Saul. When Saul presses him hard, he withdraws to the cave of Adullam, which is a rocky mountain fastness, southwest of Jerusalem, in a valley between Philistia and Hebron.

> **David therefore departed thence, and escaped to the cave of Adullam: and when his brethren and all his father's house heard it, they went down thither to him.**
>
> **And every one that was in distress, and every one that was in debt, and every one that was discontented, gathered themselves unto him; and he became a captain over them: and there were with him about four hundred men [1 Sam. 22:1-2].**

A marvelous comparison can be made between David and David's greater Son, the Lord Jesus Christ, during this period of his rejection which covered about ten years. This time in David's life compares to the present state of our Lord. You and I are living in the days of His rejection. The world has rejected Christ just as David was rejected and hunted like an animal. Saul, his enemy, was abroad; and our enemy, Satan, is abroad today. We are admonished in 1 Peter 5:8, "Be sober, be vigilant; because your adversary the devil, as a roaring lion, walketh about, seeking whom he may devour." David could say that his "soul was among lions," and we can say the same today. It is during these days that the Lord Jesus Christ is calling out of this world a people for His name. He is calling those who are in distress, those who are in debt, and those who are discontented.

These three classes of men existed in David's day. There were those who were in distress. They were persecuted and oppressed by Saul. David was a long time in breaking with Saul. There were many who were loyal to Saul, but they were finally forced to flee because their lives became endangered. Many fled to David and joined up with him.

If you have felt the whiplash of injustice in the world, if you have felt its unfairness, if you are oppressed and have no place to turn, look to the Lord Jesus Christ. Many people today are trying to find a way out of their troubles and are turning to all kinds of nostrums—some to drugs, some to drink, and some to suicide. There is one who is calling all of us today. "For the Son of man is come to seek and to save that which was lost" (Luke 19:10). He wants to help you. He can help you. "For in that he himself hath suffered being tempted, he is able to succour them that are tempted" (Heb. 2:18). Are you tested and tempted? Are you in distress? You need a Savior, and He is calling out those who will come to Him this day.

There were others who came to David during this time of rejection who were in debt. Debt is a cancer that destroys under any circumstance. In that day when a man got into debt he could lose his property and he could be sold into slavery. Men should have been protected, but they were not. This man Saul was permitting men to become slaves—he was not enforcing the Mosaic Law.

Sin has made us debtors to God. Remember that in the prayer Christ taught His disciples, it says, "Forgive us our debts." God alone can forgive us. Forgiveness always rests upon the payment of a debt, and those who were in debt had to flee. David, actually, did not pay the debt, but Christ did. He paid the debt of sin by dying on the Cross.

He set us free. That is what the Lord Jesus Christ did for you and for me. If you realize you are a debtor to God and have no means to pay, He will pay that debt for you. You can flee to Him. What a wonderful privilege that is!

The discontented also came to David. This means that they were bitter of soul. The circumstances and experiences of life had soured them. In the past few years I have noticed a restlessness sweeping our land and the world. In some areas it has become a great flood. Masses of people march in the street and protest about this, that, and the other thing. There is an undercurrent of dissatisfaction and discontentment. My friend, life will make you bitter unless you see the hand of God, as did Joseph whose story is told in the final chapters of Genesis.

There is One to whom you can go today. He is the Lord Jesus Christ, the rejected King. He is fairer than ten thousand, and He says, "Come unto me, all ye that labour and are heavy laden, and I will give you rest" (Matt. 11:28). He also says, ". . . If any man thirst, let him come unto me, and drink" (John 7:37). As David in exile receives these four hundred distressed, debt-ridden, and discontented men, what a picture he is of the Lord Jesus Christ in this age of His rejection as he is calling out of this world a people to His name.

> **And David went thence to Mizpeh of Moab: and he said unto the king of Moab, Let my father and my mother, I pray thee, come forth, and be with you, till I know what God will do for me.**
>
> **And he brought them before the king of Moab: and they dwelt with him all the while that David was in the hold [1 Sam. 22:3–4].**

Fleeing to Moab is what another Bethlehem family had done several generations before David. Elimelech, you recall, had taken his family to Moab during a period of famine in Israel. Because of this, Ruth the Moabitess is in the Bible story. The father of David would be the grandson of Ruth the Moabitess, which is undoubtedly the reason the king of Moab grants the couple asylum in Moab. The very fact that

David leaves the land of Israel and goes to Moab means he is really a frightened man. Personally, I do not think he should have left Israel, as God would have protected him if he had stayed. His faith wavered a bit as had Abraham's when he went down to Egypt.

SAUL SLAYS THE PRIESTS OF GOD

And the prophet Gad said unto David, Abide not in the hold; depart, and get thee into the land of Judah. Then David departed, and came into the forest of Hareth.

When Saul heard that David was discovered, and the men that were with him, (now Saul abode in Gibeah under a tree in Ramah, having his spear in his hand, and all his servants were standing about him;)

Then Saul said unto his servants that stood about him, Hear now, ye Benjamites; will the son of Jesse give every one of you fields and vineyards, and make you all captains of thousands, and captains of hundreds;

That all of you have conspired against me, and there is none that sheweth me that my son hath made a league with the son of Jesse, and there is none of you that is sorry for me, or sheweth unto me that my son hath stirred up my servant against me, to lie in wait, as at this day [1 Sam. 22:5–8].

It sounds like Saul is developing some paranoic tendencies. He has developed a persecution complex. Maybe he is entitled to this complex, because he has discovered that his own son has not been loyal to him. He is wondering why these men in his cabinet have not revealed this fact to him—as apparently they had not. There is one man, however, who knows where David has fled and he tells Saul what he knows. We have met him before. He was at the tabernacle when David and his men ate the showbread.

Then answered Doeg the Edomite, which was set over
the servants of Saul, and said, I saw the son of Jesse
coming to Nob, to Ahimelech the son of Ahitub.

And he inquired of the LORD for him, and gave him vict-
uals, and gave him the sword of Goliath the Philistine
[1 Sam. 22:9–10].

After Doeg gives Saul his information, Saul decides to go after Ahimelech the priest.

Then the king sent to call Ahimelech the priest, the son
of Ahitub, and all his father's house, the priests that
were in Nob: and they came all of them to the king.

And Saul said, Hear now, thou son of Ahitub. And he
answered, Here I am, my lord.

And Saul said unto him, Why have ye conspired against
me, thou and the son of Jesse, in that thou hast given
him bread, and a sword, and hast inquired of God for
him, that he should rise against me, to lie in wait, as at
this day?

Then Ahimelech answered the king, and said, And who
is so faithful among all thy servants as David, which is
the king's son in law, and goeth at thy bidding, and is
honourable in thine house? [1 Sam. 22:11–14].

Saul sent for Ahimelech the priest and the other priests who were in
Nob. Saul demanded that Ahimelech explain why he had helped
David escape. The priest gave the king a truthful answer. He had the
highest motives and was totally unaware that David was not being
honest with him. Later on David felt very bad that he had deceived
Ahimelech into thinking that he was on a mission for Saul.

Did I then begin to inquire of God for him? be it far from me: let not the king impute any thing unto his servant, nor to all the house of my father: for thy servant knew nothing of all this, less or more.

And the king said, Thou shalt surely die, Ahimelech, thou, and all thy father's house.

And the king said unto the footmen that stood about him, Turn, and slay the priests of the LORD; because their hand also is with David, and because they knew when he fled, and did not shew it to me. But the servants of the king would not put forth their hand to fall upon the priests of the LORD [1 Sam. 22:15–17].

In his anger, Saul did not listen to reason but commanded his servants to slay the priests. They hesitated to carry out his order. But Saul had gone so far in his rebellion and sin that he would not stop at anything. So he commanded Doeg to do his dirty work for him.

And the king said to Doeg, Turn thou, and fall upon the priests. And Doeg the Edomite turned, and he fell upon the priests, and slew on that day fourscore and five persons that did wear a linen ephod [1 Sam. 22:18].

This was a serious and awful crime that Saul committed. If God had not rejected him before this, He certainly would have rejected him at this point.

And Nob, the city of the priests, smote he with the edge of the sword, both men and women, children and sucklings, and oxen, and asses, and sheep, with the edge of the sword [1 Sam. 22:19].

The bitterness and vengeance of this man Saul was terrible. Bitterness is something that we need to beware of today. We are warned about it in Hebrews 12:15 which says, "Looking diligently lest any man fail of

1 SAMUEL 21 AND 22   123

the grace of God; lest any root of bitterness springing up trouble you, and thereby many be defiled." When bitterness gets into the hearts of God's people, it is a vicious and an awful thing. I have seen it in churches. I have seen officers of the church use their positions, not to bring glory to Christ, but to vent their spleens, bitterness, vengeance, and hatred against someone else. It is a terrible thing when bitterness takes over, and this is what happened in Saul's case. He was definitely Satan's man. You and I cannot be too sure about a person's salvation—even when he is active in the Lord's service—when you see him motivated by a vicious bitterness of heart and soul. It is indeed difficult to cull out the tares from the wheat at a time like that. Such was the case here.

CHAPTERS 23 AND 24

THEME: God's protection and care of David in exile

David continues to flee with his six hundred men. Jonathan contacts David and "strengthens his hand in God." David spares Saul's life in En-gedi.

DAVID FIGHTS THE PHILISTINES

Then they told David, saying, Behold, the Philistines fight against Keilah, and they rob the threshingfloors.

Therefore David inquired of the LORD, saying, Shall I go and smite these Philistines? and the LORD said unto David, Go, and smite the Philistines, and save Keilah.

And David's men said unto him, Behold, we be afraid here in Judah: how much more then if we come to Keilah against the armies of the Philistines?

Then David inquired of the LORD yet again. And the LORD answered him and said, Arise, go down to Keilah; for I will deliver the Philistines into thine hand.

So David and his men went to Keilah, and fought with the Philistines, and brought away their cattle, and smote them with a great slaughter. So David saved the inhabitants of Keilah [1 Sam. 23:1–5].

The Philistines, the perpetual enemies of Israel, were robbing the people of Keilah of their grain supply. Notice that David seeks God's will before he attempts to deliver Keilah. David is acting to protect these people, God's people, although he continues to flee from Saul.

When Saul learns that David and his men are contained in a walled city, he rushes his army down to capture them. Again David inquires of the Lord what his course of action should be. The Lord warns him to flee because the men of Keilah will not protect him from Saul—in spite of the fact that he has been their deliverer.

> Then David and his men, which were about six hundred, arose and departed out of Keilah, and went whithersoever they could go. And it was told Saul that David was escaped from Keilah; and he forbare to go forth [1 Sam. 23:13].

That is, David's men scattered—they didn't move out as an organized army.

SAUL PURSUES DAVID, AND JONATHAN AND DAVID MAKE A COVENANT

> And David abode in the wilderness in strong holds, and remained in a mountain in the wilderness of Ziph. And Saul sought him every day, but God delivered him not into his hand.
>
> And David saw that Saul was come out to seek his life: and David was in the wilderness of Ziph in a wood.
>
> And Jonathan Saul's son arose, and went to David into the wood, and strengthened his hand in God [1 Sam. 23:14–16].

Notice how faithful and true Jonathan is to his friend David and the things he says to encourage him.

> And he said unto him, Fear not: for the hand of Saul my father shall not find thee; and thou shalt be king over Israel, and I shall be next unto thee; and that also Saul my father knoweth.

> And they two made a covenant before the LORD: and
> David abode in the wood, and Jonathan went to his
> house [1 Sam. 23:17–18].

In essence Jonathan is telling David that Saul knows what is going to
happen but is fighting it. Saul is, of course, going against God's will.
He is in complete rebellion against God. Jonathan, however, is willing
to execute God's will. Jonathan's actions reveal that he is a great man.
His attitude reminds me of John the Baptist who said of the Lord Jesus
Christ, "He must increase, but I must decrease" (John 3:30).

> Then came up the Ziphites to Saul to Gibeah, saying,
> Doth not David hide himself with us in strong holds in
> the wood, in the hill of Hachilah, which is on the south
> of Jeshimon? [1 Sam. 23:19].

Saul is determined to ferret out David and is aided by the Ziphites
who promise to deliver David to him.

> And Saul went on this side of the mountain, and David
> and his men on that side of the mountain: and David
> made haste to get away for fear of Saul; for Saul and his
> men compassed David and his men round about to take
> them [1 Sam. 23:26].

Saul has David surrounded at this point and would surely have captured him if Saul had not been called home to fight off an invasion of
the Philistines. This reveals God's perfect timing, which again saves
David's life.

DAVID SPARES SAUL'S LIFE AT EN-GEDI

In chapter 24 David is still on the run. He is being hounded continually by Saul. I think this period of testing in David's life changed
him from an innocent shepherd boy to a rugged man who became
God's man and ruled over his people.

And it came to pass, when Saul was returned from following the Philistines, that it was told him, saying, Behold, David is in the wilderness of En-gedi.

Then Saul took three thousand chosen men out of all
Israel, and went to seek David and his men upon the
rocks of the wild goats [1 Sam. 24:1–2].

David had gone to a rugged place to hide. Saul went looking for David
with an army of three thousand men while David had only six hundred men. Saul's army greatly outnumbered David's, but David made
up for this imbalance by using strategy. Also, he knew the area and his
men were rugged men, indeed.

And he came to the sheepcotes by the way, where was a
cave; and Saul went in to cover his feet: and David and
his men remained in the sides of the cave [1 Sam. 24:3].

Saul entered the very cave in which David was hiding and went to
sleep. Saul's men were on guard, of course, but they were outside the
cave, not inside. They permitted the king to have privacy in order that
he might have a good nap. So this is the situation: David and his men,
and Saul, are inside the cave. Saul's soldiers are outside the cave.

And the men of David said unto him, Behold the day of
which the LORD said unto thee, Behold, I will deliver
thine enemy into thine hand, that thou mayest do to him
as it shall seem good unto thee. Then David arose, and
cut off the skirt of Saul's robe privily [1 Sam. 24:4].

David quietly slipped up to the sleeping king and trimmed off the
lower part of his garment.

And it came to pass afterward, that David's heart smote
him, because he had cut off Saul's skirt [1 Sam. 24:5].

Right away David regretted his act because it would be a source of embarrassment to Saul. Imagine what would happen when Saul awakened, stood up, and found out he was wearing a mini-skirt!

And he said unto his men, The LORD forbid that I should do this thing unto my master, the LORD's anointed, to stretch forth mine hand against him, seeing he is the anointed of the LORD [1 Sam. 24:6].

David respected the *office* of king, although he may not have respected the man.

May I interject a thought at this particular point. I personally do not feel that the President of the United States, regardless of his party or character, should be made the subject of a cartoon or the object of ridicule. In a democracy, of course, he can be criticized, but to make our president a subject of ridicule, as do some cartoonists and some comedians, is entirely wrong. Now this is just my personal opinion, but I think that we ought to have more respect for the office than we do. We live in a country that has its faults, but it has been a great country for most of us, and its offices and officers should be respected.

It is interesting to note that although David is being hunted by Saul, David will not lay a hand on him. Why? Because Saul is God's anointed. David is going to let God deal with the king. My, if we could only come to the place where we would let God handle our enemies! As a rule *we* want to take care of them, but God can do a much better job. We are told in Romans 12:19, "Dearly beloved, avenge not yourselves, but rather give place unto wrath: for it is written, Vengeance is mine; I will repay, saith the Lord." When we take things in our own hands, we are no longer walking by faith. We are not trusting God. What we are really saying is, "Lord, we cannot trust You to handle this the way we want it handled, so we are going to do it ourselves." David, however, is going to let God handle Saul.

David is sorry he has cut off Saul's skirt. His conscience disturbs him because he has made the king an object of ridicule.

So David stayed his servants with these words, and suffered them not to rise against Saul. But Saul rose up out of the cave, and went on his way [1 Sam. 24:7].

Several of David's men had no use for Saul and would have killed him in a minute, but David would not permit it.

David also arose afterward, and went out of the cave, and cried after Saul, saying, My lord the king. And when Saul looked behind him, David stooped with his face to the earth, and bowed himself [1 Sam. 24:8].

Notice once again that although David may not respect Saul personally, he does have respect for Saul's office.

And David said to Saul, Wherefore hearest thou men's words, saying, Behold, David seeketh thy hurt?

Behold, this day thine eyes have seen how that the LORD had delivered thee to-day into mine hand in the cave: and some bade me kill thee: but mine eye spared thee; and I said, I will not put forth mine hand against my lord; for he is the LORD's anointed [1 Sam. 24:9–10].

David had demonstrated to Saul that he was not seeking his life. Saul had been told, and wrongly so, that David was out to get him. Nothing could have been further from the truth. I think David was very much misunderstood, maligned, and misrepresented by both friend and enemy. David's act of mercy in sparing Saul's life should have made it abundantly clear that he was not seeking the king's life.

As David continues to reason with him, Saul actually weeps.

And it came to pass, when David had made an end of speaking these words unto Saul, that Saul said, Is this thy voice, my son David? And Saul lifted up his voice, and wept.

> And he said to David, Thou art more righteous than I:
> for thou hast rewarded me good, whereas I have re-
> warded thee evil [1 Sam. 24:16–17].

Now notice Saul's amazing statement.

> And now, behold, I know well that thou shalt surely be
> king, and that the kingdom of Israel shall be established
> in thine hand [1 Sam. 24:20].

This is an amazing confession coming from Saul. Saul realizes that
what David has said is true and is greatly moved by the fact that he has
spared his life. Then Saul acknowledges the fact that one day David
will be king.

> Swear now therefore unto me by the LORD, that thou wilt
> not cut off my seed after me, and that thou wilt not de-
> stroy my name out of my father's house.

> And David sware unto Saul. And Saul went home; but
> David and his men gat them up unto the hold [1 Sam.
> 24:21–22].

After their conversation Saul returns home, but David and his men go
to their stronghold. David still does not trust Saul. David goes farther
and farther into the wilderness to hide, because he knows there will
come a day when Saul will come after him again. I am of the opinion
that Saul is actually demon-possessed at this time. We are told that an
evil spirit had come upon him.

CHAPTER 25

THEME: Samuel dies; David meets Abigail

In this chapter Samuel dies in his retirement. David encounters Nabal and Abigail. David in anger is prevented from the rash act of murdering Nabal and his servants by the presence and diplomacy of Abigail, Nabal's beautiful wife. Nabal dies after a night of drunkenness, and David takes Abigail to wife. She was a good influence in his life.

SAMUEL DIES

And Samuel died: and all the Israelites were gathered together, and lamented him, and buried him in his house at Ramah. And David arose, and went down to the wilderness of Paran [1 Sam. 25:1].

Scripture is quite brief concerning Samuel's death. It simply says that "all the Israelites were gathered together, and lamented him." Samuel had been a great man of God; there is no question about that. He was outstanding. He was the bridge between the judges and the kings. He was the last of the judges and the first in the office of prophets. There were, of course, many prophets before Samuel, but he represented the office that continued on through the Old Testament and into the New Testament.

Samuel was also a force for good and probably prevented the full force of Saul's bitterness and hatred from being vented upon David. Samuel was a buffer between David and Saul. When Samuel died, David went a great distance into the wilderness—he went farther away from Saul than Elijah ever did from Jezebel.

DAVID AND ABIGAIL

As someone has said, "To be great is to be misunderstood." This certainly applies to David. He was great, and he was misunderstood. Because the world does not know David, it misjudges him. When the name of David is mentioned, immediately there is called to mind his sins of murder and adultery. There are those who inquire, "How could David commit such sin, and yet the Scriptures say that he was a man after God's own heart?" We will have an occasion to answer that question. But instead of questioning God's choice, we ought to investigate David's character. We will find that only those who are small will be critical of David. He is one of the outstanding characters in Scripture. To know him is to love him. I know of no man who presents such nobility of character.

David had a checkered career. He was born a peasant boy in Bethlehem, a son of Jesse of the tribe of Judah. He was brought up a little shepherd boy among seven fine-looking brothers who were older than he. He was passed by. Then one day his life changed. God had not passed him by. God knew his heart.

God does not look on the outward side of a man. God knew David's heart. He was anointed Israel's future king by Samuel. He slew the giant Goliath. As a musician he is called the "sweet psalmist of Israel." He penned the most beautiful poetry written in any language or sung in any tongue. If you have any doubt about it, have you anything to compare with Psalm 23? David married the princess Michal, the daughter of Saul. He was loved by Jonathan, the son of Saul. Never did a man have a friend like Jonathan. David became an outlaw. He gathered together a band of men during this time, and they lived in mountain strongholds. He pretended he was mad, like Hamlet, on one occasion. He finally became king of Judah and then of the entire nation of Israel. We are going to see that his own son led a rebellion against him, and once again he was forced to flee. He lived to see Solomon, his son, anointed king.

Instead of looking at David and Bathsheba and seeing David's sin, I want you to look at something else. Let's forget for the moment Goliath and David's heroic accomplishment and Jonathan's loyal friendship. Instead I want you to see the very simple story of life in this chapter. It reveals the innermost recesses of his soul. It is a story about David and Abigail, and it reveals how human David really was.

> **And there was a man in Maon, whose possessions were in Carmel; and the man was very great, and he had three thousand sheep, and a thousand goats: and he was shearing his sheep in Carmel.**

> **Now the name of the man was Nabal; and the name of his wife Abigail: and she was a woman of good understanding, and of a beautiful countenance: but the man was churlish and evil in his doings; and he was of the house of Caleb [1 Sam. 25:2–3].**

It seems that not all of Caleb's offspring turned out well, as we can see from this man Nabal. The name *Nabal* means "fool." I don't know how he got that name, but he certainly lived up to it. But then, aren't we all born fools? The Scriptures say that man is born like a wild ass's colt (Job 11:12). Look at your own life for a moment. Have you ever done anything foolish? I think all of us have done foolish things that we would rather not think about.

Nabal was a fool, but he was a rich man. He had neither honor nor honesty. He was a drunken beast. But he had a beautiful and intelligent wife. That is a rare combination in a woman but a pleasing one. The question is—how did this man get such a jewel for a wife? Dr. McConkey called the story of Nabal and Abigail "Beauty and the Beast." Frankly, I think her parents made the match. They were impressed by this man's wealth, and it was a case of beauty being sold for gold—traffic in a human soul. Perhaps you are saying, "That's terrible." It is terrible, but it happens all the time in our contemporary culture. How often it happens we do not know. It *is* an awful thing.

> **And David heard in the wilderness that Nabal did shear his sheep.**

> **And David sent out ten young men, and David said unto the young men, Get you up to Carmel, and go to Nabal, and greet him in my name [1 Sam. 25:4–5].**

David had been protecting Nabal's property. He had quite an army
with him, and he could have robbed this man and taken his sheep for
food, but he did not. Instead he kept thieves and marauders from getting the sheep. He did many things to assist Nabal. Now that David
needs food, he sends his young men to ask for help.

> And when David's young men came, they spake to Na-
> bal according to all those words in the name of David,
> and ceased.

> And Nabal answered David's servants, and said, Who is
> David? and who is the son of Jesse? there be many ser-
> vants now a days that break away every man from his
> master [1 Sam. 25:9–10].

Nabal is saying that David has betrayed Saul and that he is disloyal.

> Shall I then take my bread, and my water, and my flesh
> that I have killed for my shearers, and give it unto men,
> whom I know not whence they be?

> So David's young men turned their way, and went again,
> and came and told him all those sayings [1 Sam.
> 25:11–12].

I told you at the beginning that David is redheaded and hot-headed.
He is angry now.

> And David said unto his men, Gird ye on every man his
> sword. And they girded on every man his sword; and
> David also girded on his sword: and there went up after
> David about four hundred men; and two hundred abode
> by the stuff [1 Sam. 25:13].

Someone in Nabal's household learned of this and informed Abigail.

> But one of the young men told Abigail, Nabal's wife, say-
> ing, Behold, David sent messengers out of the wilder-
> ness to salute our master; and he railed on them [1 Sam.
> 25:14].

When Abigail heard what had happened between her husband and
David's young men, she knew what David would do. So she got together a great deal of food.

> Then Abigail made haste, and took two hundred loaves,
> and two bottles of wine, and five sheep ready dressed,
> and five measures of parched corn, and an hundred
> clusters of raisins, and two hundred cakes of figs, and
> laid them on asses.
>
> And she said unto her servants, Go on before me; be-
> hold, I come after you. But she told not her husband Na-
> bal.
>
> And it was so, as she rode on the ass, that she came
> down by the covert of the hill, and, behold, David and
> his men came down against her; and she met them
> [1 Sam. 25:18–20].

Abigail went out to meet David with food before he could get to Nabal
because David would have killed him.

> Now David had said, Surely in vain have I kept all that
> this fellow hath in the wilderness, so that nothing was
> missed of all that pertained unto him: and he hath re-
> quited me evil for good [1 Sam. 25:21].

David's intention was to kill every man that belonged to Nabal.

> And when Abigail saw David, she hasted, and lighted
> off the ass, and fell before David on her face, and bowed
> herself to the ground,

> And fell at his feet, and said, Upon me, my lord, upon
> me let this iniquity be: and let thine handmaid, I pray
> thee, speak in thine audience, and hear the words of
> thine handmaid [1 Sam. 25:23–24].

Around the hill David came, riding at full tilt, flushed with anger, and
probably saying to himself, "I'll get that fellow. He can't treat me that
way." Then he looks down the road and sees a woman coming on a
little donkey. He sees all the foodstuff, and his men are hungry. He
halts his band of men before this beautiful woman. For the first time
David, God's anointed, is face to face with a noble woman who means
well by him. She bows before David. She gets right down in the dust
and asks David to take his revenge upon her because she is Nabal's
wife. She is wise in what she does because David is not about to do
anything to a beautiful woman with an appeal like she made! Then
she apologizes for the fact that her husband is a fool and a brute.

> Let not my lord, I pray thee, regard this man of Belial,
> even Nabal: for as his name is, so is he; Nabal is his
> name, and folly is with him: but I thine handmaid saw
> not the young men of my lord, whom thou didst send
> [1 Sam. 25:25].

A "man of Belial" is a worthless person.

> Now therefore, my lord, as the LORD liveth, and as thy
> soul liveth, seeing the LORD hath withholden thee from
> coming to shed blood, and from avenging thyself with
> thine own hand, now let thine enemies, and they that
> seek evil to my lord, be as Nabal.
>
> And now this blessing which thine handmaid hath
> brought unto my lord, let it even be given unto the young
> men that follow my lord.
>
> I pray thee, forgive the trespass of thine handmaid:
> for the LORD will certainly make my lord a sure house;

because my lord fighteth the battles of the LORD, and evil hath not been found in thee all thy days [1 Sam. 25:26–28].

This was just the beginning of David's career. Sin came into his life later on, but up to this point David's life was as clean as a hound's tooth. He has lived for God, and he is attempting to please God. Abigail admires him for it.

Yet a man is risen to pursue thee, and to seek thy soul: but the soul of my lord shall be bound in the bundle of life with the LORD thy God; and the souls of thine enemies, them shall he sling out, as out of the middle of a sling [1 Sam. 25:29].

Although she does not mention him by name, Abigail is speaking about Saul as the one who is pursuing David. Then she says one of the most remarkable things about David, "But the soul of my lord shall be bound in the bundle of life with the LORD thy God."

Friend, that is exactly the position of the believer in Christ Jesus. John, in his first epistle, calls Christ "Eternal Life." He says, "For the life was manifested, and we have seen it, and bear witness, and shew unto you that eternal life, which was with the Father, and was manifested unto us" (1 John 1:2). When you and I trust Him as Savior, the Holy Spirit baptizes us into the body of believers. Paul says, "For by one Spirit are we all baptized into one body, whether we be Jews or Gentiles, whether we be bond or free; and have been all made to drink into one Spirit" (1 Cor. 12:13). You and I are brought into the body of believers—the body of Christ—by our faith in Christ. We are said to be in Christ. And there is no condemnation to those who are in Christ. So we are bound in the bundle of life with the Lord Jesus Christ.

Then Abigail said, "The souls of thine enemies God shall sling out." David knew all about slingshots, and what he had done to Goliath was well known in Israel.

Then Abigail continues.

> And it shall come to pass, when the LORD shall have
> done to my lord according to all the good that he hath
> spoken concerning thee, and shall have appointed thee
> ruler over Israel;

> That this shall be no grief unto thee, nor offence of heart
> unto my lord, either that thou hast shed blood causeless,
> or that my lord hath avenged himself: but when the LORD
> shall have dealt well with my lord, then remember thine
> handmaid [1 Sam. 25:30–31].

Abigail is saying to David, "Don't hold what my husband has done against us. You are going to be king." I can just see David sitting astride his horse, looking down at this woman who is actually down in the dust. She is a beautiful and noble woman.

> And David said to Abigail, Blessed be the LORD God of
> Israel, which sent thee this day to meet me:

> And blessed be thy advice, and blessed be thou, which
> hast kept me this day from coming to shed blood, and
> from avenging myself with mine own hand [1 Sam.
> 25:32–33].

David was thankful to this woman for her wisdom in keeping him from an act that would have caused him regret.

> So David received of her hand that which she had
> brought him, and said unto her, Go up in peace to thine
> house; see, I have hearkened to thy voice, and have ac-
> cepted thy person [1 Sam. 25:35].

David accepted Abigail's food, advice, and person.

> And Abigail came to Nabal; and, behold, he held a feast
> in his house, like the feast of a king; and Nabal's heart
> was merry within him, for he was very drunken: where-

fore she told him nothing, less or more, until the morning light.

But it came to pass in the morning, when the wine was gone out of Nabal, and his wife had told him these things, that his heart died within him, and he became as a stone.

And it came to pass about ten days after, that the LORD smote Nabal, that he died [1 Sam. 25:36–38].

Nabal had a big party that night—he was a swinger. He had sobered up the next morning, and Abigail told him what had transpired the day before with David. Then "his heart died within him, and he became as a stone." He not only had a headache, he had a heartache too. What happened to him? Did he have a heart attack? It is well that God moved Abigail to intervene. David's hands would have been red with blood, and God didn't want them that way.

Now what is David going to do? There is a beautiful widow who lives in the desert of Paran. She is, actually, the only woman who has been a blessing to him.

And when David heard that Nabal was dead, he said, Blessed be the LORD, that hath pleaded the cause of my reproach from the hand of Nabal, and hath kept his servant from evil: for the LORD hath returned the wickedness of Nabal upon his own head. And David sent and communed with Abigail, to take her to him to wife [1 Sam. 25:39].

When David heard that Nabal was dead, he wanted Abigail for his wife. When she had intercepted David on the road, she had said, "When the LORD shall have dealt well with my lord, then remember thine handmaid." Well, David could not forget her. Do you know why? She had appealed to the best in him. She had advised him, and he knew her advice was right. He knew he loved her, and I think it was love at first sight.

David also recognized the hand of God. God can use beauty. That day on the road, as he thanked her for her good advice, two great souls stood in the presence of each other. Now that Nabal was dead, David asked her to become his wife, and she did. This marks the beginning of another phase of David's life.

Now something else took place of which God did not approve.

> **David also took Ahinoam of Jezreel; and they were also both of them his wives.**

> **But Saul had given Michal his daughter, David's wife, to Phalti the son of Laish, which was of Gallim [1 Sam. 25:43–44].**

Sin entered into his life, friend. He was a rugged man and he lived a rugged life, but one day he became a murderer. Since God called him a man after His own heart, does that mean He approved of his life? No. We will see that when David longed to build God a magnificent temple, God had to tell him "no." God would not permit him to build the temple because of the sin in his life.

CHAPTERS 26 AND 27

THEME: David again spares Saul's life; David retreats to the land of Philistia

D avid again spares Saul's life in the wilderness of Ziph. Note the contrast between Saul and David. Obviously Saul knows that David is God's choice, but he seeks to slay him. David recognizes that Saul is the anointed king, and he spares him.

DAVID AGAIN SPARES SAUL'S LIFE

And the Ziphites came unto Saul to Gibeah, saying, Doth not David hide himself in the hill of Hachilah, which is before Jeshimon?

Then Saul arose, and sent down to the wilderness of Ziph, having three thousand chosen men of Israel with him, to seek David in the wilderness of Ziph [1 Sam. 26:1-2].

H ere goes Saul on another campaign, another crusade, to try to destroy David. This is what happened. David fled into the wilderness, and Saul went after him. David was a great soldier and he knew the terrain, which made him an expert general. He also had loyal men who were willing to die for him and with him. Saul did not know the terrain. Added to that, his followers were not as loyal as they could be, and Saul certainly suspected them.

David therefore sent out spies, and understood that Saul was come in very deed [1 Sam. 26:4].

David could not believe that Saul would come into territory that was unfamiliar to him. It was a military blunder of such proportions that

David sent spies out to see if Saul really was in the area. His scouts reported that Saul was indeed in the wilderness.

> **And David arose, and came to the place where Saul had pitched: and David beheld the place where Saul lay, and Abner the son of Ner, the captain of his host: and Saul lay in the trench, and the people pitched round about him [1 Sam. 26:5].**

David was in a position to observe where Saul and his men were, while he and his men were able to hide in the wilderness.

> **Then answered David and said to Ahimelech the Hittite, and to Abishai the son of Zeruiah, brother to Joab, saying, Who will go down with me to Saul to the camp? And Abishai said, I will go down with thee.**
>
> **So David and Abishai came to the people by night: and, behold, Saul lay sleeping within the trench, and his spear stuck in the ground at his bolster: but Abner and the people lay round about him [1 Sam. 26:6–7].**

David and Abishai went into Saul's camp and looked around. Saul was sleeping in a trench, surrounded by his men. At the head of his bed he had stuck his spear in the ground.

> **Then said Abishai to David, God hath delivered thine enemy into thine hand this day: now therefore let me smite him, I pray thee, with the spear even to the earth at once, and I will not smite him the second time [1 Sam. 26:8].**

Abishai was saying to David, "If you just let me at him, I will strike him once. One blow is all I need, and you will be rid of your enemy."

> **And David said to Abishai, Destroy him not: for who
> can stretch forth his hand against the LORD's anointed,
> and be guiltless? [1 Sam. 26:9].**

Once again David has the opportunity to kill Saul, but he refuses. He
will not raise his hand against the Lord's anointed.

> **David said furthermore, As the LORD liveth, the LORD
> shall smite him; or his day shall come to die; or he shall
> descend into battle, and perish [1 Sam. 26:10].**

David says, "God will have to take care of him." David is acting upon
the principle found in Hebrews 10:30, ". . . Vengeance belongeth unto
me, I will recompense, saith the Lord."

> **The LORD forbid that I should stretch forth mine hand
> against the LORD's anointed: but, I pray thee, take thou
> now the spear that is at his bolster, and the cruse of wa-
> ter, and let us go.**
>
> **So David took the spear and the cruse of water from
> Saul's bolster; and they gat them away, and no man saw
> it, nor knew it, neither awaked: for they were all asleep;
> because a deep sleep from the LORD was fallen upon
> them [1 Sam. 26:11–12].**

What David did was not difficult. He took Saul's spear and cruse of
water, and no one wakened because the Lord had caused a deep sleep
to fall upon Saul and his men.

> **Then David went over to the other side, and stood on the
> top of an hill afar off; a great space being between them
> [1 Sam. 26:13].**

Now David withdrew from Saul's camp, but he did not go back to his
men. Instead he went way over on the other side of Saul's camp and

stood on the top of a hill. It was a place where he could easily escape if anyone came after him.

> **And David cried to the people, and to Abner the son of Ner, saying, Answerest thou not, Abner? Then Abner answered and said, Who art thou that criest to the king?**

> **And David said to Abner, Art not thou a valiant man? and who is like to thee in Israel? wherefore then hast thou not kept thy lord the king? for there came one of the people in to destroy the king thy lord.**

> **This thing is not good that thou hast done. As the LORD liveth, ye are worthy to die, because ye have not kept your master, the LORD's anointed. And now see where the king's spear is, and the cruse of water that was at his bolster.**

> **And Saul knew David's voice, and said, Is this thy voice, my son David? And David said, It is my voice, my lord, O king [1 Sam. 26:14–17].**

Frankly, I think David is being sarcastic with Abner, who is Saul's captain and should have been protecting him. David is ridiculing Abner. David is telling him that the king could have been destroyed. About this time the king and his men begin to wake up, and they wonder what has happened. Then David says, "Where is Saul's spear and cruse of water? They are gone." David probably held them up and said, "Look, I've got them. I could have slain Saul, but I did not." And that is the important thing: David did not slay the king. He had a wonderful attitude about the whole thing. God was going to handle this affair as far as David was concerned. It may be easy for us to criticize David, but do we today let God handle our enemies? We try to take things in our own hands and try to answer our accusers and deal with them ourselves. God says, "Let Me handle the situation, and you walk by faith. Trust Me." We are going to find out that David trusted the Lord, and He took care of Saul in time.

Then Saul said to David, Blessed be thou, my son David: thou shalt both do great things, and also shalt still prevail. So David went on his way, and Saul returned to his place [1 Sam. 26:25].

Although again Saul admitted he was wrong and gave up his pursuit of David, David knew it was only a temporary respite.

We find that David's heart is becoming very discouraged. He is weary of this continual running away and hiding in the dens of the earth.

DAVID RETREATS TO THE LAND OF PHILISTIA

And David said in his heart, I shall now perish one day by the hand of Saul: there is nothing better for me than that I should speedily escape into the land of the Philistines; and Saul shall despair of me, to seek me any more in any coast of Israel: so shall I escape out of his hand [1 Sam. 27:1].

This is obviously a departure from the high plain of faith that characterizes the life of David. It is a period of just letting down. We find that the same thing happened to Abraham. It happened to Isaac, and it happened to Jacob. In fact, it seems that most of God's men have had this low period in their lives.

There is a message for you and me in this chapter. Perhaps this very day you are faced with problems. Perhaps you have been in a dark valley for a long time, and you wonder if you will ever come through it. There seems to be no solution to your problems. Well, if it is any comfort to you, there are many others who have been in the same valley—it is a well-worn route. This man David walked that path long before you and I got here. This is one of the reasons David has been such a help to me in my own Christian life. I can certainly sympathize with him. It looks as though he may spend the rest of his life running and will finally be slain by Saul.

And David arose, and he passed over with the six hundred men that were with him unto Achish, the son of Maoch, king of Gath.

And David dwelt with Achish at Gath, he and his men, every man with his household, even David with his two wives, Ahinoam the Jezreelitess, and Abigail the Carmelitess, Nabal's wife.

And it was told Saul that David was fled to Gath: and he sought no more again for him.

And David said unto Achish, If I have now found grace in thine eyes, let them give me a place in some town in the country, that I may dwell there: for why should thy servant dwell in the royal city with thee?

Then Achish gave him Ziklag that day: wherefore Ziklag pertaineth unto the kings of Judah unto this day [1 Sam. 27:2–6].

Here is David—discouraged, despondent—doing something he should not have done. He leaves the land of Israel and goes to live among the Philistines. There is nothing in this chapter that would reveal that David is a man of God.

CHAPTER 28

THEME: Saul consults witch of En-dor

Saul's interview with the witch of En-dor poses and provokes many questions. The primary one relates to Samuel. Did she bring Samuel back from the dead? Several explanations have been forthcoming: (1) Some expositors dismiss it as a fraud, taking the position that the witch was a ventriloquist; (2) others maintain that an overwhelming desire to communicate with dead loved ones makes the bereaved victims of deceit; and (3) a third group believe that the witch actually brought Samuel back from the dead. This is untenable, and it is inconsistent with the rest of Scripture.

THE PHILISTINES PLAN AN ATTACK, AND SAUL CONSULTS THE WITCH OF EN-DOR

And it came to pass in those days, that the Philistines gathered their armies together for warfare, to fight with Israel. And Achish said unto David, Know thou assuredly, that thou shalt go out with me to battle, thou and thy men.

And David said to Achish, Surely thou shalt know what thy servant can do. And Achish said to David, Therefore will I make thee keeper of mine head for ever.

Now Samuel was dead, and all Israel had lamented him, and buried him in Ramah, even in his own city. And Saul had put away those that had familiar spirits, and the wizards, out of the land.

And the Philistines gathered themselves together, and came and pitched in Shunem: and Saul gathered all Israel together, and they pitched in Gilboa [1 Sam. 28:1–4].

Once again the Philistines were gathering their armies together to fight Israel. David gave no distinct promise that he would help them in their war with the Israelites—he certainly would avoid it if he could. Saul gathered his troops together at Gilboa.

> And when Saul saw the host of the Philistines, he was afraid, and his heart greatly trembled.
>
> And when Saul inquired of the LORD, the LORD answered him not, neither by dreams, nor by Urim, nor by prophets.
>
> Then said Saul unto his servants, Seek me a woman that hath a familiar spirit, that I may go to her, and inquire of her. And his servants said to him, Behold, there is a woman that hath a familiar spirit at En-dor [1 Sam. 28:5–7].

Since God was not speaking to Saul, he turned to Satan in desperation. The witch of En-dor was probably a ventriloquist. I think she was partly phony and partly given over to spiritism.

I would like to dwell on the subject of spiritism for a moment. We are living in a day of frills and thrills in religion. One of the avenues which thrill-seekers are exploring is modern spiritism, or ancient necromancy. Of course, the strongest argument they have is the witch of En-dor. They say she brought Samuel back from the dead. The question is, "Did Samuel really come back from the dead and communicate with Saul?" If so, it is the only instance of such a thing in the Scripture.

Before answering this question, I want you to look at some important background material. Scripture positively condemns the practice of necromancy. This is what Deuteronomy 18:9–14 says about the subject: "When thou art come into the land which the LORD thy God giveth thee, thou shalt not learn to do after the abominations of those nations. There shall not be found among you any one that maketh his son or his daughter to pass through the fire, or that useth divination, or an observer of times, or an enchanter, or a witch, or a charmer, or a consulter with familiar spirits, or a wizard, or a necromancer. For all that do these things are an abomination unto the LORD: and because of these abominations the LORD thy God doth drive them out from before thee. Thou shalt be perfect with the LORD thy God. For these nations, which thou shalt possess, hearkened unto observers of times, and unto diviners: but as for thee, the LORD thy God hath not suffered thee so to do." We are living in a day when there is a great deal of practice in the areas just mentioned.

In *Time* magazine, several years ago, two fortunetellers were listed. According to the magazine, most of the Hollywood stars consulted them in order to find out what the future held for them. We are seeing a revival of this today, but it has been going on a long time. Back in 1947 *The Guardian*, a publication of the Church of England, ran this article: "In spite of the large amount of fraud, fake, deceit, and thought-reading, conscious or unconscious, that the investigator of psychic research has to contend with, there remains a nucleus of genuine matter that cannot be explained with our present knowledge except by accepting the hypothesis that human personalities exist through death, and that certain persons have the power and gift of contacting them. Churches have nothing to fear from genuine psychic phenomena." It is amazing that since then there has been a growing interest in this matter of looking at the stars. The so-called science of ESP has also been growing. Many people have purchased horoscopes. Millions of dollars are going into the pockets of astrologers annually.

May I say to you that the Word of God absolutely condemns this sort of thing, and God has judged nations in the past because of it. He even put His own people out of the land for turning from Him to these different abominations. My friend, these are the dangerous practices of the hour. The Scriptures warn us of the danger and predict that there will be an outbreak of it.

You will find in the account of Lazarus, the beggar, and the rich man (Luke 16:19–31) that the rich man was strictly forbidden to return to the living. He was told that he could not. Paul was caught up to heaven and *silenced*—he could not tell what he had seen (2 Cor. 12:2–4). In 2 Thessalonians 2:9 Paul says, "Even him, whose coming is after the working of Satan with all power and signs and lying wonders." Paul, writing to a younger preacher, says, "Now the Spirit speaketh expressly, that in the latter times some shall depart from the faith, giving heed to seducing spirits, and doctrines of devils" (1 Tim. 4:1). We are seeing an increasing number of churches (they are *called* churches) where Satan is actually worshiped. This is something that the Word of God says will increase in the last days.

Now we find Saul going to the witch of En-dor.

> **And Saul disguised himself, and put on other raiment, and he went, and two men with him, and they came to the woman by night: and he said, I pray thee, divine unto me by the familiar spirit, and bring me him up, whom I shall name unto thee.**
>
> **And the woman said unto him, Behold, thou knowest what Saul hath done, how he hath cut off those that have familiar spirits, and the wizards, out of the land: wherefore then layest thou a snare for my life, to cause me to die?**
>
> **And Saul sware to her by the LORD, saying, As the LORD liveth, there shall no punishment happen to thee for this thing.**
>
> **Then said the woman, Whom shall I bring up unto thee? And he said, Bring me up Samuel.**
>
> **And when the woman saw Samuel, she cried with a loud voice: and the woman spake to Saul, saying, Why hast thou deceived me? for thou art Saul.**
>
> **And the king said unto her, be not afraid: for what sawest thou? And the woman said unto Saul, I saw gods ascending out of the earth [1 Sam. 28:8–13].**

Notice that this frightens the old witch. She sees supernatural creatures coming out of the ground.

> And he said unto her, What form is he of? And she said,
> An old man cometh up; and he is covered with a mantle.
> And Saul perceived that it was Samuel, and he stooped
> with his face to the ground, and bowed himself [1 Sam.
> 28:14].

If you read the account carefully, you will realize that Saul did not see Samuel. It was the witch, who may never have seen Samuel alive, who said she saw an old man covered with a mantle. Of course they jumped to the conclusion it was Samuel. When they did, he answered as Samuel—because demons can impersonate. Saul has laid himself wide open for Satan, and Satan has moved in.

> And Samuel said to Saul, Why hast thou disquieted me,
> to bring me up? And Saul answered, I am sore dis-
> tressed; for the Philistines make war against me, and
> God is departed from me, and answereth me no more,
> neither by prophets, nor by dreams: therefore I have
> called thee, that thou mayest make known unto me what
> I shall do [1 Sam. 28:15].

Saul is abandoned by God, and he is desperately afraid of the advancing Philistines.

> Then said Samuel, Wherefore then dost thou ask of me,
> seeing the LORD is departed from thee, and is become
> thine enemy?
>
> And the LORD hath done to him, as he spake by me: for
> the LORD hath rent the kingdom out of thine hand, and
> given it to thy neighbour, even to David:
>
> Because thou obeyedst not the voice of the LORD, nor ex-
> ecutedst his fierce wrath upon Amalek, therefore hath
> the LORD done this thing unto thee this day.
>
> Moreover the LORD will also deliver Israel with thee
> into the land of the Philistines: and to-morrow shalt

> thou and thy sons be with me: the LORD also shall deliver
> the host of Israel into the hand of the Philistines [1 Sam.
> 28:16–19].

It is interesting to note that nothing new is added. Saul does not get any new information. Samuel, before his death, had already pronounced the death, the destruction, and the rejection of Saul. Certainly Saul did not gain any comfort, any direction, or any new information from his excursion into the spirit world.

This reminds me of an account related by one of the friends of Job. By the way he introduces it, you would think that he had been given some tremendous revelation. Listen to him: "Now a thing was secretly brought to me, and mine ear received a little thereof. In thoughts from the visions of the night, when deep sleep falleth on men, fear came upon me, and trembling, which made all my bones to shake. Then a spirit passed before my face; the hair of my flesh stood up: it stood still, but I could not discern the form thereof: an image was before mine eyes, there was silence, and I heard a voice, saying, Shall mortal man be more just than God? shall a man be more pure than his maker?" (Job 4:12–17). After this man had this tremendous experience and went through these gyrations, what came out of it that was new? Nothing! "Shall mortal man be more just than God? shall a man be more pure than his maker?" That is a self-evident truth. The spirit revealed nothing new!

It is obvious from the account of the witch of En-dor that God was not in it. To begin with, God would not call Samuel up—Saul makes it clear that God was no longer speaking to him. Was Satan able to call up Samuel? That, of course, is the question.

In Scripture we need to understand that only Christ ever communicated with the dead. He alone can speak to the dead. This man Saul had been abandoned by God. As far as he is concerned, heaven is silent. And so Saul turns to hell. Now did Samuel appear to Saul? Several explanations have been offered. There are those who dismiss the entire incident as a fraud. They do not believe anything about it was genuine. They say the witch was a ventriloquist and put on the whole show. I think she was a fraud, too, but because she was as frightened as Saul at what happened, we can't rule out the supernatural.

Houdini, in his day, said he could duplicate 95 percent of the so-called supernatural things that spiritualism claimed it could and did do. Granted that 99 percent of it is fraud, what about the rest of it? I believe that what happened at En-dor was supernatural, but I do not believe God had a thing to do with it. There is, of course, another explanation for what happened and that is the desire of loved ones to communicate with those that have gone before. Both Sir Oliver Lodge and Sir Conan Doyle lost sons in war and wanted to see them. I believe even these men were taken in by spiritualism. Also, many others are deceived because of their strong desire to see their loved ones who are dead.

Kipling wrote a poem that I think is the answer to this.

> The road to En-dor is easy to tread
> For Mother or yearning Wife.
> There, it is sure, we shall meet our Dead
> As they were even in life.
> Earth has not dreamed of the blessing in store
> For desolate hearts on the road to En-dor.
>
> Whispers shall comfort us out of the dark—
> Hands—ah, God!—that we knew!
> Visions and voices—look and hark!—
> Shall prove that our tale is true,
> And that those who have passed to the further shore
> May be hailed—at a price—on the road to En-dor. . . .
>
> *Oh, the road to En-dor is the oldest road*
> *And the craziest road of all!*
> *Straight it runs to the Witch's abode,*
> *As it did in the days of Saul,*
> *And nothing is changed of the sorrow in store*
> *For such as go down the road to En-dor!*
> —Rudyard Kipling

There are those who say that the witch actually brought Samuel from the dead. I say to you that such an explanation is neither tenable nor consistent with the rest of Scripture. We are told in 1 Chronicles 10:13, "So Saul died for his transgression which he committed against the LORD, even against the word of the LORD, which he kept not, and also for asking counsel of one that had a familiar spirit, to inquire of it." God condemned the thing that Saul did.

There are those who use 1 Samuel 28:12 to prove that God caused Samuel to appear. "And when the woman saw Samuel, she cried with a loud voice: and the woman spake to Saul, saying, Why hast thou deceived me? for thou art Saul." I do not hold with this theory. I believe it was an impersonation by a false spirit rather than Samuel who appeared. God no longer spoke to Saul. Worse still, Saul no longer spoke to God. The dead cannot communicate with the living. This was satanic from beginning to end.

When I say that the dead cannot communicate with the living, there is one exception. Do you want to hear a voice from the dead? Well, listen to this: "And when I saw him, I fell at his feet as dead. And he laid his right hand upon me, saying unto me, Fear not; I am the first and the last: I am he that liveth, and was dead; and, behold, I am alive for evermore, Amen; and have the keys of hell and of death" (Rev. 1:17–18). It is the Lord Jesus Christ who holds the keys of the grave and of death. He has come back from the dead.

I have a question for you: Why do you want to traffic with a witch or a spirit who you think can give you inside information? If that one is actually in touch with the spirit world, the information comes from hell, not from heaven—for hell is speaking to this earth as well as heaven. Any communication coming that route which looks supernatural (and it may be supernatural) comes from the pit of hell. Why not listen to the Man who went down through the doorway of death and came back? He is the only One who made a two-way thoroughfare of it. He says, "I was dead. I am alive forevermore, and I have the keys of death and of the grave." If you want any information, go to Him. If you want help, go to Him. If you want salvation, go to Him. He went down through the portal of death for you and for me, and He came out in mighty power which He makes available to His own.

CHAPTERS 29 AND 30

THEME: David's life among the Philistines

As we saw in chapter 27, David had become so discouraged and despondent because of Saul's determination to kill him that he left the land of Israel. God had not told him to leave any more than He had told Abraham to leave the land. On the part of both these men it was a lapse in faith. So David stepped out of the land and moved over into the country of Philistia.

The Philistines were definitely the enemies of his people. David spent some time there and became a good friend of the king of Gath, who was one of the lords of the Philistines. Then when war broke out between the Israelites and the Philistines, David found himself in an awkward spot. Since he had become friends with at least one of the lords of the Philistines, he felt he should be his ally. But God intervened and prevented David from attacking his own people. This was a narrow escape for him. Had God not intervened, David would have done something that he would have regretted the rest of his life.

Christian friend, we do not realize how many times God intervenes in our lives. We sometimes overstep the boundaries God has set, and we are not where we should be, or we are not doing what we should be doing. When we make errors in judgment, many times God graciously intervenes to keep us from committing a terrible sin that we would regret the rest of our lives. I am sure you can look back upon your life and recall many such occasions.

> Now the Philistines gathered together all their armies to Aphek: and the Israelites pitched by a fountain which is in Jezreel.
>
> And the lords of the Philistines passed on by hundreds, and by thousands: but David and his men passed on in the rereward with Achish [1 Sam. 29:1–2].

When war was about to break out, David and his men marched with the Philistines. All the lords of the Philistines knew David, and when they saw him marching with them, they did not like it—and rightly so. I am sure that if you saw a person who had been your enemy suddenly turn and be on your side, you would want to make sure that he was not going to come up from the rear and attack you. That sometimes happens even among Christian brethren today. When a formerly unfriendly person suddenly becomes friendly, you wonder if he is really your friend or whether he has some ulterior motive in mind.

PHILISTINES DISTRUST DAVID TO BATTLE ISRAEL

Then said the princes of the Philistines, What do these Hebrews here? And Achish said unto the princes of the Philistines, Is not this David, the servant of Saul the king of Israel, which hath been with me these days, or these years, and I have found no fault in him since he fell unto me unto this day? [1 Sam. 29:3].

This Philistine lord, Achish, could find no fault with him because David had been a loyal fellow. He had never attempted to undermine him—David was not that kind of man. I think one of the tragedies in our Christian circles is men who attempt to undermine other Christians.

And the princes of the Philistines were wroth with him; and the princes of the Philistines said unto him, Make this fellow return, that he may go again to his place which thou hast appointed him, and let him not go down with us to battle, lest in the battle he be an adversary to us: for wherewith should he reconcile himself unto his master? should it not be with the heads of these men? [1 Sam. 29:4].

This is the way the Philistine lords reasoned, and there is a certain amount of logic in it. It could have been that David wanted to make peace with Saul, and what better way to do it than to turn and fight against the Philistines during the battle with Israel? That would certainly reconcile him to Saul. Since these men did not know David, they cannot be blamed for the position that they took.

Is not this David, of whom they sang one to another in dances, saying, Saul slew his thousands, and David his ten thousands? [1 Sam. 29:5].

These Philistine lords had heard about David; they knew he could be a formidable foe. So I believe their position was a reasonable and logical one. Achish, however, had full confidence in David.

Then Achish called David, and said unto him, Surely, as the LORD liveth, thou hast been upright, and thy going out and thy coming in with me in the host is good in my sight: for I have not found evil in thee since the day of thy coming unto me unto this day: nevertheless the lords favour thee not.

Wherefore now return, and go in peace, that thou displease not the lords of the Philistines [1 Sam. 29:6–7].

Achish is outvoted and outnumbered. The others will not have David, although Achish has confidence in him. In order to have harmony in their midst, Achish asks David to leave. This, my friend, is nothing but the providence of almighty God. It delivers David from fighting his own people.

And David said unto Achish, But what have I done? and what hast thou found in thy servant so long as I have been with thee unto this day, that I may not go fight against the enemies of my lord the king? [1 Sam. 29:8].

Although King Saul was David's enemy at the time, David would never turn against his own people. However, David's lapse of faith in stepping out of the land meant he was also stepping out of the will of God. This opened the way for sin to come into his life. The interesting thing is, Christian friend, that when a child of God steps out of the will of God, he will not lose his salvation, but he will have trouble.

In California, after World War II, a man came to see me. He was a young man when he was discharged from the service and was out of the will of God. While in this condition, he married an unsaved girl. His life had been a living hell from that day until the day I talked to him. His only solution to the problem was to get a divorce. I told him, "Don't get a divorce. Let her go if she wants to leave you, but stick it out, brother. This is what happened to you when you stepped out of God's will." You see, the child of God will not lose his salvation when he steps out of God's will, but he may get something he will wish he did not have. You will always get into trouble when you step out of the will of God. David stepped out of God's will and was about to commit an awful sin when God intervened.

So David and his men rose up early to depart in the morning, to return into the land of the Philistines. And the Philistines went up to Jezreel [1 Sam. 29:11].

Jezreel is in the north. If you have a good map, you ought to take a look at the geography at this point. It will make clearer a great deal of what is happening. Jezreel is near the Valley of Esdraelon. In fact, I would say it is part of it. It is here that the Scriptures tell us the last great War of Armageddon will be fought. It is being used as a wonderful fertile valley today.

As the Philistines go on up to Jezreel, David and his men start back home to Ziklag. It will not be a joyful homecoming, as we shall see.

DAVID FIGHTS AMALEKITES
FOR DESTROYING ZIKLAG

While David and his men were away for home, an enemy from the south, the Amalekites, invaded the Philistine country and destroyed

Ziklag. You will note by your map that Ziklag is way down in the south—even south of Beer-sheba—in the Philistine country.

> **And it came to pass, when David and his men were come to Ziklag on the third day, that the Amalekites had invaded the south, and Ziklag, and smitten Ziklag, and burned it with fire;**
>
> **And had taken the women captives, that were therein: they slew not any, either great or small, but carried them away, and went on their way.**
>
> **So David and his men came to the city, and, behold, it was burned with fire; and their wives, and their sons, and their daughters, were taken captives [1 Sam. 30:1–3].**

Can you appreciate the position of David and his six hundred followers? They had returned to Ziklag, the city which had become their home, expecting to be reunited with their families. They returned to find it burned with fire and deserted. David and his men were distraught. They had lost their wives and children! As far as they knew, their loved ones had been slain.

> **Then David and the people that were with him lifted up their voice and wept, until they had no more power to weep.**
>
> **And David's two wives were taken captives, Ahinoam the Jezreelitess, and Abigail the wife of Nabal the Carmelite [1 Sam. 30:4–5].**

This came as a great blow and a sorrow to David. Among the missing loved ones was his wife Abigail. You remember that Abigail had been married to a very rich man whose name was Nabal (meaning "fool"). After he had died, David had taken her to wife. She was the good part of David's life, and she was the only woman who was a blessing to him.

> And David was greatly distressed; for the people spake
> of stoning him, because the soul of all the people was
> grieved, every man for his sons and for his daughters:
> but David encouraged himself in the LORD his God
> [1 Sam. 30:6].

David was greatly distressed, not only because he lost his loved ones,
but because his men spoke of stoning him. Because David was the
leader, they blamed him for leaving Ziklag and going with the Philistines. David had made a blunder, a great blunder.

Most folk think of David as the shepherd boy who slew Goliath.
Also they remember the black side of his life, the great sin he committed with Bathsheba. What they don't realize is that David was very
much a human being like the rest of us. He made many blunders just
like we do. He made a mistake when he left Israel to live among the
Philistines. Now his men are ready to stone him "because the soul of
all the people was grieved, every man for his sons and for his daughters." Notice they do not seem to be grieving for their wives. Do you
know why? They think their wives have been slain but that their children are still alive. As the common colloquialism says it, David was
between a rock and a hard place. He was between the devil and the
deep blue sea. He was in a bad spot. He has lost his loved ones. His
own followers, under this great emotional strain of having lost their
loved ones, want to stone him. "But David encouraged himself in the
LORD his God." This is one of the most wonderful statements ever
made.

Friend, there are times in our lives when the circumstances will
not produce any joy or happiness. There are times when we find ourselves in dark places, like David. We look about, and the situation
looks hopeless. What should we do? Be discouraged? Give up? Say
we are through? Friend, if we are children of God, we will encourage
ourselves in the Lord. We will turn to Him at times like this. Sometimes the Lord puts us in such a spot so we will turn to Him. He wants
to make Himself real to us. It was during times like these that David
wrote some of his most helpful psalms. When troubles come, you can

thumb your way through the Psalms and find where David is encouraging himself in the Lord. Several times he says, "The LORD is good . . . Let the redeemed of the LORD say so." David found this to be true.

> **And David said to Abiathar the priest, Ahimelech's son,**
> **I pray thee, bring me hither the ephod. And Abiathar**
> **brought thither the ephod to David [1 Sam. 30:7].**

The ephod was a portion of the high priest's garments which speaks of prayer. This garment went over the garment that the regular priest wore. The ephod set the high priest apart. It was the garment he wore when he went into the golden altar of prayer. It had two stones, one on each shoulder, on which were engraved the names of the twelve tribes of Israel: six on one shoulder and six on the other. In other words, the high priest came to the altar of prayer bearing Israel on his shoulders. This is a picture of Christ, our Great High Priest, who carries us on His shoulders. Do you remember His story of that little sheep which got lost? What did the shepherd do? He put that lamb on his shoulders and brought him back. I do not know who you are or where you are, my friend, but I do know that the Lord is prepared to come and get you, put you on His shoulders, and bring you back to the fold. "Wherefore he is able also to save them to the uttermost that come unto God by him, seeing he ever liveth to make intercession for them" (Heb. 7:25).

> **And David inquired at the LORD, saying, Shall I pursue**
> **after this troop? shall I overtake them? And he an-**
> **swered him, Pursue: for thou shalt surely overtake**
> **them, and without fail recover all [1 Sam. 30:8].**

With the ephod, the garment of prayer, David went to God for direction. He talked to his High Priest, the One who was his Shepherd. David appealed to his Lord, and the Lord encouraged him to go after the enemy.

> So David went, he and the six hundred men that were
> with him, and came to the brook Besor, where those that
> were left behind stayed.

> But David pursued, he and four hundred men: for two
> hundred abode behind, which were so faint that they
> could not go over the brook Besor [1 Sam. 30:9–10].

All provisions had been taken, and these men were absolutely faint.
Two hundred of them could not make the trip because they had
marched double time.

> And they found an Egyptian in the field, and brought
> him to David, and gave him bread, and he did eat; and
> they made him drink water [1 Sam. 30:11].

On their way after the enemy, they found an Egyptian in the field. He
was sick and told David he was the servant of one of the Amalekite
leaders. When he got sick, they left him to die. David had overtaken
this man, but he has yet to overtake the enemy. He wants to know
where they are. The Egyptian servant says he will tell David what he
wants to know if David promises not to return him to his master.
David assures him that he will not be sent back to his master. The
Egyptian tells David what had happened at the burning of Ziklag,
then leads him to the Amalekites.

David makes a surprise attack upon the Amalekites as they are in
revelry, enjoying the victory and the spoils they have taken.

> And when he had brought him down, behold, they were
> spread abroad upon all the earth, eating and drinking,
> and dancing, because of all the great spoil that they had
> taken out of the land of the Philistines, and out of the
> land of Judah.

> And David smote them from the twilight even unto the
> evening of the next day: and there escaped not a man of

them, save four hundred young men, which rode upon camels, and fled [1 Sam. 30:16–17].

Only four hundred of the young men had transportation and were able to get away from David and his men. When the battle was over, David returned to Ziklag, along with the wives and children and all the flocks and herds that had been captured.

There was an argument among David's men as to whether the men who has not participated in the battle were entitled to any of the spoils. David put down a principle here, revealing his fairness which made him the kind of man God could use. The two hundred men who were not able to make the trip and do battle were to share equally in the booty. That revealed justice on the part of David.

CHAPTER 31

THEME: Saul and Jonathan die in battle

We have now come to the final chapter of 1 Samuel. The Philistines are fighting against Israel. Thank the Lord that David is not engaged in this battle. As you recall, the providence of God intervened to keep him out of it. Because the Philistines did not trust him to fight with them, he had withdrawn and returned to Ziklag. There he found his city looted and burned and the women and children taken captive. While David and his men are hunting down the Amalekites, Israel is fleeing before the Philistines. They are being defeated in this battle because they are out of the will of God. As we have seen, when the Philistines came against Saul and he asked God for direction, God was silent. That is the reason Saul resorted to the witch of En-dor. Because of his rebellion and sinfulness, God did not answer him and is not protecting him now.

> **Now the Philistines fought against Israel: and the men of Israel fled from before the Philistines, and fell down slain in mount Gilboa [1 Sam. 31:1].**

The battle goes against Israel from the very first.

> **And the Philistines followed hard upon Saul and upon his sons; and the Philistines slew Jonathan, and Abinadab, and Melchi-shua, Saul's sons.**
>
> **And the battle went sore against Saul, and the archers hit him; and he was sore wounded of the archers [1 Sam. 31:2–3].**

It is the beginning of the end for Saul. First he was hit in battle by an archer. Apparently it was someone who did not recognize that he had

hit the king. It was, shall we say, a real bull's-eye. It is also tragic that
Jonathan was slain in this battle. This is remarkable because on another occasion when Jonathan was fighting the Philistines, he slew
250 of the enemy at one time. This shows how hopelessly outnumbered Israel was at this time. This could well have been a battle in
which David and Jonathan would have been on opposite sides, but
God had intervened.

So we find that Saul is wounded.

> **Then said Saul unto his armour-bearer, Draw thy
> sword, and thrust me through therewith; lest these un-
> circumcised come and thrust me through, and abuse
> me. But his armour-bearer would not; for he was sore
> afraid. Therefore Saul took a sword, and fell upon it
> [1 Sam. 31:4].**

When Saul saw that he was mortally wounded, he felt that the enemy
would come and abuse him and taunt him. I think he was right. As we
have seen, Saul was a proud, egotistical man, and he did not feel that
such an end was becoming to him. His armor-bearer was afraid to lay
a hand on the king when Saul asked him to thrust him through with a
sword. So Saul took a sword and fell upon it. It looks as if Saul was a
suicide case.

Was it really a suicide?

> **And when his armour-bearer saw that Saul was dead,
> he fell likewise upon his sword, and died with him.**

> **So Saul died, and his three sons, and his armour-
> bearer, and all his men, that same day together.**

> **And when the men of Israel that were on the other side of
> the valley, and they that were on the other side Jordan,
> saw that the men of Israel fled, and that Saul and his
> sons were dead, they forsook the cities, and fled; and the
> Philistines came and dwelt in them.**

> And it came to pass on the morrow, when the Philistines
> came to strip the slain, that they found Saul and his
> three sons fallen in mount Gilboa.
>
> And they cut off his head, and stripped off his armour,
> and sent into the land of the Philistines round about, to
> publish it in the house of their idols, and among the peo-
> ple [1 Sam. 31:5–9].

We begin to see now, with Saul's armour being sent around, why he
tried to get David to wear it when he fought Goliath. Had David won
the battle wearing Saul's armor, the king would have gotten the credit
for the victory. A case in point involves one of his sons. When Jonathan won a victory, instead of giving him credit for it, Saul blew the
trumpet in the land and took the credit himself.

> And they put his armour in the house of Ashtaroth: and
> they fastened his body to the wall of Beth-shan.
>
> And when the inhabitants of Jabesh-gilead heard of that
> which the Philistines had done to Saul;
>
> All the valiant men arose, and went all night, and took
> the body of Saul and the bodies of his sons from the wall
> of Beth-shan, and came to Jabesh, and burnt them there.
>
> And they took their bones, and buried them under a tree
> at Jabesh, and fasted seven days [1 Sam. 31:10–13].

This concludes the Book of 1 Samuel. Someone says, "Well, there
wasn't such a mystery about the death of Saul after all." We are not
through with this story yet. We will pick it up again in the book of
2 Samuel. We are going to find that Saul spared the Amalekites, and
Samuel rebuked him for it. He told Saul, "To obey is better than sacrifice and to hearken than the fat of rams." God wanted obedience, and
Saul's heart never bowed to almighty God. It is interesting that Saul
spared the Amalekites, and we are going to find that it may have been
the Amalekites who actually killed Saul. "But," someone says, "we

have already read the record that says the Philistines killed Saul. An archer shot him, and he was mortally wounded. He tried to get his armor-bearer to kill him, but the man would not. Finally, Saul fell on his own sword. Isn't that the explanation? Isn't it a closed case? Wasn't it all wrapped up by the Beth-shan police department?" I don't think so. Second Samuel is going to give us some more information.

(For Bibliography to 1 Samuel, see Bibliography at the end of 2 Samuel.)

The Book of
2 SAMUEL

(For introductory material to 2 Samuel, see the Book of 1 Samuel.)

OUTLINE

I. **Triumphs of David, Chapters 1—10**
   A. David Mourns the Death of Saul and Jonathan, Chapter 1
   B. David Made King over Judah, Chapter 2
   C. Civil War—Abner Joins with David but Is Murdered by Joab, Chapter 3
   D. Ish-bosheth, the Son of Saul, Killed, Chapter 4
   E. David Made King over All Israel; Moves His Capital to Jerusalem, Chapter 5
   F. David's Wrong and Right Attempts to Bring the Ark to Jerusalem, Chapter 6
   G. God's Covenant to Build the House of David, Chapter 7
   H. David Consolidates His Kingdom, Chapter 8
   I. David Befriends Mephibosheth, Chapter 9
   J. David Wars against Ammon and Syria, Chapter 10

II. **Troubles of David, Chapters 11—24**
   A. David's Two Great Sins, Chapter 11
   B. Nathan Faces David with His Sins; David Repents, Chapter 12
   C. David's Daughter Tamar Raped by Amnon, David's Son; Amnon Is Murdered by Absalom, David's Son, Chapter 13
   D. David Permits Absalom to Return with Half-hearted Forgiveness, Chapter 14
   E. Absalom Rebels against David, Chapter 15
   F. Ziba, Mophibosheth's Servant, Deceives David; Shimei Curses David, Chapter 16
   G. Absalom's Advisers (Ahithophel and Hushai) Disagree on Attack against David, Chapter 17
   H. Absalom Is Slain and David Mourns, Chapter 18
   I. David Is Restored to Throne, Chapter 19
   J. Sheba Revolts against David, Chapter 20
   K. Three-Year Famine; Gibeonites Take Vengeance on House of Saul; War with Philistines, Chapter 21

CHAPTER 1

THEME: David mourns the deaths of Saul and Jonathan

In this chapter David mourns the deaths of Saul and Jonathan. The question of who killed Saul may not be answered completely in this chapter, but another suspect is added. A young Amalekite, who came out of the camp of Israel, reported to David the death of Saul and claimed credit for slaying him. David executed the young man for the crime. David's grief over the deaths of Saul and Jonathan is touching, poetic, and dramatic. It is a striking lamentation.

Here we are introduced to another suspect in the death of Saul.

> **Now it came to pass after the death of Saul, when David was returned from the slaughter of the Amalekites, and David had abode two days in Ziklag;**
>
> **It came even to pass on the third day, that, behold, a man came out of the camp from Saul with his clothes rent, and earth upon his head: and so it was, when he came to David, that he fell to the earth, and did obeisance [2 Sam. 1:1–2].**

This was a dark day in the history of Israel. War and defeat had come to these people because they were out of the will of God. There is a lesson for us in this. At the end of World War II we thought we had brought peace to the world, and we expected to rest on our laurels from then on and to enjoy life in sin, far from God. That, I am sure, is one of the reasons the world has not had a day of peace since the end of World War II. It has been continual war for us ever since. There will be turmoil and warfare for a nation, a people, or an individual who is out of the will of God. "There is no peace, saith my God, to the wicked" (Isa. 57:21). Isaiah said that three times. I wonder if that might not be applicable to us today.

As I have said, it was a dark day for Israel. You can see their position. King Saul was dead. Jonathan and his three sons were dead. Israel had lost the battle. The Philistines had taken all the northern area around Galilee, and now they had gained ground in the south.

David did not know what had happened in the battle. He and his men had been recovering their own loved ones from the Amalekite marauders. They had been back in Ziklag for two days without hearing a word. Finally, a man all disheveled, covered with mud and dirt and wearing torn clothes, stumbled into David's camp. He said he had come from the war. He told David that the Philistines had won the war and that Saul was dead. Then he told David what had happened.

And David said unto him, From whence comest thou? And he said unto him, Out of the camp of Israel am I escaped.

And David said unto him, How went the matter? I pray thee, tell me. And he answered, That the people are fled from the battle, and many of the people also are fallen and dead; and Saul and Jonathan his son are dead also.

And David said unto the young man that told him, How knowest thou that Saul and Jonathan his son be dead?

And the young man that told him said, As I happened by chance upon mount Gilboa, behold, Saul leaned upon his spear; and, lo, the chariots and horsemen followed hard after him.

And when he looked behind him, he saw me, and called unto me. And I answered, Here am I.

And he said unto me, Who art thou? And I answered him, I am an Amalekite.

He said unto me again, Stand, I pray thee, upon me, and slay me: for anguish is come upon me, because my life is yet whole in me.

> So I stood upon him, and slew him, because I was sure
> that he could not live after that he was fallen: and I took
> the crown that was upon his head, and the bracelet that
> was on his arm, and have brought them hither unto my
> lord [2 Sam. 1:3–10].

Is this Amalekite speaking the truth? Or did he come upon the body of
Saul and, finding him dead, take the crown and bracelet and bring
them to David? I am of the opinion that when this Amalekite found
Saul, after he had fallen on his sword, he was still alive. When this
Amalekite came by, Saul asked him to finish the job. The interesting
thing is that this young man confessed to David what he had done,
and it sounds as though he expected David to give him a medal for his
deed and put him on a life pension.

> Then David took hold on his clothes, and rent them; and
> likewise all the men that were with him:
>
> And they mourned, and wept, and fasted until even, for
> Saul, and for Jonathan his son, and for the people of the
> LORD, and for the house of Israel; because they were
> fallen by the sword.
>
> And David said unto the young man that told him,
> Whence art thou? And he answered, I am the son of a
> stranger, an Amalekite.
>
> And David said unto him, How wast thou not afraid to
> stretch forth thine hand to destroy the LORD's anointed?
> [2 Sam. 1:11–14].

If this man did slay Saul, it was because Saul had disobeyed God
when he refused to slay all of the Amalekites back in the Book of
1 Samuel. Had Saul obeyed God, this man would not have been alive
to kill him, and perhaps Saul would have survived. David asked this
young man how it was that he was unafraid to touch the Lord's

anointed. David, you remember, would not take Saul's life even though he had opportunity. It is well sometimes to see things from God's viewpoint. As long as Saul was king, David would not touch him. No one else had better touch him either because God is the one who put the crown on his head, and God should be the one to take it off when the time comes.

There is danger in interfering with God's work. I could tell you some very interesting stories about folk who have attempted to interfere with God's work, God's program, and God's man. God moves in and judges. He has always done it. That is why David said to this young Amalekite, "Weren't you afraid to stretch forth your hand to destroy the Lord's anointed?"

And David called one of the young men, and said, Go near, and fall upon him. And he smote him that he died [2 Sam. 1:15].

David judged the Amalekite for touching the Lord's anointed.

And David said unto him, Thy blood be upon thy head; for thy mouth hath testified against thee, saying, I have slain the LORD's anointed [2 Sam. 1:16].

If this man made up his story and confession, it certainly was a fatal thing to do. David told him, "If you have lied to me, then your blood is upon you, because you confessed that you killed the Lord's anointed." I believe the young man really did kill Saul. He did what David would never have done, and David judged him for it.

And David lamented with this lamentation over Saul and over Jonathan his son [2 Sam. 1:17].

David's grief for Saul and Jonathan is revealed here, and it is genuine.

**(Also he bade them teach the children of Judah the use
of the bow: behold, it is written in the book of Jasher.)
[2 Sam. 1:18].**

Saul had taught Israel something. He made a contribution. You see,
the Israelites had no iron weapons of war, so Saul taught them to be
bowmen. The bow and arrow was a formidable weapon. Many of our
ancestors would testify to that. The Indians used the bow and arrow to
hold back their enemies and win many battles.

**The beauty of Israel is slain upon thy high places: how
are the mighty fallen! [2 Sam. 1:19].**

His lamentation is written in the poetic form which came so naturally
to the "sweet psalmist of Israel."

**Tell it not in Gath, publish it not in the streets of Aske-
lon; lest the daughters of the Philistines rejoice, lest the
daughters of the uncircumcised triumph [2 Sam. 1:20].**

"Tell it not in Gath"—Gath was the capital of the Philistines. "Publish
it not in the streets of Askelon." Askelon is in the Gaza strip and is one
of the five cities of the Philistines.

**Ye mountains of Gilboa, let there be no dew, neither let
there be rain, upon you, nor fields of offerings: for there
the shield of the mighty is vilely cast away, the shield of
Saul, as though he had not been anointed with oil.**

**From the blood of the slain, from the fat of the mighty,
the bow of Jonathan turned not back, and the sword of
Saul returned not empty [2 Sam. 1:21–22].**

No one could say that either Saul or Jonathan was a coward.

> Saul and Jonathan were lovely and pleasant in their
> lives, and in their death they were not divided: they
> were swifter than eagles, they were stronger than lions.
>
> Ye daughters of Israel, weep over Saul, who clothed you
> in scarlet, with other delights, who put on ornaments of
> gold upon your apparel [2 Sam. 1:23–24].

Saul had brought prosperity to the land.

> How are the mighty fallen in the midst of the battle! O
> Jonathan, thou wast slain in thine high places [2 Sam.
> 1:25].

David and Jonathan were bosom friends. They loved each other.
David's grief is sincere.

> I am distressed for thee, my brother Jonathan; very
> pleasant hast thou been unto me: thy love to me was
> wonderful, passing the love of women [2 Sam. 1:26].

It is interesting that David says, "passing the love of women," because
he was married to Jonathan's sister. Later we will find that she betrays
David. I think Michal loved him as a hero in the beginning, but the
day came when she despised him.

David was not very successful in his love affairs. Abigail is the
only noble woman that I have found in his retinue. I disagree with
those who think Bathsheba was outstanding. I do not think she was.
Although his relations with her were absolutely David's sin, and God
judged him for it, why was she parading around on the roof like that?
David had his problems with women, but he could say of Jonathan
that he was a man who was true and loyal to him unto death. It is
interesting to note that the men who were David's followers were loyal
to him through thick and thin. He had that charisma which caused his
men to stick with him. David was that type of man.

How are the mighty fallen, and the weapons of war perished! [2 Sam. 1:27].

This is a tremendous tribute to Jonathan in particular. David's grief over the deaths of Saul and Jonathan is touching. It is one of the most striking lamentations in the Word of God.

We are going to see in the next chapter that David is made king over Judah. We will also meet Abner, who was Saul's captain. Now, not all of Saul's sons had been killed, though all of them that fought in the battle were killed. But Saul had a younger son named Ish-bosheth. Abner made him king over the eleven remaining tribes and, of course, civil war broke out. David defeated Abner and the army, and after a long civil war had weakened the nation, David finally became king of all twelve tribes. He made Hebron his home at first. Later he moved to Mt. Zion in Jerusalem, which was the place that he loved above all others.

We are coming to a section that is historical. Although many people find it uninteresting, we are going to find some of the most thrilling accounts in the entire Word of God in this section. Also we find some marvelous spiritual lessons there.

CHAPTERS 2 AND 3

THEME: David made king over Judah

David, by God's direction, goes up to Hebron where he is made king over the tribe of Judah. Abner, the captain of Saul's army, makes Saul's son Ish-bosheth the king over the other eleven tribes of Israel. Civil war ensues.

> **And it came to pass after this, that David inquired of the Lord, saying, Shall I go up into any of the cities of Judah? And the Lord said unto him, Go up. And David said, Whither shall I go up? And he said, Unto Hebron [2 Sam. 2:1].**

"After this" refers to the time after the deaths of Saul and Jonathan and the period of mourning for them. Now that Saul is out of the picture, David wants to know what to do. He asks the Lord, "Shall I go up into any of the cities of Judah?" Why did he ask that question? He is in Philistine country. Saul is dead, and David is to be the next king. What should his next move be? He waited until he received his instructions from the Lord. David had learned that he must wait on the Lord for direction.

God told him to go up to Hebron. Hebron is located in the south of the land, not too far from the Philistine border. God is telling him to move cautiously. He is not to go up and arbitrarily take over Israel, but to move up into the land to make himself available.

> **So David went up thither, and his two wives also, Ahinoam the Jezreelitess, and Abigail Nabal's wife the Carmelite [2 Sam. 2:2].**

When David headed for Hebron, he took with him the two women who were his wives at this time. Perhaps you are asking, "Does God approve of a man having two wives?" No. This matter will cause David a great deal of trouble—and later he will have other wives.

> **And his men that were with him did David bring up, every man with his household: and they dwelt in the cities of Hebron [2 Sam. 2:3].**

David's loyal followers came with him and settled their families in the cities of Hebron.

> **And the men of Judah came, and there they anointed David king over the house of Judah. And they told David, saying, That the men of Jabesh-gilead were they that buried Saul [2 Sam. 2:4].**

Now that David has made himself available, the men of his own tribe come to anoint him king over Judah.

> **And David sent messengers unto the men of Jabesh-gilead, and said unto them, Blessed be ye of the LORD, that ye have shewed this kindness unto your lord, even unto Saul, and have buried him [2 Sam. 2:5].**

David does a very wise thing. The men who buried Saul were devoted to him, and now David thanks them for it. David has a great respect for the anointed of the Lord—he had two opportunities to slay him and make himself king, but he did not do it. David's good points are often passed over, because his sin seems to obscure them. It is like a cloud that covers the sky and shuts out the sunshine of his life. In many respects David was a wonderful man. Afterward he paid for his great sin every day of his life.

David complimented the men of Jabesh-gilead.

> **And now the LORD shew kindness and truth unto you: and I also will requite you this kindness, because ye have done this thing.**

> Therefore now let your hands be strengthened, and be ye
> valiant: for your master Saul is dead, and also the house
> of Judah have anointed me king over them [2 Sam.
> 2:6-7].

Then he asked for their support and devotion to him as king, even as
they had given it to Saul. Notice that he is moving in a diplomatic and
commendable manner at this time. We should recognize the fact that
both Saul and Jonathan had sons, and one of them would have been
the normal one to come to the throne had not God intervened. Abner,
who had been captain of Saul's hosts, moved immediately to make
one of them king. Notice what he did.

> But Abner the son of Ner, captain of Saul's host, took
> Ish-bosheth the son of Saul, and brought him over to
> Mahanaim;
>
> And made him king over Gilead, and over the Ashur-
> ites, and over Jezreel, and over Ephraim, and over Ben-
> jamin, and over all Israel [2 Sam. 2:8-9].

Here is the beginning of the division of the kingdom which will come
after the reign of Solomon when Jeroboam leads a rebellion. This is
the first fracture. At first David is made king over the southern kingdom of Judah, but the northern tribes make Ish-bosheth, a son of Saul,
their king.

> Ish-bosheth Saul's son was forty years old when he be-
> gan to reign over Israel, and reigned two years. But the
> house of Judah followed David.
>
> And the time that David was king in Hebron over the
> house of Judah was seven years and six months [2 Sam.
> 2:10-11].

This was an interval of civil war: war between the northern kingdom
and David's kingdom, Judah, in the south. It depleted the resources
and energy of the nation. It was indeed a tragic thing.

> **And Abner the son of Ner, and the servants of Ish-bosheth the son of Saul, went out from Mahanaim to Gibeon.**
>
> **And Joab the son of Zeruiah, and the servants of David, went out, and met together by the pool of Gibeon: and they sat down, the one on the one side of the pool, and the other on the other side of the pool [2 Sam. 2:12–13].**

Abner and Joab were attempting to negotiate a solution to prevent civil war. But as you well know (and certainly we in this country ought to know by now), when you have folk on one side who are determined on one course and people on the other side who are determined on another course, negotiation is practically valueless. It is generally an exercise in futility, and that is what happens here.

> **And Abner said to Joab, Let the young men now arise, and play before us. And Joab said, Let them arise.**
>
> **Then there arose and went over by number twelve of Benjamin, which pertained to Ish-bosheth the son of Saul, and twelve of the servants of David.**
>
> **And they caught every one his fellow by the head, and thrust his sword in his fellow's side; so they fell down together: wherefore that place was called Helkath-hazzurim, which is in Gibeon [2 Sam. 2:14–16].**

Abner said, "Let the young men come together in battle." Joab agreed. This was the way they were going to settle the issue.

> **And there was a very sore battle that day; and Abner was beaten, and the men of Israel, before the servants of David [2 Sam. 2:17].**

David is a veteran of many campaigns now. He is not the innocent little shepherd we met at first. He has spent time hiding in the caves and dens of the earth, and he has collected men of war around him. He is rugged and adept at this type of warfare. So his men are able to win a victory over Abner and his "host," an army of superior numbers.

Now I want to call your attention to something that took place which will play a prominent part later on. Abner was followed by Asahel. Asahel was a brother of Joab, who was David's captain. Abner was Saul's captain.

> And there were three sons of Zeruiah there, Joab, and Abishai, and Asahel: and Asahel was as light of foot as a wild roe [2 Sam. 2:18].

Zeruriah, by the way, was a sister of David. She had three outstanding sons.

> And Asashel pursued after Abner; and in going he turned not to the right hand nor to the left from following Abner [2 Sam. 2:19].

Asahel took out after Abner. He is not a match for him at all, and Abner warns him.

> And Abner said again to Asahel, Turn thee aside from following me: wherefore should I smite thee to the ground? how then should I hold up my face to Joab thy brother?

> Howbeit he refused to turn aside: wherefore Abner with the hinder end of the spear smote him under the fifth rib, that the spear came out behind him; and he fell down there, and died in the same place: and it came to pass, that as many as came to the place where Asahel fell down and died stood still [2 Sam. 2:22–23].

Abner warned him to stop his pursuit. Asahel refused, and finally Abner turned around and drove a spear through him. Abner killed the brother of Joab. That means that in Joab's heart there will be bitterness, hatred, and the desire to get revenge. His revenge will come later, as we shall see.

And they took up Asahel, and buried him in the sepulchre of his father, which was in Beth-lehem. And Joab and his men went all night, and they came to Hebron at break of day [2 Sam. 2:32].

Asahel's funeral closes this chapter. After the funeral Joab and his men "went all night" and came to Hebron at the break of day. They reported to David all that had taken place.

CIVIL WAR CONTINUES

Chapter 3 continues the account of the long civil war that weakened the nation. Gradually David gained in strength. Abner, after a falling-out with Ish-bosheth, deserted to David. Joab, David's captain, suspected Abner and, seeking revenge for his brother Asahel's death, murdered him.

Now there was long war between the house of Saul and the house of David: but David waxed stronger and stronger, and the house of Saul waxed weaker and weaker [2 Sam. 3:1].

The condition of the land is one of internal strife. There is civil war. The nation's energies are being depleted, and their resources are being exhausted. David has been in Hebron for seven and one-half years.

And unto David were sons born in Hebron: and his first-born was Amnon, of Ahinoam the Jezreelitess;

And his second, Chileab, of Abigail the wife of Nabal the Carmelite; and the third, Absalom the son of Maacah the daughter of Talmai king of Geshur;

> And the fourth, Adonijah the son of Haggith; and the
> fifth, Shephatiah the son of Abital;
>
> And the sixth, Ithream, by Eglah David's wife. These
> were born to David in Hebron [2 Sam. 3:2–5].

You can see that David had more than two wives. He had others, and
this will cause a great problem for David. God did not approve, and
David did not get by with this. Among the list of David's sons is one
by the name of Absalom. I am sure you are familiar with his story.
Later on we will see him lead a rebellion against David. This is the son
that David apparently wanted to follow him as king, but he was brutally killed by Joab in battle. It broke David's heart when he was slain.
Who is the mother of Absalom? Maacah who was the daughter of Talmai, king of Geshur. Who was the king of Geshur? If you go back to
1 Samuel 27:8, you will find that David and his men invaded the
Geshurites, and the Gezrites, and the Amalekites. I believe David was
wrong in doing this. He slew these people, including the king of
Geshur, and apparently took his daughter captive. She eventually became his wife. They had a son, and it was this young man who led the
rebellion against David. My friend, God saw to it that David did not
get away with his sin. It is important for us to note this.

ABNER JOINS WITH DAVID

This chapter tells us about a long period of civil war that in many
ways is uninteresting as far as you and I are concerned. Abner, who
had been the chief captain of Saul's army, had pushed Ish-bosheth,
Saul's son, onto the throne. Being an older man who had had such a
high position, he was not apt to listen to the young king. He did something he should not have done.

> And Saul had a concubine, whose name was Rizpah,
> the daughter of Aiah: and Ish-bosheth said to Abner,
> Wherefore hast thou gone in unto my father's concu-
> bine?

Then was Abner very wroth for the words of Ish-bosheth, and said, Am I a dog's head, which against Judah do shew kindness this day unto the house of Saul thy father, to his brethren, and to his friends, and have not delivered thee into the hand of David, that thou chargest me to-day with a fault concerning this woman? [2 Sam. 3:7-8].

It was the exclusive right of the man who was the successor to the throne to cohabit with the deceased king's concubines. Abner infringed on the rights of Ish-bosheth and became angry when the king rebuked him for taking Rizpah, one of Saul's concubines, into his own harem. Candidly, the young king was justified in rebuking Abner, but Abner became so enraged that he immediately began to make overtures to David.

So do God to Abner, and more also, except, as the Lord hath sworn to David, even so I do to him;

To translate the kingdom from the house of Saul, and to set up the throne of David over Israel and over Judah, from Dan even to Beer-sheba.

And he could not answer Abner a word again, because he feared him [2 Sam. 3:9-11].

In other words, Abner made known his intention of abandoning the house of Saul and allying himself with David. He was going to help David become king over the twelve tribes. Now Ish-bosheth did not say a word to Abner. He was a son of Saul, but he had no army and no training whatsoever. He was not a warrior like his brother Jonathan. He had been brought up in the king's palace. And he feared Abner.

And Abner sent messengers to David on his behalf, saying, Whose is the land? saying also, Make thy league with me, and, behold, my hand shall be with thee, to bring about all Israel unto thee.

> And he said, Well; I will make a league with thee: but
> one thing I require of thee, that is, Thou shalt not see my
> face, except thou first bring Michal Saul's daughter,
> when thou comest to see my face [2 Sam. 3:12–13].

David told Abner he could come only if he brought Saul's daughter,
Michal, with him. You remember that Michal was David's first wife.
Saul had taken her away from David. Believe me, David had a checkered career. This is the reason he suffered—he let sin enter his life. But
above it all was a faith in God that never failed. He wanted more than
all else to have a wonderful relationship with God.

> And Ish-bosheth sent, and took her from her husband,
> even from Phaltiel the son of Laish.

> And her husband went with her along weeping behind
> her to Bahurim. Then said Abner unto him, Go, return.
> And he returned [2 Sam. 3:15–16].

Abner's overture was accepted by David. We will find now that David
will become king of all twelve tribes because of Abner's treachery.

JOAB MURDERS ABNER

All of this time Joab has not forgotten that Abner had slain his
brother.

> And when Abner was returned to Hebron, Joab took him
> aside in the gate to speak with him quietly, and smote
> him there under the fifth rib, that he died, for the blood
> of Asahel his brother [2 Sam. 3:27].

So Joab avenged his brother's death. When David heard that Joab had
murdered Abner, he did not approve of it at all. In fact, he accused
Joab of doing a very terrible thing. Concerning Abner's death he said a
very interesting thing.

And the king lamented over Abner, and said, Died Abner as a fool dieth? [2 Sam. 3:33].

Why did David say that? It certainly is a strange epitaph to give a person. Abner was in Hebron. Hebron was one of the cities of refuge where a murderer was safe. In that city Joab could not have touched him. But Joab quietly took Abner aside and said to him, "Come out here. I want to talk with you. You are the captain on one side, and I am the captain on the other side. It would be nice if we could get together." So Abner stepped outside the city of refuge, and Joab killed him. That is why David said Abner died as a fool dies. He was a fool to leave Hebron.

Isn't that a message for us today? There is a refuge for every sinner in Christ. Regardless of how high a man's IQ is or what his position in life might be, if he is outside the place of refuge, he is lost. If the truth were told at many funerals today, the preachers would have to say about the departed person, "A fool has just died. He would not turn to Jesus Christ who is the place of refuge." Are you resting in Christ?

CHAPTERS 4 AND 5

THEME: David is made king over all of Israel

ISH-BOSHETH, THE SON OF SAUL, IS KILLED

Troubled times for the nation Israel continue in this chapter. Internal strife and civil war followed the deaths of Saul and Jonathan. It was a time of great heartache and heartbreak for God's people.

This section of the Word of God is usually passed over. I am confident, however, that it has been given to us for at least two reasons: (1) To show us the family of the Lord Jesus Christ and to give us His genealogy; and (2) to give us an example. Paul tells us, "Now all these things happened unto them for ensamples: and they are written for our admonition . . ." (1 Cor. 10:11). It has been given to us that it might minister to us in a spiritual way.

We have already seen that there had been a rebellion against David, who had been made king of the tribe of Judah. He had moved to Hebron, which was situated just at the edge of the kingdom in the south. Abner had led a rebellion by putting Ish-bosheth, Saul's son, on the throne. But because Ish-bosheth reprimanded and rebuked him for taking one of Saul's concubines into his own harem, Abner left the house of Saul and allied himself with David. This was a mistake, because Joab was waiting to kill Abner in revenge for the slaying of his brother Asahel.

Now that Ish-bosheth has lost Abner, his military captain, his army is weak. He knows he cannot maintain his kingdom against David without an army. Abner has been murdered. What is he going to do?

> And when Saul's son heard that Abner was dead in Hebron, his hands were feeble, and all the Israelites were troubled.
>
> And Saul's son had two men that were captains of bands: the name of the one was Baanah, and the name of

> the other Rechab, the sons of Rimmon a Beerothite, of
> the children of Benjamin: (for Beeroth also was reck-
> oned to Benjamin:
>
> And the Beerothites fled to Gittaim, and were sojourners
> there until this day.) [2 Sam. 4:1-3].

The Beerothites were ejected by Saul and they fled to Gittaim.
Beeroth, their town, passed into the possession of Benjamin.

> And Jonathan, Saul's son, had a son that was lame of his
> feet. He was five years old when the tidings came of Saul
> and Jonathan out of Jezreel, and his nurse took him up,
> and fled: and it came to pass, as she made haste to flee,
> that he fell, and became lame. And his name was Me-
> phibosheth [2 Sam. 4:4].

Mephibosheth is an unusual name, but please remember it. The story
about Mephibosheth and David is one of the most beautiful stories
ever told. This boy was Jonathan's son. As long as he lived, he was a
constant danger to David because he had throne rights. Since he was
Jonathan's son, however, David would never harm a hair of his head.
Later on David will go looking for family members of Saul and Jonathan, not to slay them, but to show them kindness.

> And the sons of Rimmon the Beerothite, Rechab and
> Baanah, went, and came about the heat of the day to the
> house of Ish-bosheth, who lay on a bed at noon.
>
> And they came thither into the midst of the house, as
> though they would have fetched wheat; and they smote
> him under the fifth rib: and Rechab and Baanah his
> brother escaped [2 Sam. 4:5-6].

These two underlings, Rechab and Baanah, were petty officers under
Abner in the army of Saul. When they discovered that Abner was
dead—and they recognized the strength and power of David—they

conspired to put Ish-bosheth, the son of Saul, to death. When Ish-bosheth was in bed, they slipped in upon him and slew him. It was a bloody, ugly thing that they did. It was also a mistake, by the way. By killing this man they expected to make peace with David. In fact, they thought David would reward them for their act.

> For when they came into the house, he lay on his bed in his bedchamber, and they smote him, and slew him, and beheaded him, and took his head, and gat them away through the plain all night.

> And they brought the head of Ish-bosheth unto David to Hebron, and said to the king, Behold the head of Ish-bosheth the son of Saul thine enemy, which sought thy life; and the LORD hath avenged my lord the king this day of Saul, and of his seed [2 Sam. 4:7-8].

They took the head of Ish-bosheth (imagine that!) to David. David was not about to accept it. David would never approve a thing like that.

> And David commanded his young men, and they slew them, and cut off their hands and their feet, and hanged them up over the pool in Hebron. But they took the head of Ish-bosheth, and buried it in the sepulchre of Abner in Hebron [2 Sam. 4:12].

Rechab and Baanah were murderers—murderers of a king. David executed them summarily for their dastardly deed.

The eleven tribes in the north recognize that they no longer have any leadership and that it is foolish to carry on rebellion against David at this time. So they attempt to make overtures of peace.

DAVID IS MADE KING OVER ALL OF ISRAEL

> Then came all the tribes of Israel to David unto Hebron, and spake, saying, Behold, we are thy bone and thy flesh [2 Sam. 5:1].

The tribes sent representatives to David. They said, "Behold we are thy bone and thy flesh." That was true. This civil war was terrible, especially because the tribes were fighting each other.

Personally, I think the worst war that this country fought was the Civil War. Looking back at it, that war seemed almost unnecessary. Certainly slavery is wrong, but it should have been abolished by means other than war. The hotheads and the protesters in that day were the ones who got the country in trouble. That is the reason I am opposed to all hot headed protesters—regardless of what side they are on. They are typical of the crowd that got this nation into the trouble during the Civil War. Men like General Grant, Abraham Lincoln, and Robert E. Lee simply found themselves in an awkward situation. In the city of Atlanta you can still see the scars of the Civil War.

The nation of Israel, after more than seven years of civil war, is reunited under David. Now it enters the greatest period it has ever enjoyed. This period foreshadows the day when Christ will come and rule.

> **Also in time past, when Saul was king over us, thou wast he that leddest out and broughtest in Israel: and the LORD said to thee, Thou shalt feed my people Israel, and thou shalt be a captain over Israel [2 Sam. 5:2].**

The tribes are rather late in acknowledging David as the legitimate and God-appointed ruler over them. They should have recognized him long before this, but they did not.

> **So all the elders of Israel came to the king to Hebron; and king David made a league with them in Hebron before the LORD: and they anointed David king over Israel.**

> **David was thirty years old when he began to reign, and he reigned forty years.**

> **In Hebron he reigned over Judah seven years and six months: and in Jerusalem he reigned thirty and three years over all Israel and Judah [2 Sam. 5:3–5].**

Israel is about to enter its greatest period of prosperity and expansion. David is thirty years old when he begins to reign—still a young man. He had reigned over the single tribe of Judah for seven years and six months in Hebron. He will reign thirty-three years in Jerusalem over all Israel, all twelve tribes. David will reign for a total of forty years and six months.

DAVID MOVES HIS CAPITAL TO JERUSALEM

Notice the first move that David makes to consolidate the kingdom: he moved the capital of Israel from Hebron to Jerusalem.

> **And the king and his men went to Jerusalem unto the Jebusites, the inhabitants of the land: which spake unto David, saying, Except thou take away the blind and the lame, thou shalt not come in hither: thinking, David cannot come in hither.**

> **Nevertheless David took the strong hold of Zion: the same is the city of David [2 Sam. 5:6–7].**

Once again, here are men who underestimated David. He was a great military leader, political leader, and king, and most and best of all he was a man of God.

Now Zion was David's favorite spot. Mark that in your Bible. I have marked it in mine. If you have ever been to that land, you will recognize that it is the high point of the city. Actually, in David's day, Jerusalem was down near the Kidron valley. The walls that surrounded the city in that day have been excavated down in that area. The present city of Jerusalem is nearer Mount Zion, where the palace of David was built. Later on, below Mount Zion, the temple was erected. David chose all of this. Jerusalem was David's city. In many of his psalms he speaks of Mount Zion and Jerusalem. Frankly, it would not be my favorite city. I agree with David on many things, but not on Jerusalem. Pilate hated that city. He went there only during the feast days. That is why he was in Jerusalem when Jesus was arrested; he was there for the

Passover. He was there to keep order and, when the Passover was over, he retired to Caesarea, which was located on the Mediterranean. I think I would prefer Caesarea to Jerusalem, too. As far as the Bible is concerned, however, Jerusalem is to be the great capital of this earth. I am delighted to know that I will not be living there throughout eternity. I am going to be in the New Jerusalem, which has a much greater vantage point than the earthly Jerusalem.

We need to note here that "David took the strong hold of Zion." He took the top of the hill and not the city proper. From that vantage point he was able to take this city of the Jebusites. The Jebusites found themselves overwhelemed before they even knew that there was a battle going on.

> And David said on that day, Whosoever getteth up to the gutter, and smiteth the Jebusites, and the lame and the blind, that are hated of David's soul, he shall be chief and captain. Wherefore they said, The blind and the lame shall not come into the house [2 Sam. 5:8].

This verse is a source of controversy. Some Bible commentators hold that this is David's retort to taunt the Jebusites. Others believe it has a deeper meaning. Since Scripture gives us no explanation, we cannot know the exact meaning.

> So David dwelt in the fort, and called it the city of David. And David built round about from Millo and inward [2 Sam. 5:9].

David first captured Mount Zion and established it as his fort; then he took the city.

> And David went on, and grew great, and the LORD God of hosts was with him.

> And Hiram king of Tyre sent messengers to David, and cedar trees, and carpenters, and masons: and they built David an house.

And David perceived that the LORD had established him king over Israel, and that he had exalted his kingdom for his people Israel's sake [2 Sam. 5:10–12].

He grew great, and God was with him. Hiram, the king of Tyre, recognized that David was an outstanding man, and so he worked out an arrangement with David whereby he supplied materials and workmen to build a palace.

And David took him more concubines and wives out of Jerusalem, after he was come from Hebron: and there were yet sons and daughters born to David [2 Sam. 5:13].

That is the record of the facts. God did not put his stamp of approval upon what David did. We will find that God definitely disapproves of polygamy. In David's son Solomon it resulted in the splitting of the kingdom and finally brought on the Babylonian captivity. Why? Because David and Solomon were kings and in places of leadership. Their actions were wrong. Who says they were wrong? God says they were wrong! After all, it is His universe, and He makes the rules. Although you may not like them, God's rules are good. God not only created us, but He laid down rules and regulations for our lives which would bring to the human family the ultimate in happiness and blessing.

And these be the names of those that were born unto him in Jerusalem; Shammuah, and Shobab, and Nathan, and Solomon,

Ibhar also, and Elishua, and Nepheg, and Japhia,

And Elishama, and Eliada, and Eliphalet [2 Sam. 5:14–16].

I know nothing about the first two boys mentioned in these verses, but I do know something about Nathan and Solomon. From the line of

Nathan came Mary the mother of Jesus. From Solomon came Joseph, Mary's husband. The Lord Jesus Christ received the blood line and the legal title to the throne of David through Nathan and Solomon. That is the reason this information is recorded for us here.

WAR WITH THE PHILISTINES

But when the Philistines heard that they had anointed David king over Israel, all the Philistines came up to seek David; and David heard of it, and went down to the hold.

The Philistines also came and spread themselves in the valley of Rephaim [2 Sam. 5:17–18].

When David was escaping from Saul and went to live in the Philistine country, at least Achish considered David their man. Now that David has returned to his own nation and has been anointed king over all Israel, the Philistines are out to get him.

And David inquired of the LORD, saying, Shall I go up to the Philistines? wilt thou deliver them into mine hand? And the LORD said unto David, Go up: for I will doubtless deliver the Philistines into thine hand.

And David came to Baal-perazim, and David smote them there, and said, The LORD hath broken forth upon mine enemies before me, as the breach of waters. Therefore he called the name of that place Baal-perazim.

And there they left their images, and David and his men burned them [2 Sam. 5:19–21].

Some time after this defeat, the Philistines returned. Again God delivered them into David's hand. Throughout David's reign there never was any peace with this enemy.

CHAPTER 6

THEME: David's wrong and right attempts to bring the ark to Jerusalem

In this chapter David does a right thing in a wrong way. He tried to bring up the ark to Zion on a cart, although God had given explicit directions for moving it. The Kohathites of the tribe of Levi were to carry the ark on their shoulders (Num. 7:9). Uzzah was smitten dead because he should have known better than to touch it. "Hands off" was made abundantly clear in God's instructions concerning the ark. David then brought the ark up in a right way. Michal rebukes David for his enthusiasm and devotion to God in bringing up the ark.

This chapter can be labeled, "Doing a Right Thing in a Wrong Way." I suppose this would be another way of putting the negative in that ancient epigram, "The end justifies the means." There have been many organizations and individuals who have used that as their philosophy of life. I do not mean to suggest that this was David's philosophy of life—it was not—but as far as this particular incident in chapter 6 is concerned, it was certainly true. I believe this is a page from one of the greatest days in the life of David.

Suppose you wanted to choose the greatest day in the life of David. What day would you choose? Would it be the day that Samuel poured the anointing oil on him as a young shepherd boy? How about the day that he slew the giant Goliath? Certainly his first romance with Michal, Saul's daughter, who was given to him in marriage, deserves consideration. Perhaps you might choose the day David escaped from Saul. Then again you might choose the day Saul died, because that meant that David would ascend the throne. You might think it was the day that he was made king of all Israel and the crown was placed upon his head. You might even want to suggest it was the day his son Absalom rebelled against him and was slain. Or perhaps you might choose the day his son Solomon was anointed king. All of these were great days in the life of a great man.

However, I believe there are two events that stand out above all others in the life of David: the day that David brought the ark of God to Jerusalem (recorded in ch. 6) and the day David purposed in his heart to build God a house (recorded in ch. 7). These are probably the two greatest days in David's life.

Now the ark of the covenant denoted the presence of God among His people. If you are not acquainted with the floor plan of the tabernacle, I would like to recommend my book about the tabernacle entitled *God's Portrait of Christ*. I emphasize the articles of furniture and their location in the tabernacle and then in the temple. In the outer court was the burnt altar and the brazen laver. Sin was dealt with there. Then there was the Holy Place which contained three articles of furniture, all of which spoke of worship and the person of Christ: the golden lampstand, the golden altar, and the table of showbread. Then inside the Holy of Holies was the ark and over it the mercy seat. This was where God met with His people. The ark is possibly the best picture of Christ we have in the Old Testament. It is the only picture, actually, that God ever painted.

Personally I do not care for the paintings of Christ, especially the way the artists of the Middle Ages pictured Him. No one knows how the Lord Jesus looked. There are those who say He was a white man, some say He was a black man, and others say He was a swarthy man with a dark complexion. Probably His skin was bronze, but we don't know because we have not been told. There is a picture of Him, however, in the tabernacle and especially in the ark, which was just a box made of acacia wood, of precise dimensions, and overlaid with gold inside and outside. Bezaleel was given a special ministry by the Spirit of God that he might make the ark. The ark, denoting the presence of God, became a hindrance to Israel because they looked upon it in a superstitious way. They thought there was some merit in that box, and there was not. It was just a symbol, a picture of the Lord Jesus Christ. It was made of gold, which speaks of His deity, and of wood, which speaks of His humanity. It was not two boxes; it was one box. It was a wooden box; it was a gold box. It was both. As such, it was a marvelous example of the hypostatical union of Jesus Christ. He is the God-man, or as one of the oldest creeds says: He is very man of very man, and He is very God of very God.

You will recall that during the time of Samuel the Philistines captured the ark and became very superstitious about it. They sent it back to Israel on a wagon and left it in the field of Abinadab. It stayed in that area for seventy years. When David captured Jerusalem, he wanted to move the ark up there because he felt that was the proper place for it, and apparently it was the place which God had chosen. One of the things the king was told was, "Three times a year shall all thy males appear before the LORD thy God in the place which he shall choose . . ." (Deut. 16:16). When David took Jerusalem, he made it the capital—and in Kirjath-jearim, eight miles west of Jerusalem, was the ark.

David had a passion and love for God that is seldom found today. I do not go along with these folk who are everlastingly criticizing David. I only wish in my own heart that I had that love and passion for God that he had. Listen to what he says in Psalm 9:1: "I will praise thee, O LORD, with my whole heart. . . ." David expressed his devotion from the depths of his heart in a most wonderful way. In Psalm 108:1 he declared, "O God, my heart is fixed; I will sing and give praise, even with my glory." Then in Psalm 103:1 he says, "Bless the LORD, O my soul: and all that is within me, bless his holy name." What a passion and love for God this man had! That is why he wanted to bring the ark of God to Jerusalem. We will see in this chapter that he will attempt to do it, but he goes about it in the wrong way.

The ark is mentioned fifteen times in the first seventeen verses. After you read this section (and I hope that you will read it carefully), you realize that the subject is the ark of the Lord. It seemed to be a rather important subject to David and to the Lord.

At least eleven of the psalms were composed around the great event of bringing the ark to Jerusalem. You can be sure of one thing: David did not have some peculiar superstition about the ark. He knew where the Lord was, and he knew He was not in that box. In Psalm 123:1 David says, "Unto thee lift I up mine eyes, O thou that dwellest in the heavens." David knew where God was, but he knew that the approach to God was made through the ark which spoke of a mediator between God and man.

This has been a rather lengthy introduction, because I believe this is an important chapter. Now notice what David wants to do.

> **Again, David gathered together all the chosen men of Israel, thirty thousand.**

> **And David arose, and went with all the people that were with him from Baale of Judah, to bring up from thence the ark of God, whose name is called by the name of the LORD of hosts that dwelleth between the cherubims.**

> **And they set the ark of God upon a new cart, and brought it out of the house of Abinadab that was in Gibeah: and Uzzah and Ahio, the sons of Abinadab, drave the new cart [2 Sam. 6:1–3].**

This is where David made his mistake. God had given specific instructions about moving the tabernacle and its furniture, but David did not follow those instructions. Someone might say, "Well, the Philistines didn't either, and they got away with it." They got away with it because they were ignorant. Light creates responsibility. If men have the light of the gospel, they are held responsible for rejecting it. I am not going to argue with you about the heathen in Africa, but I would like to argue with you about the heathen in my town and your town because they can hear the gospel, and their responsibility is great. If you turn your back on Jesus Christ, my friend, you can argue about the heathen all you want to, but you are lost and doomed and judged and are bound for eternal hell. That is the teaching of the Word of God. You may not like it; and, if you don't, you ought to move out of this universe into another one. This is God's universe and these are His rules.

So David goes to bring up the ark to Jerusalem, but he does it in the wrong way. The ark was constructed with rings on the four corners. Staves were put through those rings, and the ark was carried on the shoulders of the Levites. On the wilderness march the Kohathites put that ark on their shoulders and carried it. David simply did not follow God's instructions.

Friend, in just such a way God wants the gospel to go out today. I sometimes wonder why He doesn't get a better instrument than I am and why He doesn't write the gospel in the skies. But Jesus Christ has to be carried through this world on the shoulders of those who are His own. That is God's way of doing it today. That was God's way of doing it in David's day. David was wrong, so wrong. He is going to get into trouble, just as God's people today get in trouble when they do wrong.

> **And David and all the house of Israel played before the Lord on all manner of instruments made of fir wood, even on harps, and on psalteries, and on timbrels, and on cornets, and on cymbals [2 Sam. 6:5].**

David was a musician. He believed in having lots of music, and he is going to bring the ark to Jerusalem with a great deal of it.

> **And when they came to Nachon's threshingfloor, Uzzah put forth his hand to the ark of God, and took hold of it; for the oxen shook it.**

> **And the anger of the Lord was kindled against Uzzah; and God smote him there for his error; and there he died by the ark of God [2 Sam. 6:6–7].**

This is a pretty serious situation. The ark was on the cart, and the oxen were shaking the cart. When Uzzah tried to steady the ark with his hand, the Lord smote him and he died. Some might say that it was a small breach of conduct for such extreme punishment. Uzzah's death so affected David that he stopped the procession and left the ark in the house of Obed-edom the Gittite. David was shaken and angry with the Lord. The Lord was angry too. God was angry because David was moving the ark in the wrong way.

> And David was displeased, because the LORD had made
> a breach upon Uzzah: and he called the name of the
> place Perez-uzzah to this day.
>
> And David was afraid of the LORD that day, and said,
> How shall the ark of the LORD come to me? [2 Sam.
> 6:8–9].

You and I would do well, friend, to be afraid of the Lord. Psalm 111:10
tells us that "The fear of the LORD is the beginning of wisdom. . . ."
Many people need to recognize that fact today. God is going to judge. I
do not know about you, but I am a little weary of hearing all this love,
love, lovey-dovey stuff. Sure, God is love. Certainly God loves you,
but you can go on in sin, you can turn your back on Him, and you are
lost. There is no way out of it. There is no other alternative. John 14:6
says, ". . . I am the way, the truth, and the life: no man cometh unto the
Father, but by me." Jesus Christ spoke those words, and they are truth.
We should fear Him and do as He tells us to do. David was afraid of the
Lord that day, and he finally asked, "How shall the ark of the LORD
come to me?"

> So David would not remove the ark of the LORD unto him
> into the city of David: but David carried it aside into the
> house of Obed-edom the Gittite.
>
> And the ark of the LORD continued in the house of Obed-
> edom the Gittite three months: and the LORD blessed
> Obed-edom, and all his household.
>
> And it was told king David, saying, The LORD hath
> blessed the house of Obed-edom, and all that pertaineth
> unto him, because of the ark of God. So David went and
> brought up the ark of God from the house of Obed-edom
> into the city of David with gladness [2 Sam. 6:10–12].

He was determined to bring the ark to the city of David. Has he learned
his lesson? How is he going to bring it up now? On the shoulders of
the priests.

> And it was so, that when they that bare the ark of the
> LORD had gone six paces, he sacrificed oxen and fat-
> lings.
>
> And David danced before the LORD with all his might;
> and David was girded with a linen ephod [2 Sam.
> 6:13–14].

I know there are going to be many arched eyebrows at the fact that
David danced, but God is the One who put it in His Word. David
danced by himself. It had nothing in the world to do with sex. Any
kind of a dance today (and I do not care how you try to cover it up with
culture and refinement) is a sex dance. David's dance was one of worship. Now if you could have a worshipful dance, I would be all for it,
but I don't think you can, my friend. I do not find people in love with
God like this man David was. David is rejoicing before God. Personally, I would like to see more people rejoicing and praising God today.
I am concerned when I see believers with long faces. God doesn't like
it, my friend. We are to come into His presence with joy. David did,
you may be sure of that.

> So David and all the house of Israel brought up the ark
> of the LORD with shouting, and with the sound of the
> trumpet.
>
> And as the ark of the LORD came into the city of David,
> Michal Saul's daughter looked through a window, and
> saw king David leaping and dancing before the LORD;
> and she despised him in her heart [2 Sam. 6:15–16].

Michal did not like to see anyone who was in love with God like that,
and she despised David for it. Remember, Michal is David's wife. Her
attitude is a very serious thing as far as her relationship with David is
concerned.

> And they brought in the ark of the LORD, and set it in his
> place, in the midst of the tabernacle that David had

pitched for it: and David offered burnt offerings and peace offerings before the LORD [2 Sam. 6:17].

Those burnt offerings speak of the person of Christ. The peace offerings speak of the peace that He made by the blood of His cross and of the relationship—the wonderful relationship—which was between God and David.

My friend, let's push aside the extraneous arguments we hear about David's dancing before the Lord and about Uzzah being smitten dead. The record is here in the Word of God; let's accept it as it is written. The important thing is to see the lesson that is here for us. What about your relationship to God? Let me give a personal testimony at this point. Driving down to the office this morning, feeling rather weary since I have just returned from a trip, I thanked God that He had brought me to another day. I thanked Him that I've confessed all my sins and am in a right relationship with Him. And I told Him that I love Him. How He deserves our love and adoration! The important thing to see in this chapter is David's relationship with God. Here is a man who is in love with his God. He is rightly related to Him and thrilled to be able to serve Him. Oh, that you and I might have the same *joy* of the Lord in our lives!

Then David returned to bless his household. And Michal the daughter of Saul came out to meet David, and said, How glorious was the king of Israel to-day, who uncovered himself to-day in the eyes of the handmaids of his servants, as one of the vain fellows shamelessly uncovereth himself! [2 Sam. 6:20].

David "uncovered himself" in the sense that he took off his royal garments which set him apart as the king. He mingled and mixed with the people, and thanked God, and rejoiced in the fact that the ark was being brought to the city of David. Michal did not like that. She liked dignity and reverence in worship. I am always afraid of these super-duper pious folk who talk everlastingly about dedication and piety.

Watch those folk, my friend. They are dangerous. I fear them like David did. What a man of God he was!

> **And David said unto Michal, It was before the LORD, which chose me before thy father, and before all his house, to appoint me ruler over the people of the LORD, over Israel: therefore will I play before the LORD [2 Sam. 6:21].**

David is saying, "Because God chose me, I will rejoice." My, I wish folk had a better time when they went to church. They would enjoy the services more.

> **And I will yet be more vile than thus, and will be base in mine own sight: and of the maidservants which thou hast spoken of, of them shall I be had in honour [2 Sam. 6:22].**

When he says he will make himself "more vile," he means that he will come down to the level of the most humble worshiper. He doesn't mind being informal in his worship of God.

Because of her attitude, David "put her aside." That is, he became permanently estranged from her, and she was childless. Obviously, Michal did not share David's love and enthusiasm for God.

CHAPTER 7

THEME: *God's covenant to build the house of David*

God's covenant with David makes this one of the great chapters of the Bible. The message of the Bible from this point on rests upon this promise that God makes to David. David desired deeply to build a temple to house the ark of God, and Nathan the prophet concurred with him in the plan. God appeared to Nathan to correct him, for God would not let David build the temple because he was "a bloody man." However, God gave him credit for his desire, and in turn He promised to build David a house. God promised a king and a kingdom to come in the line of David. He was referring not only to Solomon but to Christ, great David's greater Son, and His eternal Kingdom. God confirmed this promise with an oath (Ps. 89:34–37). David understood that a King was coming in his line who would be more than a man.

Frankly, it is very difficult to understand the prophets from this point on without knowing about this covenant. One of the reasons many people find themselves so hopelessly confused in the study of prophecy is because they do not pay attention to a chapter like this. Second Samuel 7 is by far the most significant chapter thus far in the Old Testament. The New Testament opens with: "The book of the generation of Jesus Christ, the son of David. . . ." That is important because the promises God made to David are to be fulfilled in prophecy.

When the angel Gabriel appeared to Mary, he said, ". . . Fear not, Mary: for thou hast found favour with God. And, behold, thou shalt conceive in thy womb, and bring forth a son, and shall call his name JESUS. He shall be great, and shall be called the Son of the Highest: and the Lord God shall give unto him the throne of his father *David*" (Luke 1:30–32). You see, God is fulfilling His promise to David.

Peter began in 2 Samuel 7 when he preached on the day of Pentecost: "Men and brethren, let me freely speak unto you of the patriarch David, that he is both dead and buried, and his sepulchre is with us unto this day. Therefore being a prophet, and knowing that God had sworn with an oath to him, that of the fruit of his loins, according to the flesh, he would raise up Christ to sit on his throne" (Acts 2:29-30; see also Acts 2:25-31, 34-36). Peter is making reference to that which God promised to David.

Paul, in the Book of Romans, says, "Paul, a servant of Jesus Christ, called to be an apostle, separated unto the gospel of God, (Which he had promised afore by his prophets in the holy scriptures,) Concerning his Son Jesus Christ our Lord, which was made of the seed of David according to the flesh" (Rom. 1:1-3).

The New Testament closes with the Lord Jesus Christ saying, "I Jesus have sent mine angel to testify unto you these things in the churches. I am the root and the offspring of David, and the bright and morning star" (Rev. 22:16). These are only a few of the fifty-nine references to David in the New Testament.

The Old Testament prophets based their message of the kingdom on the promise God gave to David in 2 Samuel 7. You will find that each of the Old Testament prophets goes back to David and God's promises to him concerning the kingdom. After all, what is the Kingdom of Heaven but the kingdom that God vouchsafed to David? For example, listen to Jeremiah 23:5, "Behold, the days come, saith the LORD, that I will raise unto David a righteous Branch, and a King shall reign and prosper, and shall execute judgment and justice in the earth." The Kingdom became the theme song of the prophets.

DAVID'S DESIRE TO BUILD THE TEMPLE

And it came to pass, when the king sat in his house, and the LORD had given him rest round about from all his enemies;

That the king said unto Nathan the prophet, See now, I dwell in an house of cedar, but the ark of God dwelleth within curtains.

And Nathan said to the king, Go, do all that is in thine heart; for the LORD is with thee [2 Sam. 7:1-3].

Let us look at the background of these verses. We have seen that David took Jerusalem and made it his capital. Then Hiram, the king of Tyre, built David a palace on Mount Zion. Finally David brought the ark up to the city of Jerusalem. One night when David was in his palace, he began to think about the ark. I think it must have been a rainy night in Jerusalem. The first night I ever spent in that city, it rained, and I thought, *It must have been a rainy night when David awakened and heard the pitter-patter of rain on that lovely palace that his friend Hiram had built for him.* Then he thought of God's ark in a tent. Perhaps he could even hear the flapping of the tent, and he thought, *I want to build God a house.*

David called in Nathan, his prophet, and divulged to him the desires of his heart. He said, "I dwell in a house of cedar, but the ark of God dwelleth within curtains." Nathan told David to go ahead with his plans. And here is a case where a prophet was wrong, and I mean *wrong.* Nathan said, "Go, do all that is in thine heart; for the LORD is with thee." I would have said the same thing. The fact of the matter is, if someone came to me and said, "Dr. McGee, we want to underwrite your radio ministry on a certain station," I'll be frank with you, I would not say, "Well, let me go and pray about this and see whether this is what ought to be done." I would say, "Yes, this is what we want." But my decision might not be the will of God. I understand how Nathan felt. David's plans sounded good. Nathan could not think of anything better than building a house for God. But he was wrong. David, as we have indicated before, was a bloody man. Long before he committed his great sin, he was a bloody man. God said, "You cannot build me a temple." It was in the heart of David, however, and God gives him credit for it. I think we make a mistake by calling it Solomon's temple, because it was David who gathered all of the materials and made all of the arrangements with the contractor. Solomon just carried out the plans. The only temple Solomon ever had was on the side of his head. It should be called David's temple.

And it came to pass that night, that the word of the LORD came unto Nathan, saying,

> Go and tell my servant David, Thus saith the LORD,
> Shalt thou build me an house for me to dwell in?
>
> Whereas I have not dwelt in any house since the time
> that I brought up the children of Israel out of Egypt,
> even to this day, but have walked in a tent and in a taber-
> nacle [2 Sam. 7:4–6].

God had to correct Nathan. God said to him, "You are going to have to
correct the word you gave to David. You go tell David that I appreciate
the fact that he wants to build Me a house. I never asked him to do it. I
never asked any of My people to build Me a house." God had met with
His people in a tent. In other words, God identified Himself with His
people. That is why 1900 years ago Jesus Christ came to earth and
took upon Himself our humanity. John says, "And the Word was made
flesh, and dwelt among us, (and we beheld his glory, the glory as of
the only begotten of the Father,) full of grace and truth" (John 1:14).
That word *dwelt* means "pitched His tent" here among us. Instead of
meeting man in a flimsy tent made of linen, God met man in a flimsy
tent made of flesh. He came to earth and identified Himself with us.
God has always identified Himself with His people.

> In all the places wherein I have walked with all the chil-
> dren of Israel spake I a word with any of the tribes of
> Israel, whom I commanded to feed my people Israel,
> saying, Why build ye not me an house of cedar? [2 Sam.
> 7:7].

In other words, building the temple was David's idea—not God's commandment. God gives him credit for building the temple.

> Now therefore so shalt thou say unto my servant David,
> Thus saith the LORD of hosts, I took thee from the sheep-
> cote, from following the sheep, to be ruler over my peo-
> ple, over Israel [2 Sam. 7:8].

God says, "You were a little shepherd boy when I chose you. And I've made you ruler over My people."

> **And I was with thee whithersoever thou wentest, and have cut off all thine enemies out of thy sight, and have made thee a great name, like unto the name of the great men that are in the earth [2 Sam. 7:9].**

In God's book David ranks as one of the greatest men who has lived on this earth. Compare David with any man who has ever ruled, and he is outstanding. If I understand the prophets correctly, it is God's intention, when David is raised from the dead in the resurrection, to let him rule on this earth as regent to the Lord Jesus Christ during the Millennium.

> **Moreover I will appoint a place for my people Israel, and will plant them, that they may dwell in a place of their own, and move no more; neither shall the children of wickedness afflict them any more, as beforetime [2 Sam. 7:10].**

This is what God is *going to do*. Notice the "I will's" of God. (1) "I will appoint a place for my people Israel; (2) I will plant them, that they may dwell in a place of their own, and move no more." Friend, that was a long time ago—actually, God said this over three thousand years ago, and it has not yet come to pass. But God is going to make good His promise.

> **And as since the time that I commanded judges to be over my people Israel, and have caused thee to rest from all thine enemies. Also the LORD telleth thee that he will make thee an house [2 Sam. 7:11].**

God says to Nathan, "You go tell David that I will make *him* a house." David said, "I want to build God a house." God says, "David, you

can't do it. Your hands are bloody. You can't build Me a house, but I
know the desire is in your heart. I will give you credit for building Me
a house, and I will build you a house." Isn't that just like the Lord? You
can't out do the Lord, friend.

One of the reasons so many of us are so poor today is because we
do so little for the Lord. We never get in a position where He can do
much for us. We can learn a lesson from David. David wanted to do
something great for God and God did something far greater for him.

> **And when thy days be fulfilled, and thou shalt sleep
> with thy fathers, I will set up thy seed after thee, which
> shall proceed out of thy bowels, and I will stablish his
> kingdom [2 Sam. 7:12].**

This is tremendous! We have read from the New Testament that the
Lord Jesus Christ was made of the seed of David (Rom. 1:3). God said
to David, "I am going to set up thy seed after thee, and He will establish the Kingdom." God was not talking about Solomon. God was referring to the Lord Jesus Christ.

> **He shall build an house for my name, and I will estab-
> lish the throne of his kingdom for ever [2 Sam. 7:13].**

Solomon is the subject here; he is the next in line. The Kingdom, however, goes beyond Solomon and looks on to the future. "I will stablish
the throne of his kingdom for ever." This speaks of the throne of David.
The Lord Jesus Christ will one day sit on the throne of David. That was
the angel Gabriel's message to Mary. He said, "He shall be great, and
shall be called the Son of the Highest: and the Lord God shall give
unto him the throne of his father David" (Luke 1:32).

> **I will be his father, and he shall be my son. If he commit
> iniquity, I will chasten him with the rod of men, and
> with the stripes of the children of men [2 Sam. 7:14].**

Listen again to God's "I will." In a unique way God says, "I will be his father." At His resurrection the Lord Jesus Christ said to Mary Magdalene, "Touch me not; for I am not yet ascended to my Father: but go to my brethren, and say unto them, I ascend unto my Father, and your Father; and to my God, and your God" (John 20:17). God is the Father of Jesus Christ because of His position in the Trinity. God is my Father by regeneration—"But as many as received him, to them gave he power to become the sons of God, even to them that believe on his name" (John 1:12). When I received Christ as my Savior, He gave me the right (the *exousia*) to become His son. That right is given to those who do neither more nor less than simply believe in His name. God says, "I will be his father, and he shall be my son."

The last part of verse 14 is a very strange statement. "If he commit iniquity, I will chasten him with the rod of of men, and with the stripes of the children of men." Bishop Horsley gives an interesting translation of this: "When guilt is laid upon him, I will chasten him with the rod of men." That is exactly what God is saying now. God says, "When guilt is laid upon Him, I am going to be His Father, and He will be My Son." That is the unique relationship between God the Father and God the Son. But "if he commit iniquity," that is, when iniquity is laid upon Him—when your sin and my sin were put upon Him—it is with His stripes that we are healed. He died on the Cross for you and me. He was delivered for our offenses. That is the reason He died on the Cross. "Who his own self bare our sins in his own body on the tree, that we, being dead to sins, should live unto righteousness: by whose stripes ye were healed" (1 Pet. 2:24)—healed from sin. Isaiah the prophet says concerning Christ, "Yet it pleased the LORD to bruise him; he hath put him to grief . . ." (Isa. 53:10). The One coming in David's line would bear the sins of the world. Isaiah continues to speak of the Lord Jesus when he says, "Surely he hath borne our griefs, and carried our sorrows: yet we did esteem him stricken, smitten of God, and afflicted. But he was wounded for our transgressions, he was bruised for our iniquities: the chastisement of our peace was upon him; and with his stripes we are healed. All we like sheep have gone astray; we have turned every one to his own way; and the LORD

hath laid on him the iniquity of us all" (Isa. 53:4–6). "With his stripes
we are healed." Healed of what? We are healed of sin. Sin is the awful
disease that afflicts mankind, my beloved. That is why God says, "I
will chasten him with the rod of men, and with the stripes of the children of men."

**But my mercy shall not depart away from him, as I took
it from Saul, whom I put away before thee [2 Sam. 7:15].**

In other words, though the line of David sinned grievously, God would
carry through to the end of His purpose with David and his line. And
God did just that. He brought the Lord Jesus Christ into the world.

**And thine house and thy kingdom shall be established
for ever before thee: thy throne shall be established for
ever [2 Sam. 7:16].**

God considered this important because Psalm 89:34–37 says, "My
covenant will I not break, nor alter the thing that is gone out of my
lips. Once have I sworn by my holiness that I will not lie unto David.
His seed shall endure for ever, and his throne as the sun before me. It
shall be established for ever as the moon, and as a faithful witness in
heaven. Selah."

"Established for ever as the moon." Scientists are saying, after
studying the rocks brought back from the moon, that the universe is
probably from three to five billion years old—that's a long time. God
said He would establish David's throne just as He established the
moon. God made a covenant with David, and He will not break it.

**According to all these words, and according to all this
vision, so did Nathan speak unto David [2 Sam. 7:17].**

DAVID'S PRAYER

**Then went king David in, and sat before the Lord, and
he said, Who am I, O Lord God? and what is my house,
that thou hast brought me hitherto?**

**And this was yet a small thing in thy sight, O Lord GOD;
but thou hast spoken also of thy servant's house for a
great while to come. And is this the manner of man, O
Lord GOD? [2 Sam. 7:18–19].**

Once again consider Bishop Horsley's translation of this verse: "O
Lord God, thou hast spoken of your servant's house for a great while to
come, and hast regarded me in the arrangement about the man that is
to be from above, O God Jehovah." That is a remarkable statement.
They were looking for One to come. He was to be of the seed of the
woman. He was to be from Abraham; He was to come from the tribe of
Judah; now we are told that He will be in the family of David. David is
overwhelmed by the fact that Jesus Christ will be in his line.

**And what can David say more unto thee? for thou, Lord
GOD, knowest thy servant [2 Sam. 7:20].**

Have you ever poured out your heart to God until you didn't have
anything left to say? That was David's state. He had poured out his
heart and was empty; he was just sitting there before Him. I like to
pray while I am driving alone in my car. I tell Him everything in my
heart until I can't even think of anything else to say. How wonderful
He is. How wonderful is our God.

**For thy word's sake, and according to thine own heart,
hast thou done all these great things, to make thy servant know them [2 Sam. 7:21].**

Did God do all of this for David because he was a nice boy? He wasn't
a nice boy, friend, as we are going to see. Neither did God save you or
me because we were nice girls or boys. He saved us because of His
marvelous, infinite grace. He does so many special things for us, not
because of our goodness, but because of *His* goodness. He is wonderful. We are not. We ought to praise His name. David is overwhelmed
by what God has told him. It is no wonder that he could sing those
beautiful psalms.

> Wherefore thou art great, O Lord God: for there is none
> like thee, neither is there any God beside thee, accord-
> ing to all that we have heard with our ears [2 Sam.
> 7:22].

Doesn't this verse do you good just to read it? My, what a privilege to
have a God like this!

> And now, O Lord God, the word that thou hast spoken
> concerning thy servant, and concerning his house, es-
> tablish it for ever, and do as thou hast said [2 Sam.
> 7:25].

Did you know that this became David's salvation? Listen to what he
says in 2 Samuel 23:5, "Although my house be not so with God; yet
he hath made with me an everlasting covenant, ordered in all things,
and sure: for this is all my salvation, and all my desire, although he
make it not to grow." David rested upon what God had promised.

God has also made a promise to you. It is recorded in John 3:16. It
says, "For God so loved the world, that he gave his only begotten Son,
that whosoever believeth in him should not perish, but have everlasting life." Will you believe God? David believed God. Also we have
seen that Abraham believed God. Moses believed God. Joshua believed God. And He wants you to believe God. Whatever your name is,
He is saying to you today, "Believe Me. I'll save you if you will trust
Christ as your Savior." That is His covenant with you and with me.

CHAPTERS 8—10

THEME: David consolidates his kingdom

Now that David has established Jerusalem as his capital and has brought the ark of God there, he consolidates his kingdom and befriends the only living son of Jonathan, Mephibosheth. Also he gains victories over the old enemies of Israel and enlarges Israel's borders.

DAVID CONSOLIDATES HIS KINGDOM

And after this it came to pass, that David smote the Philistines, and subdued them: and David took Methegammah out of the hand of the Philistines [2 Sam. 8:1].

The "after this" refers to the time after God made His covenant with David. David is now being fully established in the kingdom, and we find that he has a great victory over the Philistines. They were the perpetual and inveterate enemies of Israel. David drives them back, not only out of the land of Israel, but even beyond their own borders. The Philistines inhabited a great section of that land, especially in the southern part.

In recounting David's conquest of the king of Zobah, it is said:

And David took from him a thousand chariots, and seven hundred horsemen, and twenty thousand footmen: and David hocked all the chariot horses, but reserved of them for an hundred chariots [2 Sam. 8:4].

Hadadezer, the king of Zobah, had a kingdom that went as far as the river Euphrates. We are told that David took a thousand chariots from him. David got rid of all but a few of the horses. In the Book of Deuteronomy God made a rule for the kings that they were not to multiply horses or wives. Although David multiplied wives (Solomon multiplied both horses and wives), he is apparently trying to follow the Lord's instructions in this matter concerning the horses.

There is a great deal of detail in this chapter. If you like to explore new areas and new lands, you will enjoy studying this chapter and tracing on a map the different areas in which David moved. He enlarged the borders of Israel. He extended them to the south in the land of the Philistines, and to the east in the land of the Moabites. He established garrisons in Syria and Edom. So we find that Syria, Moab, Ammon, the Philistines, and the Amalekites all became subject to David and apparently paid tribute.

> **And David gat him a name when he returned from smiting of the Syrians in the valley of salt, being eighteen thousand men.**
>
> **And he put garrisons in Edom; throughout all Edom put he garrisons, and all they of Edom became David's servants. And the LORD preserved David withersoever he went [2 Sam. 8:13–14].**

In the southwest, the southeast, and now to the north, David was able to push back the borders of Israel and enlarge the kingdom. There is no use to say that the borders were enlarged in the west because the border in the west was the Mediterranean Sea.

> **And David reigned over all Israel; and David executed judgment and justice unto all his people [2 Sam. 8:15].**

David was noted for his judgment and justice to his people. There has been a tremendous expansion and extension of the kingdom. David has brought the kingdom to its zenith and made it a world power corresponding to other kingdoms of that day.

DAVID BEFRIENDS MEPHIBOSHETH

This chapter records one of the most beautiful stories in the Scriptures. It is a story that reveals what a great man David really was. We usually think of David in connection with the sin he committed, and that is probably a natural thing to do. Suppose I had a large white screen before me. On that screen is one little black spot—some ink got on the screen. As I look at it, what is the most impressive thing about it? There is a vast area of white, but that one little black spot stands out. Or suppose you ride down the highway, as I have done in west Texas, and you see a couple of thousand sheep in a field. All of the sheep are white but one. Which sheep do you really see? So it is in the life of David. We always concentrate on his big sin, and it was big. The trouble is that we give sparse attention to the noble life and exploits of David. Someone has said, "There is so much good in the worst of us, and so much bad in the best of us, that it behooves most of us not to talk about the rest of us." Maybe we ought to reevaluate our viewpoint of David. There are so many bright spots in the long life of David, from that young shepherd boy who slew a giant, to an old man wise in experience who could write, "The LORD is my shepherd, I shall not want." In this chapter we shall see the gracious side of David's character.

Chapter 9 records the story of Mephibosheth. He is the son of Jonathan and the grandson of Saul. It is important at this point to recall some of the background of Saul. He had been the pitiless foe and bitter enemy of David. At the death of Saul, David began to marshal his forces. According to oriental custom of that day, a new king would naturally put to death all contenders to the throne of a former dynasty. Any claimant would be removed by execution. That would protect the new king from any threat. According to the code of that day, David would have been justified in putting to death any of the offspring of Saul. When Saul and Jonathan had been killed in the same battle, a little son of Jonathan's was hidden lest David find him and kill him. The name of this boy was Mephibosheth. David could more firmly establish his throne by slaying this boy and thus remove the last vestige of danger.

> And David said, Is there yet any that is left of the house of Saul, that I may shew him kindness for Jonathan's sake?
>
> And there was of the house of Saul a servant whose name was Ziba. And when they had called him unto David, the king said to him, Art thou Ziba? And he said, Thy servant is he.
>
> And the king said, Is there not yet any of the house of Saul, that I may shew the kindness of God unto him? And Ziba said unto the king, Jonathan hath yet a son, which is lame on his feet.
>
> And the king said unto him, Where is he? And Ziba said unto the king, Behold, he is in the house of Machir, the son of Ammiel, in Lo-debar [2 Sam. 9:1–4].

Ziba, a servant of Saul, betrayed the hiding place of Mephibosheth, and David could have easily killed him.

> Then king David sent, and fetched him out of the house of Machir, the son of Ammiel, from Lo-debar.
>
> Now when Mephibosheth, the son of Jonathan, the son of Saul, was come unto David, he fell on his face, and did reverence. And David said, Mephibosheth. And he answered, Behold thy servant! [2 Sam. 9:5–6].

When Mephibosheth is brought before David, he falls on his face before him, expecting to be executed. Instead, David speaks kindly to him, calling him by his name.

> And David said unto him, Fear not: for I will surely shew thee kindness for Jonathan thy father's sake, and will restore thee all the land of Saul thy father; and thou shalt eat bread at my table continually [2 Sam. 9:7].

David quickly puts him at ease and explains the reason he has sent for him. He restores his inheritance to him and gives him a permanent place at the king's table—honoring him as one of his own sons!

> **And he bowed himself, and said, What is thy servant, that thou shouldest look upon such a dead dog as I am? [2 Sam. 9:8].**

Notice the reaction of Mephibosheth to all of this. Had there been another king on the throne, he would have been slain. It would have been an entirely different story. Realizing this, Mephibosheth counts himself as "a dead dog." But David does not call him that. He says, "You are no dead dog. You are Mephibosheth, the son of Jonathan. I intend to show kindness to you."

> **Then the king called to Ziba, Saul's servant, and said unto him, I have given unto thy master's son all that pertained to Saul and to all his house.**
>
> **Thou therefore, and thy sons, and thy servants, shall till the land for him, and thou shalt bring in the fruits, that thy master's son may have food to eat: but Mephibosheth thy master's son shall eat bread alway at my table. Now Ziba had fifteen sons and twenty servants [2 Sam. 9:9–10].**

That is quite a household! So this property and land of Saul's was turned over to Mephibosheth. It rightfully belonged to him, and David sees to it that he gets it.

> **Then said Ziba unto the king, According to all that my lord the king hath commanded his servant, so shall thy servant do. As for Mephibosheth, said the king, he shall eat at my table, as one of the king's sons.**

> **And Mephibosheth had a young son, whose name was Micha. And all that dwelt in the house of Ziba were servants unto Mephibosheth.**
>
> **So Mephibosheth dwelt in Jerusalem: for he did eat continually at the king's table; and was lame on both his feet [2 Sam. 9:11–13].**

What David did for Mephibosheth was wonderful, but there are some other impressive lessons with great spiritual truths which I don't want you to miss.

1. *A child of God recognizes that he is also a cripple in God's sight.* We are told in Romans 3:15–16: "Their feet are swift to shed blood: Destruction and misery are in their ways." That is the report from God's clinic on the human race. Our feet lead us astray. "All we like sheep have gone astray; we have turned every one to his own way; and the LORD hath laid on him the iniquity of us all" (Isa. 53:6). Then the writer of the Book of Proverbs says, "There is a way that seemeth right unto a man, but the end thereof are the ways of death" (Prov. 16:25). Our feet get us into trouble. The way that the soul and the feet are so closely connected in Scripture is quite interesting. I do not mean to make a bad pun; I am not talking about the sole of the foot.

Remembering that David for the rest of his life had a crippled boy who ate at his table, listen to the words of Psalm 56:13, "For thou hast delivered my soul from death: wilt not thou deliver my feet from failing, that I may walk before God in the light of the living?" Then in Psalm 73:2 David says, "But as for me, my feet were almost gone; my steps had well nigh slipped." David knew what it was to have lame feet! In Psalm 116:8 he says, "For thou hast delivered my soul from death, mine eyes from tears, and my feet from falling." My friend, all of us are actually cripples before God.

Modern philosophy and humanism present another picture of man. I once heard a liberal say that Christ came to reveal the splendors of the human soul! God says, "The heart is deceitful above all things, and desperately wicked: who can know it?" (Jer. 17:9). Out of the heart proceed evil thoughts, and it is a mess of bad things. You cannot expect any good from human nature. Paul could say, "For I know that in me (that is, in my flesh,) dwelleth no good thing: for to will is present with me; but how to perform that which is good I find not" (Rom. 7:18). Paul had no confidence in the flesh. The Law is condemnation. John 14:6 says, "Jesus saith unto him, I am the way, the truth, and the life: no man cometh unto the Father, but by me." When we come that way, He will receive us.

2. *David extended kindness to Mephibosheth for the sake of Jonathan.* This is another facet of this amazing incident. You see, David did not know the boy. He did what he did for the sake of Jonathan whom he loved. When David looked upon this boy, he did not see a cripple; he saw Jonathan. He had made a covenant with Jonathan. The kindness, mercy, and grace extended to a helpless person were for the sake of another.

We have seen how much Jonathan meant to David. When the news of his death reached him, he said: "How are the mighty fallen in the midst of the battle! O Jonathan, thou wast slain in thine high places. I am distressed for thee, my brother Jonathan: very pleasant hast thou been unto me: thy love to me was wonderful, passing the love of women" (2 Sam. 1:25–26). Now God has saved you and me because of Another—the Lord Jesus Christ. When we accept Jesus Christ as Savior, Ephesians 1:6 tells us that we are "accepted in the beloved." When God sees you and me in Christ, He accepts us and saves us.

3. *David said nothing about the lame feet of Mephibosheth.* There is no record that David ever mentioned it or made an allusion to it. He never said to him, "It is too bad that you are crippled." He treated him like a prince. He sat at the king's table, and his feet were covered with a linen cloth. My friend, God forgets our sin because it is blotted out by the blood of the Lord Jesus Christ. That is the *only* way God can forgive our sins. The writer of Hebrews put it this way: "And their sins and iniquities will I remember no more" (Heb. 10:17).

4. *Mephibosheth said nothing about his lame feet.* What do you think David and Mephibosheth talked about when they sat at the table? They talked about another person. Do you know who it was? It

was Jonathan. David loved Jonathan. Mephibosheth loved Jonathan—he was his father. Jonathan was the subject of conversation.

What should you and I talk about? Some Christians take a keen delight in talking about the old days when they lived in sin. It is too bad that when we get together we don't talk about Another. The Lord Jesus Christ should be the main subject of our conversation.

5. *Others said nothing about Mephibosheth's lame feet.* There was a large company that ate at the king's table. One day they saw David bringing this crippled boy to the table. The gossips did not say, "Did you hear how it happened?" Instead they listened to the king. They heard David praise Mephibosheth. They had no time to indulge in cheap talk. Their hearts went out in love to this boy. You see, love "beareth all things, endureth all things." Love "never fails" (1 Cor. 13:7–8).

As far as I can tell, David was never able to make this boy walk. If you see that you cannot walk well-pleasing to God, turn to the Lord Jesus Christ. Christ said to the man with palsy, whose friends had let him down through the roof, ". . . Son, be of good cheer; thy sins be forgiven thee. . . . Arise, and walk" (Matt. 9:2–5). The apostle Paul urged: "I therefore, the prisoner of the Lord, beseech you that ye walk worthy of the vocation wherewith ye are called, with all lowliness and meekness, with longsuffering, forbearing one another in love" (Eph. 4:1–2). If you are failing in your walk, turn to Christ for help.

Christ is sending out an invitation today into the highways and byways and out into the streets of your town. He is saying, "Come to my table of salvation just as you are, crippled, and I will feed you." He says, "Come unto me, all ye that labour and are heavy laden, and I will give you rest" (Matt. 11:28). He also says, ". . . If any man thirst, let him come unto me, and drink" (John 7:37).

What a wonderful picture of God's love is presented in this chapter!

DAVID WARS AGAINST AMMON AND SYRIA

And it came to pass after this, that the king of the children of Ammon died, and Hanun his son reigned in his stead.

Then said David, I will shew kindness unto Hanun the
son of Nahash, as his father shewed kindness unto me.
And David sent to comfort him by the hand of his servants for his father. And David's servants came into the
land of the children of Ammon.

And the princes of the children of Ammon said unto
Hanun their lord, Thinkest thou that David doth honour
thy father, that he hath sent comforters unto thee? hath
not David rather sent his servants unto thee, to search
the city, and to spy it out, and to overthrow it? [2 Sam.
10:1–3].

You can see that these people had no confidence at all in David. They
believed that he intended to attack them. His friendly gesture was
completely misunderstood.

Wherefore Hanun took David's servants, and shaved off
the one half of their beards, and cut off their garments
in the middle, even to their buttocks, and sent them
away [2 Sam. 10:4].

My friend, that was an insult! I can't think of a way to more thor-
oughly humiliate David's ambassadors than this. Some commentators
believe that this was Hanun's challenge to war—whereas David had
meant it as a gesture of goodwill and peace.

When they told it unto David, he sent to meet them, because the men were greatly ashamed: and the king said,
Tarry at Jericho until your beards be grown, and then
return.

And when the children of Ammon saw that they stank
before David, the children of Ammon sent and hired the
Syrians of Beth-rehob, and the Syrians of Zoba, twenty
thousand footmen, and of king Maacah a thousand men,
and of Ish-tob twelve thousand men [2 Sam. 10:5–6].

The Ammonites see that they have made themselves odious to David and prepare for war. They hire mercenaries from Syria—at considerable cost, we learn from the account in 1 Chronicles 19:6-7.

> And when David heard of it, he sent Joab, and all the host of the mighty men.
>
> And the children of Ammon came out, and put the battle in array at the entering in of the gate: and the Syrians of Zoba, and of Rehob, and Ish-tob, and Maacah, were by themselves in the field.
>
> When Joab saw that the front of the battle was against him before and behind, he chose of all the choice men of Israel, and put them in array against the Syrians:
>
> And the rest of the people he delivered into the hand of Abishai his brother, that he might put them in array against the children of Ammon [2 Sam. 10:7-10].

The Israelites were now veterans in warfare. Joab, apparently, is throwing his best forces between the approaching Syrian mercenaries and the forces of the Ammonites to prevent their joining together.

> And the Syrians fled before Israel; and David slew the men of seven hundred chariots of the Syrians, and forty thousand horsemen, and smote Shobach the captain of their host, who died there.
>
> And when all the kings that were servants to Hadarezer saw that they were smitten before Israel, they made peace with Israel, and served them. So the Syrians feared to help the children of Ammon any more [2 Sam. 10:18-19].

It was a tremendous victory for Israel. This establishes David, without doubt, as the great ruler of that day.

CHAPTER 11

THEME: David's two great sins

We have now come to the second and last section of the Book of 2 Samuel, which I have labeled "The Troubles of David." We have seen the "Triumphs of David" in the first section. Under the blessing of God, David has become one of the great kings of the earth. However, the sin recorded in this chapter places David under the judgment of God. From here on David will have trouble. His life will be a series of heartbreaks.

This sin causes the enemies of God to blaspheme—until this day. Leering and suggestive, they exclaim, "This is the 'man after God's own heart'!"

The sin of David stands out like a tar-baby in a field of snow, like a blackberry in a bowl of cream. It may cause us to miss the greatness of the man. Remember that sin was the exception in David's life—not the pattern of it.

The Word of God does not play down the sin of David; it does not whitewash the man. God doesn't say it is not sin. God is going to call it sin, and David will be punished for it.

> **And it came to pass, after the year was expired, at the time when kings go forth to battle, that David sent Joab, and his servants with him, and all Israel; and they destroyed the children of Ammon, and besieged Rabbah. But David tarried still at Jerusalem [2 Sam. 11:1].**

It was the time of the year when kings went forth to war. In other words, in that day the nations had an "open season" on each other like we do today on birds and animals. At a certain season you can shoot them; at other seasons you cannot. But, after all, isn't that true even in modern warfare today? During the monsoons in Vietnam, the war came to a standstill because they got bogged down in the swamps, and the rain kept the planes out of the air. After the monsoons let up, the war was on again. The approach to war in David's day may have been a great deal more modern than we think. The unfortunate thing about the two world wars is that the greatest suffering was caused by the winter weather rather than by the enemy, but they attempted to carry on the fighting. At least in David's day there was a season for warfare. Maybe they were a little more civilized than we are. At least they recognized a time when they could enjoy comparative peace.

Now David sent Joab and the army to fight the children of Ammon. David did not go with them. Instead he tarried at Jerusalem. That was unlike David. Why did he stay? I have only a suggestion to make. After David built his palace he found it very comfortable. It was quite different from the cave of Adullam where he had spent his youth. His palace was a place of luxury and comfort. Also David loved Mount Zion and wanted to stay around that place. Prosperity is one of the things that has trapped so many men and women. Our great comfort has become a curse in our nation. David tarried in Jerusalem. That was his first mistake. He should have gone to war with his men.

> **And it came to pass in an eveningtide, that David arose from off his bed, and walked upon the roof of the king's house: and from the roof he saw a woman washing herself; and the woman was very beautiful to look upon [2 Sam. 11:2].**

In that day the roof was the place where people spent their evenings. They had no front porches or patios in the rear of their homes. Even today the old city of righteousness is very compact, and the flat roof is the place where the family gathers. David went up to the roof of his palace and walked back and forth, apparently a little nervous. I suppose he had a great many problems on his mind. His men were in the field fighting and it may be that his conscience was bothering him. As he walked, he looked around and saw this woman bathing on the roof of her home. Although it was David's sin—God put the blame right on David—it seems that Bathsheba was a contributing factor. She could have been a little bit more modest.

At the risk of sounding like a prude, let me say we are living in a day when women's dress has become a great temptation to men. I wonder how many women, even Christian women, realize what they are doing when they wear certain types of apparel. I have attended services in many churches in which the soloist would get up and carry you to the gates of heaven. Then I have seen her sit down and carry you to the gates of hell. It is my opinion that this woman Bathsheba was partially guilty. What was she doing bathing in public? When I say "public," certainly David was able to see her from his palace. I wonder if she thought there was a chance that David might see her, and she was purposely bathing on the roof.

> **And David sent and inquired after the woman. And one said, Is not this Bath-sheba, the daughter of Eliam, the wife of Uriah the Hittite? [2 Sam. 11:3].**

Uriah was actually a foreigner.

> **And David sent messengers, and took her; and she came in unto him, and he lay with her; for she was purified from her uncleanness: and she returned unto her house [2 Sam. 11:4].**

This is the ugly story, and it is put in plain and simple language so that we cannot miss the point. If David had been out in the field with his men, this would never have happened. If Bathsheba had taken her bath inside her house, this would not have happened.

> **And the woman conceived, and sent and told David, and said, I am with child [2 Sam. 11:5].**

David has a real problem. What is he going to do? Uriah, Bathsheba's husband, is one of David's mighty men. He is one of David's loyal followers.

> And David sent to Joab, saying, Send me Uriah the Hit-
> tite. And Joab sent Uriah to David.
>
> And when Uriah was come unto him, David demanded
> of him how Joab did, and how the people did, and how
> the war prospered [2 Sam. 11:6–7].

David pretended that he had brought Uriah back from the war for consultation to find out how the war was going.

> And David said to Uriah, Go down to thy house, and
> wash thy feet. And Uriah departed out of the king's
> house, and there followed him a mess of meat from the
> king [2 Sam. 11:8].

David is doing everything he can, in this particular instance, to try to
absolve himself of any guilt.

> But Uriah slept at the door of the king's house with all
> the servants of his lord, and went not down to his house
> [2 Sam. 11:9].

Uriah slept at the door of the king's house. At a time of war this man
would not go to his own home. This really surprised David. Also it
was a rebuke to David who was enjoying the luxury of his palace.

> And when they had told David, saying, Uriah went not
> down unto his house, David said unto Uriah, Camest
> thou not from the journey? why then didst thou not go
> down unto thine house? [2 Sam. 11:10].

You can see that David is trying to get Uriah in the position where
David will not be blamed for the pregnancy.

> And Uriah said unto David, The ark, and Israel, and
> Judah, abide in tents; and my lord Joab, and the servants

> **of my lord, are encamped in the open fields; shall I then
> go into mine house, to eat and to drink, and to lie with
> my wife? as thou livest, and as thy soul liveth, I will not
> do this thing [2 Sam. 11:11].**

Uriah was a great man. Although he was a foreigner, he was loyal to
Israel. That made David's double sin all the greater. Uriah said, "The
army and my commander are out in the field. They are in danger. I am
not about to come back home and enjoy luxury and comfort."

> **And David said to Uriah, Tarry here to-day also, and to-
> morrow I will let thee depart. So Uriah abode in Jerusa-
> lem that day, and the morrow.**

> **And when David had called him, he did eat and drink
> before him; and he made him drunk: and at even he
> went out to lie on his bed with the servants of his lord,
> but went not down to his house [2 Sam. 11:12–13].**

Now David tries something else to trick Uriah into going home. David
gets Uriah drunk! Yet the man still did not go home.

> **And it came to pass in the morning, that David wrote a
> letter to Joab, and sent it by the hand of Uriah.**

> **And he wrote in the letter, saying, Set ye Uriah in the
> forefront of the hottest battle, and retire ye from him,
> that he may be smitten, and die [2 Sam. 11:14–15].**

In my judgment this is the worst part of David's sin. He deliberately
plotted the murder of Uriah. This is inexcusable. The Word of God
records what David did. God did not cover it up; He brought it right
out in the open. These are the facts. David is guilty.

> **And it came to pass, when Joab observed the city, that he
> assigned Uriah unto a place where he knew that valiant
> men were.**

> And the men of the city went out, and fought with Joab:
> and there fell some of the people of the servants of
> David; and Uriah the Hittite died also [2 Sam. 11:16–
> 17].

This chills your blood, does it not?

> Then Joab sent and told David all the things concerning
> the war;
>
> And charged the messenger, saying, When thou hast
> made an end of telling the matters of the war unto the
> king,
>
> And if so be that the king's wrath arise, and he say unto
> thee, Wherefore approached ye so nigh unto the city
> when ye did fight? knew ye not that they would shoot
> from the wall? [2 Sam. 11:18–20].

Joab's anticipation of David's reaction may be a cover-up to hide from
the messenger the true significance of the message.

> Who smote Abimelech the son of Jerubbesheth? did not a
> woman cast a piece of a millstone upon him from the
> wall, that he died in Thebez? why went ye nigh the wall?
> then say thou, Thy servant Uriah the Hittite is dead also.
>
> So the messenger went, and came and shewed David all
> that Joab had sent him for.
>
> And the messenger said unto David, Surely the men pre-
> vailed against us, and came out unto us into the field,
> and we were upon them even unto the entering of the
> gate.
>
> And the shooters shot from off the wall upon thy ser-
> vants; and some of the king's servants be dead, and thy
> servant Uriah the Hittite is dead also.

> Then David said unto the messenger, Thus shalt thou
> say unto Joab, Let not this thing displease thee, for the
> sword devoureth one as well as another: make thy battle
> more strong against the city, and overthrow it: and en-
> courage thou him [2 Sam. 11:21–25].

This is very pious talk from David. Aren't you ashamed of him? He is
a real sinner, friend. He has done an awful thing. What should be done
to him? We shall see that God is going to punish him.

> And when the wife of Uriah heard that Uriah her hus-
> band was dead, she mourned for her husband.

> And when the mourning was past, David sent and
> fetched her to his house, and she became his wife, and
> bare him a son. But the thing that David had done dis-
> pleased the Lord [2 Sam. 11:26–27].

"The thing that David had done *displeased* the Lord"—don't miss
that. David did not get by with his sin. Up to this point in his life
David has had many triumphs, but from now on, to his dying day, he
will have trouble.

    May I say to you, Christian friend, that you can sin. Someone
asked me, "Can a Christian get drunk?" I replied, "Yes, a Christian
can get drunk." This person was shocked, but then he asked, "Can he
get by with it?" That is where the rub comes. The man of the world
can get by with it; the Lord does not whip the Devil's children. But He
sure takes His own children to the woodshed. Will you take it from
one who has been to the woodshed? I happen to know that you cannot
get by with sin. David did not get by with it. The thing he did displeased the Lord. When a thing displeases the Lord, friend, He is going to do something about it.

    David thinks he has gotten by with his sin, although there are a few
people who know the facts. Joab, David's captain, knows the facts. A
few of David's intimate counselors in Jerusalem who brought Bathsheba to the palace know the facts. Beyond that, no one knows, and

the lips of these men are closed. They would not dare talk. David, however, wonders as he sits on his throne and looks around him. When David held court, there were probably two hundred people around him, and he undoubtedly looked into each face and silently asked himself, *Do they know?* After a time David probably sat back in satisfaction and said to himself, *Well, I got by with it. Nobody knows.*

My friend, whether it was known in Jerusalem or not, David's secret sin and our secret sins are open before God. Someone has put it this way, "Secret sin on earth is open scandal in heaven." God knows all about what we do.

CHAPTER 12

THEME: Nathan faces David with his sins; David repents

NATHAN FACES DAVID WITH HIS SINS

The critics who say that God allows David to get by with his great sin apparently haven't read the whole story. Friend, we need to keep on reading. When Nathan confronts David with his sin, David repents. In spite of that, Nathan pronounces God's judgment upon David. David must learn that a man reaps what he sows.

God's man may get in sin, but he will not stay in sin. That is what distinguishes God's man from the man of the world. A sheep may fall in the mud, but he will struggle out of it as soon as he can. A pig will stay in the mud and enjoy it.

God has said that men, like pieces of pottery, can be marred. One flaw can ruin a valuable piece of pottery. A valuable article is put on sale because the merchant sees a flaw in it. I am a great one for sales as I go about the country. When I see that a sale is on, I rush down to the store. Usually I find that first-grade merchandise has become second-grade merchandise because of a flaw. It is marked down because of a little defect. Now David will have to be marked down because of his sin. In chapter 11 we saw David's sin in all of its blackness and ugliness. The Word of God does not soft-pedal it. The Word of God does not whitewash David's actions. His sin is as black as ink, and as dark as night, and as low as the underside of Satan and the bottomless pit, and as deep as hell. David sinned.

What David did displeased the Lord, and God is going to do something about it. You see, God did something about man's sin. He gave Jesus Christ to die on the Cross and pay the penalty—sin is that heinous. It is God who says that sin is so black that it required the death of His Son. If you turn your back on God, you are lost. However, if you are God's man and you drop into sin, God is going to deal with you.

In chapter 11 we left David sitting on his throne in smug complacency. He thought he had gotten away with his sin, but he was wrong. David is going to live to regret that he ever committed that awful sin.

The first verse introduces us to Nathan, one of the bravest men in Scripture. David could have merely lifted his scepter and without a word could have condemned Nathan to execution for his audacity. This, however, did not stop Nathan.

And the LORD sent Nathan unto David. And he came unto him, and said unto him, There were two men in one city; the one rich, and the other poor [2 Sam. 12:1].

Nathan is going to tell David a story. It is a story that will reveal David as though he were looking in a mirror. The Word of God is a mirror that reveals us as we really are. Nathan is going to hold up a mirror so that David can get a good look at himself. There was probably a lull in state business when Nathan came. Since Nathan was God's prophet, David said to him, "Do you have anything from the Lord for me?" He did. He told Nathan a story about two men in one city. One man was rich and the other man was poor—a typical city with its ghetto and its rich estates.

The rich man had exceeding many flocks and herds:

But the poor man had nothing, save one little ewe lamb, which he had bought and nourished up: and it grew up together with him, and with his children; it did eat of his own meat, and drank of his own cup, and lay in his bosom, and was unto him as a daughter [2 Sam. 12:2–3].

The story of the rich man and the poor man sounds very familiar. The rich had many flocks and herds. The poor man had one little lamb. It was a pet and dearly loved by the family. They fed it—it was probably a fat little fellow. It was all the poor man had. What a contrast. This has been the continual war between the rich and the poor. I personally think the outstanding problem today is not the racial problem, but the conflict between capital and labor, the rich and the poor.

> And there came a traveller unto the rich man, and he
> spared to take of his own flock and of his own herd, to
> dress for the wayfaring man that was come unto him;
> but took the poor man's lamb, and dressed it for the
> man that was come to him [2 Sam. 12:4].

Nathan is telling a story that is quite familiar, is it not? The poor man had nothing but the little ewe lamb; the rich man had everything—yet he was a skinflint. I do not often discuss politics, but I would like to put down a principle in this world of sin today. I recognize that political parties say they have the solutions for the problems of the world because they want their candidates to be elected to office. I have no confidence in men. I do not believe that any politician today is going to champion the poor. This never has been done, and it never will be done. Let us not kid ourselves about that. It is quite interesting about the government poverty programs. Do they tax the rich? No! Taxes go up for the rest of us. I tell you, they are surely taking my little ewe lamb, friends.

> And David's anger was greatly kindled against the
> man; and he said to Nathan, As the LORD liveth, the man
> that hath done this thing shall surely die [2 Sam. 12:5].

David thought Nathan had brought before him a case for someone in the kingdom and was asking for David to rule upon it. David had a sense of right and wrong. He also had a sense of justice. He is red-headed and hotheaded. When he heard Nathan's story, he probably sprang to his feet and demanded, "Where is this man? We will arrest him. We will execute him!"

It is interesting how easily you can see the sin in somebody else, but you cannot see it in your own life. That was David's problem.

> And he shall restore the lamb fourfold, because he did
> this thing, and because he had no pity [2 Sam. 12:6].

David sounds like a preacher, doesn't he? It is so easy to preach to the other person, tell him his faults, analyze him, and tell him what to do. Most of us are amateur psychologists who put other people on our own little critical couches and give them a working over. That is David. David says, "Wherever that man is, we are going to see that justice is done."

> And Nathan said to David, Thou art the man. Thus saith the LORD God of Israel, I anointed thee king over Israel, and I delivered thee out of the hand of Saul;
>
> And I gave thee thy master's house, and thy master's wives into thy bosom, and gave thee the house of Israel and of Judah; and if that had been too little, I would moreover have given unto thee such and such things [2 Sam. 12:7–8].

It took courage for Nathan to say this to David. In my judgment he is the bravest man in the Bible. I know of no one who can be compared to him. He said, "David, you are the guilty one." What is David going to do? He is going to do something unusual, I can assure you of that. Dr. Margoliouth has said this: "When has this been done—before or since? Mary, Queen of Scots, would declare that she was above the law; Charles I would have thrown over Bathsheba; James II would have hired witnesses to swear away her character; Mohammed would have produced a revelation authorizing both crimes; Charles II would have publicly abrogated the seventh commandment; Queen Elizabeth would have suspended Nathan." Years ago, the Duke of Windsor would have given up his throne for her. We have had some presidents who would have repealed the Ten Commandments and appointed Nathan to the Supreme Court. David did not do any of these things. His actions will reveal his greatness.

God would have given David anything his heart wanted, but David longed for something that was not his. The new morality today says it was not sin. God still says this is sin, and the man after God's own heart cannot get by with it.

Wherefore hast thou despised the commandment of the Lord, to do evil in his sight? thou hast killed Uriah the Hittite with the sword, and hast taken his wife to be thy wife, and hast slain him with the sword of the children of Ammon [2 Sam. 12:9].

Nathan spells out the sins in no uncertain terms.

Don't you imagine, friends, that the court was shocked when they heard what Nathan said to David? There were undoubtedly many present who did not know what had happened. They hear Nathan accuse David of the most brutal crime written in the books. David has done the things that God said, "Thou shalt not do."

Is he going to get by with it?

Now therefore the sword shall never depart from thine house; because thou hast despised me, and hast taken the wife of Uriah the Hittite to be thy wife [2 Sam. 12:10].

May I say, Christian friend, that when the question arises, "Can a Christian sin?" the answer is yes. But when you sin, you despise God. God says that that is what you do. When David took Uriah's wife to be his wife, he was despising God.

Thus saith the Lord, Behold, I will raise up evil against thee out of thine own house, and I will take thy wives before thine eyes, and give them unto thy neighbour, and he shall lie with thy wives in the sight of this sun [2 Sam. 12:11].

Evil is going to arise against David out of his own house. And friends, in the next chapter a scandal breaks out among David's children that is an awful thing. It becomes a heartbreak to this man. But you will never find him whimpering or crying out to God about it, because David knew that God was putting the lash on his back. All that David wanted was what is written in Psalm 42:1, "As the hart panteth after the water brooks, so panteth my soul after thee, O God."

> For thou didst it secretly: but I will do this thing before all Israel, and before the sun [2 Sam. 12:12].

DAVID REPENTS

> And David said unto Nathan, I have sinned against the LORD. And Nathan said unto David, The LORD also hath put away thy sin; thou shalt not die [2 Sam. 12:13].

David should have died for this crime. God spared David's life and put away his sin, but David's baby died. God is not going to let David get by with his sin.

> Howbeit, because by this deed thou hast given great occasion to the enemies of the LORD to blaspheme, the child also that is born unto thee shall surely die [2 Sam. 12:14].

And friends, the enemies of the Lord still blaspheme God because of what David did. When I was a pastor in downtown Los Angeles, there were many times when some unbeliever or skeptic came to me and said, "How could God choose a man like David?" They would actually leer at me while waiting for my reply. The enemy is still blaspheming. God is going to take David to the woodshed.

> And Nathan departed unto his house. And the LORD struck the child that Uriah's wife bare unto David, and it was very sick.

> David therefore besought God for the child; and David fasted, and went in, and lay all night upon the earth.

> And the elders of his house arose, and went to him, to raise him up from the earth: but he would not, neither did he eat bread with them [2 Sam. 12:15–17].

David went before God and pleaded for Him to spare the little fellow's life. Finally they brought word to David that the child was dead.

> **But when David saw that his servants whispered, David perceived that the child was dead: therefore David said unto his servants, Is the child dead? And they said, He is dead.**

> **Then David arose from the earth, and washed, and anointed himself, and changed his apparel, and came into the house of the LORD, and worshipped: then he came to his own house; and when he required, they set bread before him, and he did eat [2 Sam. 12:19–20].**

David's servants are astounded. When the child was alive, David was in sackcloth and ashes. When the child died, he should have been beside himself with grief. Instead, he got up, took a shower, and changed his clothes, *then went to the house of God to worship.* His servants ask for an explanation.

> **And he said, While the child was yet alive, I fasted and wept: for I said, Who can tell whether GOD will be gracious to me, that the child may live?**

> **But now he is dead, wherefore should I fast? can I bring him back again? I shall go to him, but he shall not return to me [2 Sam. 12:22–23].**

David knew that the little baby was saved. He said, "I will go to him someday." David knew that when death came to him, he would be reunited with his son.

A child dying in infancy goes to be with the Lord. Matthew 18:10 says, "Take heed that ye despise not one of these little ones; for I say unto you, That in heaven their angels do always behold the face of my Father which is in heaven." The word *angels* in this verse should be translated "spirits." When a little baby dies today, that baby goes immediately to be with the Lord. That is the teaching of the Word of God.

I don't know about you, but this means a great deal to me because I have a little one up there, and I am looking forward to one day being with her.

David could rejoice when his infant son died because he knew that one day he would see him again. That was not the case when his son Absalom died many years later. Absalom was a heartbreak to David. When he died, David wept and mourned. Why? David was not sure Absalom was saved.

THE BIRTH OF SOLOMON

And David comforted Bath-sheba his wife, and went in unto her, and lay with her: and she bare a son, and he called his name Solomon: and the LORD loved him.

And he sent by the hand of Nathan the prophet; and he called his name Jedidiah, because of the LORD [2 Sam. 12:24–25].

The name *Jedidiah* means "beloved of the Lord." This name was given by God through Nathan to Solomon.

DAVID AND JOAB TAKE RABBAH

And Joab fought against Rabbah of the children of Ammon, and took the royal city.

And Joab sent messengers to David, and said, I have fought against Rabbah, and have taken the city of waters.

Now therefore gather the rest of the people together, and encamp against the city, and take it: lest I take the city, and it be called after my name.

And David gathered all the people together, and went to Rabbah, and fought against it, and took it [2 Sam. 12:26–29].

David is now back out in the field where he should have been all along. David's kingdom continues to be extended and expanded, and David becomes a great ruler of that day. What about his sin? Did he get by with it? In the next chapter we will find out that David had a son that committed an awful crime. He raped his half sister, a daughter of David. Absalom, a full brother of the girl who was raped, killed him. Say, that was a scandal! Can you imagine how that news spread over Israel? The people said, "Look at the king ruling over us. He cannot even rule his own household!" Poor David.

Before we get through with the life of David, I feel like saying to the Lord, "You have whipped him enough. Why don't you take the lash off his back now?" But, you know, David never said that. David went into the presence of the Lord and cried: "Have mercy upon me, O God, according to thy lovingkindness: according unto the multitude of thy tender mercies blot out my transgressions. Wash me throughly from mine iniquity, and cleanse me from my sin. Restore unto me the joy of thy salvation; and uphold me with thy free spirit" (Ps. 51:1–2, 12). David wanted to be brought back into fellowship with his God.

CHAPTERS 13 AND 14

THEME: Crimes of David's sons—Amnon and
Absalom

There is that old bromide which says, "If you are going to dance,
you are going to have to pay the fiddler." If you are going to indulge in sin, you will have to suffer the consequences. The Lord gives
it to us straight in Galatians 6:7: "Be not deceived; God is not
mocked: for whatsoever a man soweth, that shall he also reap." You
are not going to get by with sin. Galatians 6:8 goes on to say, "For he
that soweth to his flesh shall of the flesh reap corruption; but he that
soweth to the Spirit shall of the Spirit reap life everlasting." There is
no question that David had sown to the flesh. Don't think for one minute that now he can walk away from his sin, make a sweet little confession, and that is it. I have heard people say, "Well, the blood of
Christ covers it." It certainly does, and you don't lose your salvation,
brother. But I want to tell you that sin causes a festering sore that has to
be lanced.

This brings us to chapter 13. David has made his confession of sin.
God has told him, "Your sin has caused My enemies to blaspheme Me.
I won't give you up, but you are not going to get by with it." Thank
God that He will not give us up, but the chickens do come home to
roost.

DAVID'S DAUGHTER RAPED BY HIS SON

**And it came to pass after this, that Absalom the son of
David had a fair sister, whose name was Tamar; and
Amnon the son of David loved her [2 Sam. 13:1].**

Although Absalom and Tamar had the same mother and father, Tamar was Amnon's half sister. David was their father, but they had different mothers.

> And Amnon was so vexed, that he fell sick for his sister Tamar; for she was a virgin; and Amnon thought it hard for him to do any thing to her.
>
> But Amnon had a friend, whose name was Jonadab, the son of Shimeah David's brother: and Jonadab was a very subtil man.
>
> And he said unto him, Why art thou, being the king's son, lean from day to day? wilt thou not tell me? And Amnon said unto him, I love Tamar, my brother Absalom's sister [2 Sam. 13:2-4].

Amnon was not eating. He was so madly in love with Tamar that he had lost his appetite. His friend could see that he was not eating, but he also recognized the problem since Tamar was Absalom's sister and Amnon was afraid of Absalom.

> And Jonadab said unto him, Lay thee down on thy bed, and make thyself sick: and when thy father cometh to see thee, say unto him, I pray thee, let my sister Tamar come, and give me meat, and dress the meat in my sight, that I may see it, and eat it at her hand.
>
> So Amnon lay down, and made himself sick: and when the king was come to see him, Amnon said unto the king, I pray thee, let Tamar my sister come, and make me a couple of cakes in my sight, that I may eat at her hand.
>
> Then David sent home to Tamar, saying, Go now to thy brother Amnon's house, and dress him meat [2 Sam. 13:5-7].

There is no use to read the next few verses which contain the sordid details of what happened next. Amnon raped Tamar. Then we are told that he hated her.

> **Then Amnon hated her exceedingly; so that the hatred wherewith he hated her was greater than the love wherewith he had loved her. And Amnon said unto her, Arise, be gone [2 Sam. 13:15].**

This awful thing had taken place in the house of David. When Amnon was through with her, he flung her out.

> **And Tamar put ashes on her head, and rent her garment of divers colours that was on her, and laid her hand on her head, and went on crying [2 Sam. 13:19].**

Tamar was thrown out of the house, and now she is in sackcloth and ashes.

> **And Absalom her brother said unto her, hath Amnon thy brother been with thee? but hold now thy peace, my sister: he is thy brother; regard not this thing. So Tamar remained desolate in her brother Absalom's house.**

> **But when king David heard of all these things, he was very wroth [2 Sam. 13:20–21].**

David is angry about what happened but does nothing about it. David was like many other men in Scripture: he was an indulgent father who raised a bunch of kids who were bad. That has happened again and again. It started with old Eli, God's high priest. His sons were not only immoral, they were godless and had a religious racket going. Then we come to Samuel. Since he was raised in the same atmosphere as Eli's sons, you would think Samuel would be more of a disciplinarian and that he would have maintained some authority and control over his sons. But his sons turned out to be corrupt and dishonest. Next we come to David. He knew Samuel, and he knew Samuel's sons. You would think he would have been more strict with his children, but he was not. He too was an indulgent father. He was angry about what Amnon did to his sister Tamar. But, after all, what kind of an example has David set for his boys? The chickens are beginning to come home to roost.

Perhaps you think I am a square because I say some old-fashioned things, but I am convinced that the main problem today in Christian homes is the lack of example and discipline on the part of the parents. My friend, if you are a Christian and you have a naughty little boy in your home, don't spend your time lecturing him. You are not going to get anywhere that way. Give him an example and discipline—and start soon, because the day will come when he will walk out.

Another strike against David is the fact that he had multiple wives and many children. As a king with many heavy responsibilities, how much time do you think he spent in rearing his children? The problem with many of us who have been in Christian work is that we probably have neglected our families for the sake of the work. We have excused our neglect on the basis that we were doing Christian work. I must confess that if I could go back and do one thing over again, it would be to spend more time with my daughter when she was growing up. Do you know why? I was too busy when she was small. Now I am not so busy and I can spend time with my grandchildren.

Christian parents need to realize that they need to spend time training their children. Don't get the impression that you are raising a little angel. There are many parents who treat a child as if he were a cross between an orchid and a piece of Dresden china. They believe that if they apply the board of education to the seat of knowledge they will break him in pieces or he will come apart. Proverbs 23:13 says, "Withhold not correction from the child: for if thou beatest him with the rod, he shall not die."

David did nothing about the problem created by Amnon. So what happened?

And Absalom spake unto his brother Amnon neither good nor bad: for Absalom hated Amnon, because he had forced his sister Tamar [2 Sam. 13:22].

This is David's home, friends. This is David's life at home. He did not get by with sin. God says that we will not get by with sin either. Absa-

lom is marking time. He is waiting for the day when he can get even
with Amnon. And that day will come.

AMNON IS MURDERED BY ABSALOM

I am not going into detail at this point, but the day came when Absalom killed Amnon. Absalom waited for two years before making his
move. He invited the king's sons to a feast in connection with sheep-
shearing time. Since Absalom had shown no signs of wanting revenge, David let Amnon go and attend the party.

> **Now Absalom had commanded his servants, saying,
> Mark ye now when Amnon's heart is merry with wine,
> and when I say unto you, Smite, Amnon; then kill him,
> fear not: have not I commanded you? be courageous,
> and be valiant [2 Sam. 13:28].**

When the day came that Amnon's "heart was merry with wine," Absalom had him killed.

The first message David received was that all his sons were dead.
Then Jonadab told him that only Amnon was slain.

> **Now therefore let not my lord the king take the thing to
> his heart, to think that all the king's sons are dead: for
> Amnon only is dead.**

> **But Absalom fled. And the young man that kept the
> watch lifted up his eyes, and, behold, there came much
> people by the way of the hill side behind him.**

> **And Jonadab said unto the king, Behold, the king's sons
> come: as thy servant said, so it is [2 Sam. 13:33–35].**

Since Absalom actually plotted Amnon's murder, he has to flee.

> **And it came to pass, as soon as he had made an end of
> speaking, that, behold, the king's sons came, and lifted**

up their voice and wept: and the king also and all his servants wept very sore.

But Absalom fled, and went to Talmai, the son of Ammihud, king of Geshur. And David mourned for his son every day [2 Sam. 13:36–37].

Absalom's mother was a daughter of the king of Geshur, and this is one reason why Absalom fled to him. As I have pointed out before, David made a mistake in marrying this foreign woman. Remember that he had married this woman during his lapse of faith when he withdrew from the land. She bore the king two very attractive children. One was Absalom and the other was Tamar. Apparently David did not discipline this wild boy, who was the son of a pagan and a Bedouin. In a way, Absalom seems to be justified in what he did, since David did not take matters into his own hands when Amnon sinned.

So Absalom fled, and went to Geshur, and was there three years.

And the soul of king David longed to go forth unto Absalom: for he was comforted concerning Amnon, seeing he was dead [2 Sam. 13:38–39].

After Absalom took Amnon's life, he fled. David wanted to bring him back, but he did not. David mourned for him and that is all he did. He mourned for him and wished for his return. Absalom, I believe, was more like David than any of his other sons. I think it was David's intention that Absalom succeed him as the next king of Israel. That ambition also lurked in the mind of Absalom, as we shall see.

DAVID PERMITS ABSALOM TO RETURN

Now Joab the son of Zeruiah perceived that the king's heart was toward Absalom.

And Joab sent to Tekoah, and fetched thence a wise woman, and said unto her, I pray thee, feign thyself to

> be a mourner, and put on now mourning apparel, and anoint not thyself with oil, but be as a woman that had a long time mourned for the dead:
>
> And come to the king, and speak on this manner unto him. So Joab put the words in her mouth [2 Sam. 14:1–3].

Joab grew up in the vicinity of Tekoah and may have known this woman from earlier days.

> And when the woman of Tekoah spake to the king, she fell on her face to the ground, and did obeisance, and said, Help, O king.
>
> And the king said unto her, What aileth thee? And she answered, I am indeed a widow woman, and mine husband is dead.
>
> And thy handmaid had two sons, and they two strove together in the field, and there was none to part them, but the one smote the other, and slew him.
>
> And, behold, the whole family is risen against thine handmaid, and they said, Deliver him that smote his brother, that we may kill him, for the life of his brother whom he slew; and we will destroy the heir also: and so they shall quench my coal which is left, and shall not leave to my husband neither name nor remainder upon the earth [2 Sam. 14:4–7].

Joab got her to play upon the feelings of David by telling him her sad story. Just as David had used deception, he was now being deceived.

> Then said she, I pray thee, let the king remember the Lord thy God, that thou wouldest not suffer the revengers of blood to destroy any more, lest they destroy my

> son. And he said, As the LORD liveth, there shall not one
> hair of thy son fall to the earth [2 Sam. 14:11].

David grants her imaginary son a full pardon. Then she makes the
application to David and Absalom.

> **And the woman said, Wherefore then hast thou thought
> such a thing against the people of God? for the king
> doth speak this thing as one which is faulty, in that the
> king doth not fetch home again his banished [2 Sam.
> 14:13].**

The widow of Tekoah was putting David in the place of her imaginary
prosecutors. What her prosecutors could do to her remaining son,
David was doing to God's people by punishing Absalom for the crime
he had committed. She is representing the people of Israel as the wid-
owed mother. She claims to be speaking in the name of all Israel, and
possibly she does express their feelings. Absalom was very popular
with the people, and they probably felt that Amnon got what he de-
served.

The final outcome of the incident is that in a half-hearted way
David is willing for Absalom to return.

> **And the king said unto Joab, Behold now, I have done
> this thing: go therefore, bring the young man Absalom
> again.**
>
> **And Joab fell to the ground on his face, and bowed him-
> self, and thanked the king: and Joab said, To-day thy
> servant knoweth that I have found grace in thy sight, my
> lord, O king, in that the king hath fulfilled the request of
> his servant.**
>
> **So Joab arose and went to Geshur, and brought Absalom
> to Jerusalem.**

> And the king said, Let him turn to his own house, and
> let him not see my face. So Absalom returned to his own
> house, and saw not the king's face [2 Sam. 14:21–24].

It is unfortunate that David did not want to see his son. It actually set
the stage for Absalom's rebellion which takes place in chapter 15. Absalom was a bad boy, but he was a good politician. We shall see this in
the next chapter.

Absalom's high-handed action of setting Joab's standing grain on
fire to force Joab to come to him is another revelation of Absalom's
personality.

> And Absalom answered Joab, Behold, I sent unto thee,
> saying, Come hither, that I may send thee to the king, to
> say, Wherefore am I come from Geshur? it had been
> good for me to have been there still: now therefore let me
> see the king's face; and if there be any iniquity in me, let
> him kill me.

> So Joab came to the king, and told him: and when he
> had called for Absalom, he came to the king, and bowed
> himself on his face to the ground before the king: and
> the king kissed Absalom [2 Sam. 14:32–33].

Absalom's prank succeeded in persuading Joab to bring him to his
father for reconciliation. Although David's kiss was a sign of complete
reconciliation and restoration of Absalom's position as the king's son,
it was given reluctantly. The fact that his father did not give him in-
stant, wholehearted forgiveness rankled in his soul.

God had not forgiven David half-heartedly. God did not say, "Well,
I forgive you, but we will not have fellowship any more. I will not
restore to you the joy of your salvation." When God forgives, He forgives completely. You and I are admonished: "And be ye kind one to
another, tenderhearted, forgiving one another, even as God for Christ's
sake hath forgiven you" (Eph. 4:32). Has God forgiven us? Yes! How

are we to forgive others? The same way that God does. David should have forgiven Absalom. He is setting the stage for rebellion.

Oh, my friend, our God is a God who forgives. Galatians 6:1 tells us, "Brethren, if a man be overtaken in a fault, ye which are spiritual, restore such an one in the spirit of meekness; considering thyself, lest thou also be tempted." It appears that many of us don't read that verse correctly. We think it says, "If any man be overtaken in a fault, take a baseball bat and hit him over the head!" We are reluctant to forgive, and we can be very mean at times, very unloving, and critical. There are times when the truth should be spoken, but when forgiveness is asked for, it should be extended immediately.

David made a blunder in not forgiving his son as God had forgiven David. He will live to regret it.

CHAPTERS 15 AND 16

THEME: Absalom rebels against David

ABSALOM REBELS AGAINST DAVID

David, after committing his terrible sin, found that trouble came to him thick and fast. The same way that he had sinned, members of his family sinned, and David is not through with the effect of it yet. God really took David to the woodshed.

In this chapter Absalom leads a rebellion against David. In a very subtle way Absalom begins to steal the hearts of the children of Israel. He is an attractive young fellow—probably like David in many ways. He is the heir apparent to the throne; that is, David would like for him to succeed him. We find now that Absalom is back in Jerusalem, beginning to move secretly to plot David's overthrow. This is a dastardly deed, but the chickens are coming home to roost for David. Actually, a formidable revolution will break out which will cause David to flee from Jerusalem.

> And it came to pass after this, that Absalom prepared him chariots and horses, and fifty men to run before him.
>
> And Absalom rose up early, and stood beside the way of the gate: and it was so, that when any man that had a controversy came to the king for judgment, then Absalom called unto him, and said, Of what city art thou? And he said, Thy servant is of one of the tribes of Israel [2 Sam. 15:1–2].

Absalom stationed himself at the busiest gate of the city. When men with complaints came to the gate requiring justice, he listened to them with a great show of sympathy.

> And Absalom said unto him, See, thy matters are good and right; but there is no man deputed of the king to hear thee.

> Absalom said moreover, Oh that I were made judge in the land, that every man which hath any suit or cause might come unto me, and I would do him justice! [2 Sam. 15:3-4].

Absalom was a bad boy but a good politician; he was clever and crooked, subtle and sly.

> And it was so, that when any man came nigh to him to do him obeisance, he put forth his hand, and took him, and kissed him.

> And on this manner did Absalom to all Israel that came to the king for judgment: so Absalom stole the hearts of the men of Israel [2 Sam. 15:5-6].

Absalom is a true politician, isn't he? This is the way many men get elected to office today. They have no qualifications other than the fact that they are good at handshaking and backslapping. There are many preachers who use this method today. They cannot preach, and they cannot teach, but they sure can slap backs. Unfortunately that is exactly what appeals to us. As far as I can tell from the Word of God, that is the way that the Antichrist will come to power. He is going to be the greatest little backslapper that the world has ever seen. Now Absalom was a good backslapper. He stood at the gate and said, "Oh, if I were only a judge. Then you would get *justice!*" You can understand the appeal that that kind of statement would make. Absalom was saying, "If you vote me into office, I can solve all of your problems. I will be able to take care of all the foreign and domestic affairs." That is what the politicians tell us today. Unfortunately, we listen to them, believe them, and vote for them. Then when they get into office, they do not produce.

Absalom, of course, is preparing for a rebellion against David, his father. This rebellion within the house of David is a terrible thing.

> **And it came to pass after forty years, that Absalom said unto the king, I pray thee, let me go and pay my vow, which I have vowed unto the LORD, in Hebron.**
>
> **For thy servant vowed a vow while I abode at Geshur in Syria, saying, If the LORD shall bring me again indeed to Jerusalem, then I will serve the LORD [2 Sam. 15:7–8].**

His request seems a little unusual—he says he wants to go south to Hebron to pay a vow he made in exile, yet he was in Syria in the north while he was in exile. However, David does not question it.

> **And the king said unto him, Go in peace. So he arose, and went to Hebron.**
>
> **But Absalom sent spies throughout all the tribes of Israel, saying, As soon as ye hear the sound of the trumpet, then ye shall say, Absalom reigneth in Hebron [2 Sam. 15:9–10].**

You will recall that Hebron is where David began his reign. He was king over Judah for seven years in Hebron. Absalom, obviously, did not go to Hebron to pay a vow. He went there to begin his rebellion.

> **And with Absalom went two hundred men out of Jerusalem, that were called; and they went in their simplicity, and they knew not any thing [2 Sam. 15:11].**

In other words, these men went along with Absalom, but they did not know that the rebellion was prepared against David.

> **And Absalom sent for Ahithophel the Gilonite, David's counsellor, from his city, even from Giloh, while he offered sacrifices. And the conspiracy was strong; for the**

people increased continually with Absalom [2 Sam. 15:12].

This is a rebellion that gains momentum. It begins to snowball as it goes along, and soon there is a great company standing with Absalom. Even Ahithophel, David's counselor, is a partner to all of this. Before David actually realizes what is happening, the rebellion surfaces.

DAVID FLEES

And there came a messenger to David, saying, The hearts of the men of Israel are after Absalom.

And David said unto all his servants that were with him at Jerusalem, Arise, and let us flee; for we shall not else escape from Absalom: make speed to depart, lest he overtake us suddenly, and bring evil upon us, and smite the city with the edge of the sword [2 Sam. 15:13-14].

David is going to flee from Jerusalem. The question arises, "Why did he flee?" David loved the city of Jerusalem. Why didn't he make a stand in this city? I am confident that David knew God was punishing him for his sin. I know this is true on the basis of 2 Samuel 15:25–26 where we are told, "And the king said unto Zadok, Carry back the ark of God into the city: if I shall find favour in the eyes of the LORD, he will bring me again, and shew me both it, and his habitation: But if he thus say, I have no delight in thee; behold, here am I, let him do to me as seemeth good unto him." David knew what was happening to him. He knew that judgment was coming from God.

You recall in 2 Samuel 13 that Amnon committed a crime against Tamar. David was disgraced by the awful thing that happened. This scandal had taken place in Jerusalem. You will also recall that David's great sin involving Uriah and Bathsheba—when David should have been out fighting with his army—took place in Jerusalem. David is leaving Jerusalem this time because he knows that God is punishing him, and he does not want to see the city he built and loved become the scene of battle. In 2 Samuel 15:30 we are told, "And David went up by the ascent of mount Olivet, and wept as he went up, and had his head covered, and he went barefoot: and all the people that was with him covered every man his head, and they went up, weeping as they went up." David loved Jerusalem. He did not want it to be a place of battle; yet this city was to be destroyed more than any other city because of its rebellion and sin.

Also David fled from Jerusalem because he was not ready to press the issue with Absalom. We will see in the next chapters that it was in David's heart to spare the life of his son. He did not want harm to come to him. I think David loved Absalom above every person on earth. Leaving Jerusalem puts David's life in grave danger, but that is nothing new for him. He had been in great danger many times. He has more concern about his relationship with God and with his son than he has about his life.

With this background, let us look at the rebellion that is taking place.

> Then said the king to Ittai the Gittite, Wherefore goest thou also with us? return to thy place, and abide with the king: for thou art a stranger, and also an exile.
>
> Whereas thou camest but yesterday, should I this day make thee go up and down with us? seeing I go whither I may, return thou, and take back thy brethren: mercy and truth be with thee [2 Sam. 15:19–20].

Ittai is a native of Gath in Philistia, probably a general in his own country since David later makes him a joint commander with Joab and Abishai. He feels such loyalty to David that he and his entire family insist upon going into exile with him.

> And Ittai answered the king, and said, As the LORD liveth, and as my lord the king liveth, surely in what place my lord the king shall be, whether in death or life, even there also will thy servant be.

And David said to Ittai, Go and pass over. And Ittai the Gittite passed over, and all his men, and all the little ones that were with him.

And all the country wept with a loud voice, and all the people passed over: the king also himself passed over the brook Kidron, and all the people passed over, toward the way of the wilderness [2 Sam. 15:21–23].

David had many loyal followers. There were many men willing to lay down their lives for him.

THE ARK IS RETURNED TO JERUSALEM

And lo Zadok also, and all the Levites were with him, bearing the ark of the covenant of God: and they set down the ark of God; and Abiathar went up, until all the people had done passing out of the city.

And the king said unto Zadok, Carry back the ark of God into the city: if I shall find favour in the eyes of the LORD, he will bring me again, and shew me both it, and his habitation [2 Sam. 15:24–25].

David sent the ark of the covenant of God back to Jerusalem where it belonged. He recognized that what was happening to him was the judgment of God. As he left the city, he went over the Mount of Olives, weeping as he went.

And one told David, saying, Ahithophel is among the conspirators with Absalom. And David said, O LORD, I pray thee, turn the counsel of Ahithophel into foolishness [2 Sam. 15:31].

Ahithophel had been a highly esteemed counselor of David. When he defected to Absalom's side, David prayed that his counsel to Absalom would be foolish, and God answered this prayer, by the way. Notice that David didn't ask for judgment upon Absalom.

HUSHAI IS SENT BACK

And it came to pass, that when David was come to the top of the mount, where he worshipped God, behold, Hushai the Archite came to meet him with his coat rent, and earth upon his head:

Unto whom David said, If thou passest on with me, then thou shalt be a burden unto me [2 Sam. 15:32–33].

He may have been elderly and would require more care.

But if thou return to the city, and say unto Absalom, I will be thy servant, O king; as I have been thy father's servant hitherto, so will I now also be thy servant: then mayest thou for me defeat the counsel of Ahithophel.

And hast thou not there with thee Zadok and Abiathar the priests? therefore it shall be, that what thing soever thou shalt hear out of the king's house, thou shalt tell it to Zadok and Abiathar the priests.

Behold, they have there with them their two sons, Ahim-aaz Zadok's son, and Jonathan Abiathar's son; and by them ye shall send unto me every thing that ye can hear.

So Hushai David's friend came into the city, and Absalom came into Jerusalem [2 Sam. 15:34–37].

When David heard of Ahithophel's defection to Absalom, he induced Hushai to go over to Absalom to defeat the counsels of this now dangerous enemy. Hushai was David's friend and would risk being a spy for him.

ZIBA, MEPHIBOSHETH'S SERVANT, DECEIVES DAVID

And when David was a little past the top of the hill, behold, Ziba the servant of Mephibosheth met him, with a couple of asses saddled, and upon them two hundred loaves of bread, and an hundred bunches of raisins, and an hundred of summer fruits, and a bottle of wine.

And the king said unto Ziba, What meanest thou by these? And Ziba said, The asses be for the king's household to ride on; and the bread and summer fruit for the young men to eat; and the wine, that such as be faint in the wilderness may drink [2 Sam. 16:1–2].

You recall that Mephibosheth was Jonathan's lame son. Because of David's great love for Jonathan, he cared for Mephibosheth.

Ziba, a servant of Mephibosheth, thought that the internal struggle within the house of David would give the house of Saul a chance to regain the throne—Mephibosheth was the sole heir to the throne. By telling his fictitious story, Ziba hoped to get something out of the estate of Mephibosheth. David, not having opportunity to check the facts, impetuously grants Ziba lands that had been Mephibosheth's.

SHIMEI CURSES DAVID

And when king David came to Bahurim, behold, thence came out a man of the family of the house of Saul, whose name was Shimei, the son of Gera: he came forth, and cursed still as he came.

And he cast stones at David, and at all the servants of king David: and all the people and all the mighty men were on his right hand and on his left.

And thus said Shimei when he cursed, Come out, come out, thou bloody man, and thou man of Belial:

> The LORD hath returned upon thee all the blood of the
> house of Saul, in whose stead thou hast reigned; and the
> LORD hath delivered the kingdom into the hand of Absa-
> lom thy son: and, behold, thou art taken in thy mischief,
> because thou art a bloody man [2 Sam. 16:5–8].

What Shimei said to David had some truth in it. David was a bloody
man, and judgment was coming upon him—there was no question
about that.

> Then said Abishai the son of Zeruiah unto the king,
> Why should this dead dog curse my lord the king? let
> me go over, I pray thee, and take off his head [2 Sam.
> 16:9].

Abishai, one of David's men, was all for silencing this man permanently.
    Notice David's reaction to what Shimei said.

> And the king said, What have I to do with you, ye sons of
> Zeruiah? so let him curse, because the LORD hath said
> unto him, Curse David. Who shall then say, Wherefore
> hast thou done so?

> And David said to Abishai, and to all his servants, Be-
> hold, my son, which came forth of my bowels, seeketh
> my life: how much more now may this Benjamite do it?
> let him alone, and let him curse; for the LORD hath bid-
> den him [2 Sam. 16:10–11].

David was saying, "I don't mind this outsider cursing me. I do not
want to take revenge on him. The thing that is happening to me is the
judgment of God. What disturbs me is that it is my own boy, Absalom,
who is leading the rebellion against me."
    We have been with David as he escaped from Jerusalem; now we go
back to Jerusalem with Hushai as he offers his services to Absalom.

And Absalom, and all the people the men of Israel, came to Jerusalem, and Ahithophel with him.

And it came to pass, when Hushai the Archite, David's friend, was come unto Absalom, that Hushai said unto Absalom, God save the king, God save the king.

And Absalom said to Hushai, Is this thy kindness to thy friend? why wentest thou not with thy friend? [2 Sam. 16:15–17].

Absalom is surprised that this trusted friend of his father's did not go with him into exile.

And Hushai said unto Absalom, Nay; but whom the LORD, and this people, and all the men of Israel, choose, his will I be, and with him will I abide.

And again, whom should I serve? should I not serve in the presence of his son? as I have served in thy father's presence, so will I be in thy presence [2 Sam. 16:18–19].

Hushai is saying that the man whom God and the people choose will be his man, although he is secretly planning to be a spy for David.

Then said Absalom to Ahithophel, Give counsel among you what we shall do.

And Ahithophel said unto Absalom, Go in unto thy father's concubines, which he hath left to keep the house; and all Israel shall hear that thou art abhorred of thy father: then shall the hands of all that are with thee be strong.

So they spread Absalom a tent upon the top of the house; and Absalom went in unto his father's concubines in the sight of all Israel [2 Sam. 16:20–22].

Ahithophel advises Absalom to do an abominable thing, but it has great significance for Israel. Absalom's act was a coarse and rude declaration that David's rights had ended and that everything he owned now belonged to his son.

> **And the counsel of Ahithophel, which he counselled in those days, was as if a man had inquired at the oracle of God: so was all the counsel of Ahithophel both with David and with Absalom [2 Sam. 16:23].**

The word of Ahithophel was obeyed without question—just as if it had been the command of God.

The act of Absalom fulfilled what the Lord had spoken to David: "Thus saith the LORD, Behold, I will raise up evil against thee out of thine own house, and I will take thy wives before thine eyes, and give them unto thy neighbour, and he shall lie with thy wives in the sight of this sun. For thou didst it secretly: but I will do this thing before all Israel, and before the sun" (2 Sam. 12:11–12).

We now find David back out in the dens and caves of the earth. What is he going to do? Absalom is going to try to win a victory over David's forces. David, however, is an old veteran and knows how to fight. Absalom is doing a very dangerous thing by going against his father. The tragic thing is that David loves him and wants to save him.

These were difficult days for David. I am sure by now that your heart goes out in sympathy to him. But David does not whimper or cry aloud. He says in substance, "Just as long as I know that things are right with God, I will bear these burdens that come upon me."

David was a great man, friend. He had committed an awful sin, but he is like a wonderful piece of statuary with one flaw in it. That is the way many Christians are today. Did you ever meet one who didn't have a flaw? We all have flaws in our lives. Thank God that He will not throw us overboard because of the flaws.

CHAPTERS 17 AND 18

THEME: Civil war between Absalom and David

In chapter 17, Absalom hears the counsel of Ahithophel and Hushai, David's friend. When Absalom accepts Hushai's argument that David and his men are veterans in the field of battle and that Absalom needs reinforcements, David is able to escape and prepare for battle. In chapter 18 the two sides engage in civil war. The battle ends with Absalom's death. The chapter concludes with the touching grief of David over his slain son.

THE CONFLICTING COUNSEL
OF AHITHOPHEL AND HUSHAI

As we have been following the different experiences of David, we saw first his triumphs, and now we are seeing his troubles. In fact, he is really in trouble right now. David's own son Absalom, whom I believe he loved above everything else in this world, is leading a rebellion against him. This was a heartbreak to the king. David withdrew from Jerusalem because he did not want it to become the scene of a battle and possibly be destroyed. Instead, David left his beloved city. He sent Hushai back to Absalom so that he might give him counsel that would be to David's advantage. Ahithophel, who had once been an advisor to David, had defected to Absalom. In chapter 17 these two advisors are giving Absalom contradictory counsel about whether or not to attack his father at this time.

> **Moreover Ahithophel said unto Absalom, Let me now choose out twelve thousand men, and I will arise and pursue after David this night:**
>
> **And I will come upon him while he is weary and weak handed, and will make him afraid: and all the people**

> that are with him shall flee; and I will smite the king
> only [2 Sam. 17:1–2].

In other words, if David could be destroyed, the rebellion would be broken and Absalom would be made king. Ahithophel's advice, of course, would be disastrous for David if it were followed. Ahithophel outlines his plan:

> And I will bring back all the people unto thee: the man
> whom thou seekest is as if all returned: so all the people
> shall be in peace.
>
> And the saying pleased Absalom well, and all the elders
> of Israel [2 Sam. 17:3–4].

Even Absalom agreed to this heartless plan.

> Then said Absalom, Call now Hushai the Archite also,
> and let us hear likewise what he saith.
>
> And when Hushai was come to Absalom, Absalom
> spake unto him, saying, Ahithophel hath spoken after
> this manner: shall we do after his saying? if not; speak
> thou [2 Sam. 17:5–6].

It was a good thing that Hushai was present, because he offers an altogether different strategy. He gives Absalom advice that is very good—but it is favorable to David. David is in a very vulnerable position and desperately needs time.

> And Hushai said unto Absalom, The counsel that
> Ahithophel hath given is not good at this time.
>
> For, said Hushai, thou knowest thy father and his men,
> that they be mighty men, and they be chafed in their
> minds, as a bear robbed of her whelps in the field: and

thy father is a man of war, and will not lodge with the people.

Behold, he is hid now in some pit, or in some other place: and it will come to pass, when some of them be overthrown at the first, that whosoever heareth it will say, There is a slaughter among the people that follow Absalom.

And he also that is valiant, whose heart is as the heart of a lion, shall utterly melt: for all Israel knoweth that thy father is a mighty man, and they which be with him are valiant men [2 Sam. 17:7–10].

Hushai is giving Absalom good advice even though it is for David's benefit. His advice is simply this: "You must recognize, Absalom, that you are not a man of war. Your father is a man of war. He is acquainted with the field. He is a veteran. He is rugged. He has his mighty men with him. David and his men are chafed by what has happened. They are licking their wounds right now and are like a mother bear who has been robbed of her whelps—that mama bear is really going to fight and will become twice as dangerous as she would be otherwise. You would be very foolish to attack David now. But suppose you did attack him. David has been pursued before—he is an expert at evading capture. Saul hunted him for years. David would not be among the people. He would know where to hide. He would know how to escape. Suppose you went into his host and did not find David. Soon word would circulate that you were losing the battle, and you would find that the people who had temporarily joined you in your cause would not stay with you."

Now that Hushai has pointed out errors in judgment in Ahithophel's counsel, he outlines another strategy.

Therefore I counsel that all Israel be generally gathered unto thee, from Dan even to Beer-sheba, as the sand that is by the sea for multitude; and that thou go to battle in thine own person.

> So shall we come upon him in some place where he
> shall be found, and we will light upon him as the dew
> falleth on the ground: and of him and of all the men that
> are with him there shall not be left so much as one
> [2 Sam. 17:11–12].

He is saying to Absalom, "The important thing is that you are not
prepared to go into battle. Ahithophel is not prepared for battle. Just
taking a few thousand men with you will not enable you to overcome
David. What you need to do is to gather all Israel together, and you
yourself lead the forces into battle. That is what is expected of a king.
That is the way your father came to the throne. He was, first of all, a
great general. We will have to overwhelm him and his men by sheer
numbers." Hushai's advice was good all right, but it was not for Absalom's benefit. It was given for David's benefit. It would give David
time to reconnoiter.

Now what did Absalom and the men of Israel think of Hushai's
counsel?

> And Absalom and all the men of Israel said, The coun-
> sel of Hushai the Archite is better than the counsel of
> Ahithophel. For the LORD had appointed to defeat the
> good counsel of Ahithophel, to the intent that the LORD
> might bring evil upon Absalom [2 Sam. 17:14].

Absalom and his advisors felt that Hushai's advice was better. Very
candidly, friend, Hushai's counsel was certainly better than that of
Ahithophel from David's standpoint. God was at work in David's behalf.

WARNING IS SENT TO DAVID

While they are attempting to gather together the nation and unite
them under Absalom, Hushai gets a warning to David. He is to escape
over Jordan quickly. In the next few verses we see the movement of the
spy system. When the message reached David, he responded quickly.

> Then David arose, and all the people that were with
> him, and they passed over Jordan: by the morning light
> there lacked not one of them that was not gone over Jor-
> dan [2 Sam. 17:22].

AHITHOPHEL'S SUICIDE

Because Ahithophel was a proud man and a highly respected advisor, when he saw that his counsel was not followed, he considered his
career over. The record says that he put his house in order, then
hanged himself.

ABSALOM PURSUES DAVID

Absalom now has gotten together a great army from all the tribes of
Israel, and they pursue David.

> Then David came to Mahanaim. And Absalom passed
> over Jordan, he and all the men of Israel with him.
>
> And Absalom made Amasa captain of the host instead
> of Joab: which Amasa was a man's son, whose name
> was Ithra an Israelite, that went in to Abigail the daugh-
> ter of Nahash, sister to Zeruiah Joab's mother.
>
> So Israel and Absalom pitched in the land of Gilead
> [2 Sam. 17:24–26].

David spent a great deal of his life running from somebody. In this
instance, of course, it is indirectly because of his own sin.

David is actually in a very difficult position. He had fled Jerusalem
without any preparation whatsoever. Those who were loyal to him
had fled with him.

> And it came to pass, when David was come to Maha-
> naim, that Shobi the son of Nahash of Rabbah of the

children of Ammon, and Machir the son of Ammiel of
Lodebar, and Barzillai the Gileadite of Rogelim,

Brought beds, and basons, and earthen vessels, and
wheat, and barley, and flour, and parched corn, and
beans, and lentiles, and parched pulse,

And honey, and butter, and sheep, and cheese of kine,
for David, and for the people that were with him, to eat:
for they said, The people is hungry, and weary, and
thirsty, in the wilderness [2 Sam. 17:27–29].

David finds that he has many allies in the people round about. They
know David and the warrior that he is. The rulers of these kingdoms
probably have very little confidence in Absalom, knowing he is deceitful and tricky. He would not be dependable. They do, however,
have confidence in David. Therefore, they bring supplies to David and
his men to ease their hardship.

Absalom's delay enables David to get supplies from his allies and
ready his troops for combat.

CIVIL WAR

And David numbered the people that were with him,
and set captains of thousands and captains of hundreds
over them.

And David sent forth a third part of the people under the
hand of Joab, and a third part under the hand of Abishai
the son of Zeruiah, Joab's brother, and a third part under the hand of Ittai the Gittite. And the king said unto
the people, I will surely go forth with you myself also
[2 Sam. 18:1–2].

David wanted to go into battle with his men.

But the people answered, Thou shalt not go forth: for if
we flee away, they will not care for us; neither if half of

**us die, will they care for us: but now thou art worth ten
thousand of us: therefore now it is better that thou succour us out of the city [2 Sam. 18:3].**

The army refused to let David go into battle.

**And the king said unto them, What seemeth you best I
will do. And the king stood by the gate side, and all the
people came out by hundreds and by thousands.**

**And the king commanded Joab and Abishai and Ittai,
saying, Deal gently for my sake with the young man,
even with Absalom. And all the people heard when the
king gave all the captains charge concerning Absalom
[2 Sam. 18:4–5].**

This is one of the saddest chapters in David's life. While the chapter of
David's sin is the most sordid chapter, this is the saddest because it
records the death of his son, Absalom. Because they have urged him
not to go with them to battle, David takes his place at the side of the
gate as the army marches out. It marches out under three leaders:
Joab, Abishai, and Ittai. As each of these three captains comes by,
David charges him to deal gently with his son. All the army heard him
give this order. I think some smiled, but others felt a bit resentful.
Absalom would always be a troublemaker, and they would like to
eliminate him. David, however, loved his son and did not want him to
die. He said to his commanders, "Deal gently with my boy Absalom."
David's men heard what he said.

**So the people went out into the field against Israel: and
the battle was in the wood of Ephraim;**

**Where the people of Israel were slain before the servants
of David, and there was there a great slaughter that day
of twenty thousand men [2 Sam. 18:6–7].**

This was a civil war. It was a terrible thing. We had a civil war in the United States, and we know the sadness of brother fighting brother. David was a strategist and a general, and Absalom did not have anyone in his group who could match David's ability or the ability of David's three captains. Therefore, the children of Israel lost the battle.

For the battle was there scattered over the face of all the country: and the wood devoured more people that day than the sword devoured [2 Sam. 18:8].

The troops of Absalom became entangled in the woods of Ephraim when they attempted to flee from David's army. They became bottled in; the forest became the cause of death for many of them rather than the sword. They had picked the wrong place to battle with David.

ABSALOM SLAIN BY JOAB

And Absalom met the servants of David. And Absalom rode upon a mule, and the mule went under the thick boughs of a great oak, and his head caught hold of the oak, and he was taken up between heaven and the earth; and the mule that was under him went away.

And a certain man saw it, and told Joab, and said, Behold, I saw Absalom hanged in an oak [2 Sam. 18:9–10].

Apparently Absalom's head got caught in the forks of an oak tree while he was riding his mule through the woods. He was fleeing, by the way; and, when he got caught in the tree, the mule keep right on going, leaving Absalom in quite a predicament. Under other circumstances this incident could be rather humorous. In this case it is not.

And Joab said unto the man that told him, And, behold, thou sawest him, and why didst thou not smite him

> there to the ground? and I would have given thee ten
> shekels of silver, and a girdle [2 Sam. 18:11].

This man is shocked that Joab would want the prince, the son of
David, killed.

> And the man said unto Joab, Though I should receive a
> thousand shekels of silver in mine hand, yet would I not
> put forth mine hand against the king's son: for in our
> hearing the king charged thee and Abishai and Ittai,
> saying, Beware that none touch the young man Absa-
> lom.
>
> Otherwise I should have wrought falsehood against
> mine own life: for there is no matter hid from the king,
> and thou thyself wouldest have set thyself against me
> [2 Sam. 18:12–13].

The soldier said, "The king told us not to touch his son, and if I had
done anything to him, you would have punished me yourself." But
Joab did not have time to argue with him. He had a matter of business
to take care of immediately.

> Then said Joab, I may not tarry thus with thee. And he
> took three darts in his hand, and thrust them through
> the heart of Absalom, while he was yet alive in the midst
> of the oak.
>
> And ten young men that bare Joab's armour compassed
> about and smote Absalom, and slew him.
>
> And Joab blew the trumpet, and the people returned
> from pursuing after Israel: for Joab held back the peo-
> ple.
>
> And they took Absalom, and cast him into a great pit in
> the wood, and laid a very great heap of stones upon

> him: and all Israel fled every one to his tent [2 Sam.
> 18:14–17].

When Absalom was dead, the rebellion was over. Joab had no right to
kill Absalom, especially after David had given the command that he
was not to be touched. However, he is weary of all the trouble Absalom
has caused, and he knows that the death of this boy will end the rebellion.

> Then said Ahimaaz the son of Zadok, Let me now run,
> and bear the king tidings, how that the Lord hath
> avenged him of his enemies.

> And Joab said unto him, Thou shalt not bear tidings this
> day, but thou shalt bear tidings another day: but this day
> thou shalt bear no tidings, because the king's son is
> dead.

> Then said Joab to Cushi, Go tell the king what thou hast
> seen. And Cushi bowed himself unto Joab, and ran.

> Then said Ahimaaz the son of Zadok yet again to Joab,
> But howsoever, let me, I pray thee, also run after Cushi.
> And Joab said, Wherefore wilt thou run, my son, seeing
> that thou hast no tidings ready? [2 Sam. 18:19–22].

Joab was reluctant to let Ahimaaz bear the news of Absalom's death to
David because he did not have all the necessary information to give
the king.

DAVID MOURNS FOR ABSALOM

> But howsoever, said he, let me run. And he said unto
> him, Run. Then Ahimaaz ran by the way of the plain,
> and overran Cushi.

> And David sat between the two gates: and the watchman
> went up to the roof over the gate unto the wall, and lifted

> up his eyes, and looked, and behold a man running
> alone [2 Sam. 18:23-24].

This, now, is one of the most touching scenes in the Word of God.
David is sitting in the gate of the city, anxiously waiting for word to be
brought to him.

> And the watchman cried, and told the king. And the
> king said, If he be alone, there is tidings in his mouth.
> And he came apace, and drew near.
>
> And the watchman saw another man running: and the
> watchman called unto the porter, and said, Behold an-
> other man running alone. And the king said, He also
> bringeth tidings.
>
> And the watchman said, Me thinketh the running of the
> foremost is like the running of Ahimaaz the son of Za-
> dok. And the king said, He is a good man, and cometh
> with good tidings.
>
> And Ahimaaz called, and said unto the king, All is
> well. And he fell down to the earth upon his face before
> the king, and said, Blessed be the LORD thy God, which
> hath delivered up the men that lifted up their hand
> against my lord the king.
>
> And the king said, Is the young man Absalom safe? And
> Ahimaaz answered, When Joab sent the king's servant,
> and me thy servant, I saw a great tumult, but I knew not
> what it was [2 Sam. 18:25-29].

David has but one question to ask Ahimaaz, "Is the young man Absalom safe?" But Ahimaaz did not have all of the necessary information
to tell the king. He did not know that Absalom was dead. And, friend,
there are many messengers running about today telling the human
family that God says all is well—but all is not well. Man is a sinner. He
needs a Savior. Man needs to know that the Son of God died on the

Cross for him. Man needs to be born again. Ahimaaz did not have the message that David should have received.

> **And, behold, Cushi came; and Cushi said, Tidings, my lord the king: for the LORD hath avenged thee this day of all them that rose up against thee [2 Sam. 18:31].**

Notice that David's first question is about Absalom. His chief concern is not for who won the battle but for the safety of Absalom.

> **And the king said unto Cushi, Is the young man Absalom safe? and Cushi answered, The enemies of my lord the king, and all that rise against thee to do thee hurt, be as that young man is [2 Sam. 18:32].**

Cushi has the correct information. He is gently telling David that Absalom is dead. Then follows David's mourning for his son. It is the most touching expression of grief in the Bible or in any other literature. It is at this point one feels like saying, "Lord, you have whipped David enough for his sin. Let up on your son David."

> **And the king was much moved, and went up to the chamber over the gate, and wept: and as he went, thus he said, O my son Absalom, my son, my son Absalom! would God I had died for thee, O Absalom, my son, my son! [2 Sam. 18:33].**

CHAPTER 19

THEME: David is restored to the throne

JOAB REPROVES DAVID

The news of Absalom's death was a real heartbreak to David. He had a tender love for his son, and he was extremely grieved when the boy died. Why? There are several reasons. First of all, I do not think that David was sure about the salvation of Absalom. You will recall that when David's first son by Bathsheba was born, he became very sick, and David fasted and prayed for him. When David heard that the little boy was dead, he arose, bathed, went to the house of God to worship, and then was ready for a good dinner. His servants could not understand his action. He made it very clear to them when he said, "I am going to him some day. He will not return to me, but it will be a great day when I go to him." He knew where the little fellow was. When Absalom died, however, David's heart broke. Why? He was not sure of the young man's salvation; he was not sure where his son was. Frankly, I believe that David felt his son was not saved, and that is why he was so stricken with grief. Also, even though David was a great king, he was a poor father; I am sure David realized this. He never quite succeeded in being the father he should have been, and Absalom was evidence of this failure.

David also recognized that trouble had come upon him because of the sin he had committed. God had told him that strife would never depart from his house because of it. That is exactly what happened, and from the time of Absalom's death I believe David was a broken man. I think part of his grief was due to his disappointment. He had really hoped that Absalom would succeed him to the throne. He did not like the idea of Absalom rebelling against him, but he did want him to be the next king.

David's grief was such that even Joab was disturbed by it and rebuked David for it.

And it was told Joab, Behold, the king weepeth and mourneth for Absalom.

And the victory that day was turned into mourning unto all the people: for the people heard say that day how the king was grieved for his son [2 Sam. 19:1–2].

It should have been a great day of victory and a day of rejoicing, because the enemy was defeated. For David, however, it was not a victory at all. Instead, it was a time of grief and sorrow beyond expression.

And the people gat them by stealth that day into the city, as people being ashamed steal away when they flee in battle [2 Sam. 19:3].

David's army should have been rejoicing because they had won the battle. Instead they left the battlefield after the victory and retreated to Jerusalem as if they had been defeated. Why? Because Absalom was slain and it had broken the heart of David.

But the king covered his face, and the king cried with a loud voice, O my son Absalom, O Absalom, my son, my son! [2 Sam. 19:4].

My, how David loved this boy! What a tender expression this is. David had been such a poor father—he had handled things so badly—but he loved his son and was broken by his death.

Now Joab was responsible for Absalom's death. I am not sure that David ever really comprehended just how his son died. I am sure that he heard quite a few stories relating how it occurred, but David probably did not want to pursue it too far.

And Joab came into the house to the king, and said, Thou hast shamed this day the faces of all thy servants,

which this day have saved thy life, and the lives of thy sons and of thy daughters, and the lives of thy wives, and the lives of thy concubines;

In that thou lovest thine enemies, and hatest thy friends. For thou hast declared this day, that thou regardest neither princes nor servants: for this day I perceive, that if Absalom had lived, and all we had died this day, then it had pleased thee well [2 Sam. 19:5-6].

Of course Joab is pushing this situation to the opposite extreme, but certainly David would have preferred others dying rather than Absalom; that is quite evident. Joab rebukes David because he is so grieved about the death of his son who had become his enemy and who would have killed David given the opportunity.

DAVID IS RESTORED TO THE THRONE

Then the king arose, and sat in the gate. And they told unto all the people, saying, Behold, the king doth sit in the gate. And all the people came before the king: for Israel had fled every man to his tent [2 Sam. 19:8].

The people needed some rallying point now. Everyone was depressed. It was a bad state of affairs: the man who had led the rebellion had been slain but, instead of rejoicing, the people witnessed the greatest grief that David ever expressed. However, after Joab talked to the king, David went up to the gate to let his men know that he deeply appreciated their loyalty to him.

And all the people were at strife throughout all the tribes of Israel, saying, The king saved us out of the hand of our enemies, and he delivered us out of the hand of the Philistines; and now he is fled out of the land for Absalom.

> **And Absalom, whom we anointed over us, is dead in battle. Now therefore why speak ye not a word of bringing the king back? [2 Sam. 19:9–10].**

What happened was simply this: there were those who had gone over to Absalom's side and now that he was dead, they didn't know what to do. They decided that the best thing was to bring the king back.

> **And king David sent to Zadok and to Abiathar the priests, saying, Speak unto the elders of Judah, saying, Why are ye the last to bring the king back to his house? seeing the speech of all Israel is come to the king, even to his house [2 Sam. 19:11].**

Apparently, even in the tribe of Judah, there had been a great defection to Absalom's side. Now David rebukes them for their action.

> **Ye are my brethren, ye are my bones and my flesh: wherefore then are ye the last to bring back the king?**
>
> **And say ye to Amasa, Art thou not of my bone, and of my flesh? God do so to me, and more also, if thou be not captain of the host before me continually in the room of Joab.**
>
> **And he bowed the heart of all the men of Judah, even as the heart of one man; so that they sent this word unto the king, Return thou, and all thy servants [2 Sam. 19:12–14].**

There was a unanimous desire to return David to his throne.

> **So the king returned, and came to Jordan. And Judah came to Gilgal, to go to meet the king, to conduct the king over Jordan.**

> And Shimei the son of Gera, a Benjamite, which was of
> Bahurim, hasted and came down with the men of Judah
> to meet king David.
>
> And there were a thousand men of Benjamin with him,
> and Ziba the servant of the house of Saul, and his fifteen
> sons and his twenty servants with him; and they went
> over Jordan before the king [2 Sam. 19:15–17].

Shimei had cursed David when he went out. Now he wants to be the
first one to welcome the king back.

> And there went over a ferry boat to carry over the king's
> household, and to do what he thought good. And Shimei
> the son of Gera fell down before the king, as he was
> come over Jordan;
>
> And said unto the king, Let not my lord impute iniquity
> unto me, neither do thou remember that which thy ser-
> vant did perversely the day that my lord the king went
> out of Jerusalem, that the king should take it to his
> heart.
>
> For thy servant doth know that I have sinned: therefore,
> behold, I am come the first this day of all the house of
> Joseph to go down to meet my lord the king.
>
> But Abishai the son of Zeruiah answered and said,
> Shall not Shimei be put to death for this, because he
> cursed the LORD's anointed? [2 Sam. 19:18–21].

David was a generous fellow. He was a man who could forgive.

> And David said, What have I to do with you, ye sons of
> Zeruiah, that ye should this day be adversaries unto me?
> shall there any man be put to death this day in Israel?
> for do not I know that I am this day king over Israel?
> [2 Sam. 19:22].

David is saying, "Why should I pay attention to this fellow? I know I am the king of Israel." David is satisfied that God has restored him to this position. "Why should I worry about a little fellow like Shimei? Why should I put him to death? What he thinks doesn't amount to anything." There are many Christians today who let little things bother them. They let little people bother them, and they should not. Is God blessing you, my friend? Perhaps you are a discouraged pastor. Are you having trouble with your board of deacons? Are you having problems with a troublemaker? My friend, forget it. You are serving God. God is on your side. Live above that small irritation and serve the Lord—make sure that is what you are doing. Forget about the other things; we need to live above them.

> **Therefore the king said unto Shimei, Thou shalt not die. And the king sware unto him [2 Sam. 19:23].**

David's final decision concerning Shimei was that he did not intend to punish him. In fact, David did not intend to deal with this man in any way.

> **And Mephibosheth the son of Saul came down to meet the king, and had neither dressed his feet, nor trimmed his beard, nor washed his clothes, from the day the king departed until the day he came again in peace [2 Sam. 19:24].**

Mephibosheth, in deep appreciation to David, would not join in the rebellion. He remained loyal to David, and during all this time he fasted and prayed for the king. It is wonderful to have friends like that, is it not?

> **And it came to pass, when he was come to Jerusalem to meet the king, that the king said unto him. Wherefore wentest not thou with me, Mephibosheth?**

And he answered, My lord, O king, my servant deceived me: for thy servant said, I will saddle me an ass, that I may ride thereon, and go to the king; because thy servant is lame.

And he hath slandered thy servant unto my lord the king; but my lord the king is as an angel of God: do therefore what is good in thine eyes.

For all of my father's house were but dead men before my lord the king: yet didst thou set thy servant among them that did eat at thine own table. What right therefore have I yet to cry any more unto the king? [2 Sam. 19:25–28].

Mephibosheth tells David, "If you think I have betrayed you, then do to me as you please. I have no right to ask any other favor of you at all."

And the king said unto him, Why speakest thou any more of thy matters? I have said, Thou and Ziba divide the land.

And Mephibosheth said unto the king, Yea, let him take all, forasmuch as my lord the king is come again in peace unto his own house [2 Sam. 19:29–30].

This, I feel, proves Mephibosheth's sincerity.

And Barzillai the Gileadite came down from Rogelim, and went over Jordan with the king, to conduct him over Jordan.

Now Barzillai was a very aged man, even fourscore years old: and he had provided the king of sustenance while he lay at Mahanaim; for he was a very great man [2 Sam. 19:31–32].

Barzillai the Gileadite was a patriarch from another nation who had been generous to David and had given him sustenance during the rebellion. Now David wanted this man to go back to Jerusalem with him so he could reward him for his generosity.

> And the king said unto Barzillai, Come thou over with me, and I will feed thee with me in Jerusalem.
>
> And Barzillai said unto the king, How long have I to live, that I should go up with the king unto Jerusalem [2 Sam. 19:33–34].

Barzillai said to David, "I have not many more years. I have had my threescore and ten, and ten more. I know my days are numbered, and I would just as soon stay home. I appreciate your generous offer of going and living in a palace, but I have reached the age where things like that do not tempt me at all."

> I am this day fourscore years old: and can I discern between good and evil? can thy servant taste what I eat or what I drink? can I hear any more the voice of singing men and singing women? wherefore then should thy servant be yet a burden unto my lord the king? [2 Sam. 19:35].

Barzillai continues, "I am an old man. I can't hear the music anymore. Food does not taste like it once did. I don't want to come and mar the party. I don't want to be the one to slow down the king and his enjoyment."

> Thy servant will go a little way over Jordan with the king: and why should the king recompense it me with such a reward? [2 Sam. 19:36].

Barzillai helped David because he knew David was God's man. He had confidence in the king. This was his motivation to assist David.

It is too bad that David had not been a little more forgiving with his own son. When Absalom sinned and came back, it might have been different if he had completely forgiven the boy. If he had received him like the father received the Prodigal Son by putting his arms around him, placing a robe on him, and killing the calf for a feast, I believe David would have spared himself the awful rebellion which took place.

CHAPTERS 20—22

THEME: Revolt, vengeance, and famine within the kingdom: war with the Philistines outside the kingdom

Chapter 20 is the record of another revolt against David. After all the troubles that have come to David, you would think the Lord would let up on him; but, as He promised, the sword will not depart from the house of David. Through all of this we do not hear a whimper from David. He recognizes it as the just punishment of his sin.

Seemingly as a result of the petty jealousy of the men of Israel—because they had not been consulted in returning David to the throne—another revolt errupts, led by Sheba of the tribe of Benjamin.

SHEBA LEADS A REVOLT

And there happened to be there a man of Belial, whose name was Sheba, the son of Bichri, A Benjamite: and he blew a trumpet, and said, We have no part in David, neither have we inheritance in the son of Jesse: every man to his tents, O Israel [2 Sam. 20:1].

Sheba is called "a man of Belial," which means he is a rabble-rouser.

So every man of Israel went up from after David, and followed Sheba the son of Bichri: but the men of Judah clave unto their king, from Jordan even to Jerusalem [2 Sam. 20:2].

It is amazing how faithless and undependable the children of Israel were. Some people might say, "Well, that was a crude day before man was developed and civilized." I would like to ask those people a question. Do you think things are any better today? It is interesting that the president of this country, or any public official, can make some little statement that should not have been said, and, when a poll is taken, they find out that his popularity has so diminished that he cannot be elected to office again. This can happen to any officeholder regardless of his party affiliation. That proves just how fickle the mob can be; it shows how fickle all of us are. God knows our hearts. Jeremiah 17:9 says, "The heart is deceitful above all things, and desperately wicked: who can know it?" Whose heart is this verse speaking about? The heart of a brutal dictator? No. It is speaking about your heart and mine. Wicked things are in the human heart. The apostle Paul could say in Romans 7:18, "For I know that in me (that is, in my flesh,) dwelleth no good thing: for to will is present with me; but how to perform that which is good I find not."

The ten tribes of Israel followed Sheba in his rebellion.

> **And David came to his house at Jerusalem; and the king took the ten women his concubines, whom he had left to keep the house, and put them in ward, and fed them, but went not in unto them. So they were shut up unto the day of their death, living in widowhood [2 Sam. 20:3].**

These are the women, you remember, that Absalom had taken.

> **Then said the king to Amasa, Assemble me the men of Judah within three days, and be thou here present [2 Sam. 20:4].**

Amasa, you may recall, was the captain of the rebel forces under Absalom. According to 2 Samuel 17:25 and 1 Chronicles 2:17, Amasa is the son of Abigail, a sister of David. This would make him a cousin of Absalom. After the defeat of the rebels under Amasa and the death of Absalom, David made Amasa captain of his army in the place of Joab.

> **So Amasa went to assemble the men of Judah: but he tarried longer than the set time which he had appointed him.**

> And David said to Abishai, Now shall Sheba the son of Bichri do us more harm than did Absalom: take thou thy lord's servants, and pursue after him, lest he get him fenced cities, and escape us.
>
> And there went out after him Joab's men, and the Cherethites, and the Pelethites, and all the mighty men: and they went out of Jerusalem, to pursue after Sheba the son of Bichri [2 Sam. 20:5–7].

In other words, this man Amasa is not moving. So Joab leads the army in pursuit of the rebel, Sheba. Also Joab brutally slays Amasa, apparently believing he also is a traitor to David.

The chapter concludes with Joab continuing after the rebel, Sheba. When Sheba sought refuge in the city of Abel, and the army was prepared to attack the city to get him, a wise woman intervened. Sheba is slain by the people of Abel. This, of course, ends the rebellion. However, it does not end the troubles of David, as we shall see.

Through all of these trials David is not crying aloud, nor is he whimpering. He knows that the Lord is dealing with him in the woodshed. Don't think that David got by with his sin, friend. He was severely punished. However, David loved God. Underneath the faith that failed was a faith that never failed. That's David, God's man, a man after God's own heart.

FAMINE FOR THREE YEARS

Chapter 21 opens with a period of famine in the land of Israel.

> Then there was a famine in the days of David three years, year after year; and David inquired of the LORD. And the LORD answered, It is for Saul, and for his bloody house, because he slew the Gibeonites [2 Sam. 21:1].

The reason God gives for the famine is rather strange, but in it there is a lesson for us.

THE GIBEONITES TAKE VENGEANCE
ON THE HOUSE OF SAUL

And the king called the Gibeonites, and said unto them; (now the Gibeonites were not of the children of Israel, but of the remnant of the Amorites; and the children of Israel had sworn unto them: and Saul sought to slay them in his zeal to the children of Israel and Judah.)

Wherefore David said unto the Gibeonites, What shall I do for you? and wherewith shall I make the atonement, that ye may bless the inheritance of the LORD?

And the Gibeonites said unto him, We will have no silver nor gold of Saul, nor of his house; neither for us shalt thou kill any man in Israel. And he said, What ye shall say, that will I do for you.

And they answered the king, The man that consumed us, and that devised against us that we should be destroyed from remaining in any of the coasts of Israel,

Let seven men of his sons be delivered unto us, and we will hang them up unto the LORD in Gibeah of Saul, whom the LORD did choose. And the king said, I will give them.

But the king spared Mephibosheth, the son of Jonathan the son of Saul, because of the LORD's oath that was between them, between David and Jonathan the son of Saul [2 Sam. 21:2-7].

This is quite a remarkable passage of Scripture. To understand it we must go back to the days of Joshua when the Gibeonites deceived him and Joshua made a treaty with them (Josh. 9). Israel had been told by God not to make a treaty with anyone.

A treaty in that day (which some folk consider "uncivilized") was inviolate. When a treaty was made, the terms of the treaty were kept.

Treaties were more than a scrap of paper. They were not made to be broken. In our day this matter of nations sitting around the conference table trying to make a treaty is almost laughable, because who will keep it? The average person has a right to be cynical about the way nations attempt to get along with each other. But when a nation is obeying God, its word is as good as its bond. Joshua made a treaty with the Gibeonites; but Saul came along and broke it. David attempted to make amends for Saul's actions, and he succeeded.

But the other side of the coin is interesting. God did not forget that Saul, representing Israel, had broken the treaty with the Gibeonites. Because the Israelites are His people, they are not going to get by with it. The three years of famine came upon them as a judgment. Now let me make this kind of an application to this incident, which I think is valid. You and I live in a day when it cannot be said that any particular nation is a Christian nation or a nation in obedience to God. But God does deal with nations; he does judge nations. God holds nations responsible—it does not make any difference what nation it is. God judged Egypt. God judged Babylon. God judged Assyria, Greece, and Rome; and God will judge America. I am of the opinion (and will you follow me now very carefully) that we are in the process of dissolution as a nation. There are several evidences of God's judgment upon us. Let me mention several things.

Since World War II it has been our intention to be a peacemaking nation yet to live in sin. Believe me, friend, after World War II Americans started plunging into sin. Also, we could not quit fighting. There has not been a moment since World War II that our troops have not been fighting somewhere. If it isn't Korea, it is Vietnam. If it isn't Vietnam, it is in Europe or on some other continent. We are talking peace today as we have never talked it before; yet there is no peace. Isaiah 57:21 says, "There is no peace, saith my God, to the wicked."

Another indication of this dissolution is that we have no great statesmen today. I recognize that there are quite a few of our boys in Washington who think that they are clever—and this type of thinking is not confined to any one party. Apparently they all feel that they could solve the problems of the world. Actually, it is rather pitiful to see this nation without great leaders. This is another evidence of God's judgment. Do you remember what God said in Isaiah 3:12? "As for my people, children are their oppressors, and women rule over them. O my people, they which lead thee cause thee to err, and destroy the way of thy paths." We see a continual movement in this direction in our own nation.

Right here in Southern California we have become the center of pornography. Also many of the "cults" and the "isms" originate in Southern California. Not long ago God gave us quite a shaking. I am of the opinion that the earthquake was a judgment of God. Now I know that there is a scientific explanation for the earthquake. Beneath us is the San Andreas fault, and we have several other faults. In fact, we have a whole lot of faults out here! I believe God is beginning to judge America. America is guilty of lawlessness and gross immorality, and God judges nations for that. If there is one thing 2 Samuel 21 reveals, it is the fact that God judges nations.

WAR WITH THE PHILISTINES

Next we find that David is engaged in continual warfare with the Philistines.

> Moreover the Philistines had yet war again with Israel; and David went down, and his servants with him, and fought against the Philistines: and David waxed faint.

> And Ishbi-benob, which was of the sons of the giant, the weight of whose spear weighed three hundred shekels of brass in weight, he being girded with a new sword, thought to have slain David.

> But Abishai the son of Zeruiah succoured him, and smote the Philistine, and killed him. Then the men of David sware unto him, saying, Thou shalt go no more out with us to battle, that thou quench not the light of Israel [2 Sam. 21:15–17].

David is a great man, and his men know that there is no one to take his place. Now David is getting to be an old man; when he goes out to battle, he finds he does not have the stamina he used to have. He is easily overcome—that is an unusual experience for David! The leaders of Israel see that David is too old to engage in battle, and they tell him so. They tell him that he is needed more at home than on the battlefield.

A great battle took place, and God gave the victory to Israel.

> **These four were born to the giant in Gath, and fell by the hand of David, and by the hand of his servants [2 Sam. 21:22].**

The giant spoken of in this verse was Goliath. You will recall that when David went out to meet Goliath he took five smooth stones. I have heard it described vividly that because David thought he might miss the first shot, he had some stones in reserve. Those who teach the story that way say that the lesson for us is that we, too, should have a reserve. However, the explanation is that Goliath had four sons. They were part of the Philistine army. David knew that when he slew the giant the four sons might want to come out and fight him. Although David did not have this experience at that time, of course the sons would want revenge. If Abishai had not come to David's aid in this his final battle with the Philistines, one of Goliath's sons, Ishbi-benob, would have had his revenge.

However, when David was a young man fighting Goliath, he had four other stones and was ready to take on Goliath's four sons. He was deadly accurate with the slingshot. He probably practiced several hours each day. I imagine he could put a stone in the hollow of a tree that was not big enough even for a squirrel to crawl into.

This chapter concludes David's career as a warrior. In a marvelous way, God has delivered David from all his enemies.

DAVID'S SONG OF DELIVERANCE

In chapter 22 we have the song David sings after God has delivered him from his enemies. It is the same as Psalm 18.

And David spake unto the LORD the words of this song in the day that the LORD had delivered him out of the hand of all his enemies, and out of the hand of Saul [2 Sam. 22:1].

This is a song that David composed, apparently, at the end of his life. As he looked back over his life, he could see how the hand of God had moved and brought him to the place of old age. I believe he composed Psalm 23 about the same time, because at this time of his life he could say, "The LORD is my Shepherd; I *shall* not want." Paul put it this way, "Being confident of this very thing, that he which hath begun a good work in you will perform it unto the day of Jesus Christ" (Phil. 1:6). God has brought you up to this moment, friend; why in the world do you think he is going to let you down now? God's loving care for David in the past gives him confidence in the future.

And he said, The LORD is my rock, and my fortress, and my deliverer;

The God of my rock; in him will I trust: he is my shield, and the horn of my salvation, my high tower, and my refuge, my saviour; thou savest me from violence [2 Sam. 22:2–3].

"The LORD is my rock." A rock is a place upon which to rest. Christ is the rock of our salvation—He is the foundation. We rest on Him. "And my fortress." That is for protection in life. "And my deliverer." He will deliver us in the time of temptation. "The God of my rock." The Lord is not only my rock, but He is the God of my rock, that is, of my faith. He is the object of my faith. "In him will I trust: he is my shield." He protects me from the enemy. "And the horn of my salvation." He is the One in whom I rest for salvation. He is "my high tower." That is where I go to view the land. He is my vision. "My refuge, my saviour." He is the One "who savest me from violence."

We are living in a day when we do not have anything that corresponds to genius in the way of writing. There is no great vision today. In our scientific age everything is run by computers. Everything is already taped. We know that two plus two equals four, but we don't seem to produce anything really original. How monotonous life is when God is left out of it. In contrast, David recognized God in all the experiences of his life, and his poetic expression of gratitude is a masterpiece of literature.

> **Thou hast also given me the shield of thy salvation: and thy gentleness hath made me great [2 Sam. 22:36].**

David was a rough and rugged man. He was hotheaded. But God is gentle, and David's love for and association with God had quieted him. It had made David a gracious man: "Thy gentleness hath made me great." You and I need to associate more with God. My, how men need God in this hour in which we are now living!

This is a great psalm. David's psalms are wonderful. They open the heart. They open up the mind. They open up life. They let you live, friend. We hear so much about people wanting to "live." We have comforts and gadgets galore today. Many young people are growing up in homes of affluence where they have every comfort. Many leave all of that and go out and live as vagrants. They say it is because they want to live. Well, my friend, "things" won't enable you to live. Running off and throwing away all the bands and cords with which God has bound us will not enable us to live either. It is only when we come into a right relationship with God that we are enabled to really live.

Second Samuel 22 is a great psalm, one which David composed as he looked back over his life. Also, when we come to Psalm 23, you will find that I take the position that it was not written by a little immature boy. Psalm 23 was not written by a college student who didn't really know what life was all about. Neither was it written by a middle-aged man who had ambition to get to the top in business or politics. It was not written by someone who wanted to become famous. Psalm 23 was written by an old king who looked back upon his life and could trace the hand of God moving in it. David was a man who had tasted everything. There was nothing that the world afforded that David had not tasted, my friend. David's conclusion was that the most wonderful thing of all was, "The LORD is my shepherd."

This beautiful song of praise is not only great literature, it opens new vistas for us and lets us see something that is much more glorious than a sunset or the rising of the moon. It speaks of the marvelous relationship one man had with the almighty God. How we need that today!

CHAPTER 23

DAVID'S LAST WORDS

Now these be the last words of David. David the son of Jesse said, and the man who was raised up on high, the anointed of the God of Jacob, and the sweet psalmist of Israel, said [2 Sam. 23:1].

David was "the son of Jesse." Jesse was a peasant, a farmer in Bethlehem—David was never ashamed of that. God lifted David "up on high". He placed him with the great men of the world. David was the "anointed of the God of Jacob." The same God who took that clever, conniving fellow Jacob and made him Israel, a prince with God, is the same God who took David and put him on the throne. He is the same God who saved me and the same God who saved you. He is gracious, good, and loving. Oh, my friend, how wonderful is our God!

David was also "the sweet psalmist of Israel." He was a musician: he wrote music, he played music, and he loved to hear music. I share David's love for music although I have no talent for reproducing music in any form. But I appreciate *good* music. I don't care for what we call "rock" music—in fact, to me it is not even music. I deeply regret that this type of music is being brought into the church. Good music, elevating music, music that thrills the soul has always contributed something beautiful to man's worship of his God.

The spirit of the LORD spake by me, and his word was in my tongue [2 Sam. 23:2].

The Spirit of God came upon David, and that is the way he wrote his psalms. Peter tells us that that is the way men wrote the Old Testament. "Knowing this first, that no prophecy of the scripture is of any private interpretation. For the prophecy came not in old time by the will of man: but holy men of God spake as they were moved by the Holy Ghost" (2 Pet. 1:20–21).

> **The God of Israel said, the Rock of Israel spake to me, He that ruleth over men must be just, ruling in the fear of God [2 Sam. 23:3].**

It is obvious that the decisions made in our government today— regardless of the party—are not made "in fear of God." They are made in fear of the voters. There is little effort being made to please God in our government. I wish it could be said that the United States of America is a Christian nation. It is not.

I was rather amused by the comments being made by some men who were out of work because of a decision made in Washington by the Senate. Each man who was out of work said, "I voted for that man because he said he was going to vote for this project, and he voted against it." Well, all the politician wanted was to be elected to office. He didn't care anything about the men and their project. We need men who will rule in the fear of God and, until we get them, we are going to have corruption in high places.

> **And he shall be as the light of the morning, when the sun riseth, even a morning without clouds; as the tender grass springing out of the earth by clear shining after rain [2 Sam. 23:4].**

This is one of the more remarkable statements David ever made. You will recall that I said 2 Samuel 7 was one of the great chapters of the Bible. In that chapter God made a covenant with David. The Davidic covenant, upon which the future kingdom of Christ was to be founded, provided for David the promise of posterity in his house, a royal throne of authority, and a kingdom on earth established forever. God promised that the Messiah would come through the Davidic line. He is the same One promised to Eve in the Garden of Eden. He is the same One promised to Abraham, Isaac, and Jacob. He is the One whom Moses talked about. Joshua also spoke of Him. Now God's covenant with David concerns Him.

> **Although my house be not so with God; yet he hath made with me an everlasting covenant, ordered in all things, and sure: for this is all my salvation, and all my desire, although he make it not to grow [2 Sam. 23:5].**

What David is saying is simply this: "My house is not worthy of this. We did not receive this by merit. It did not come because of who I am." If David had gotten his just deserts, God would never have made a covenant with him. Neither would God have saved you or me if it had been on the basis of merit. And yet He made an everlasting covenant with David. God has made a covenant with us, too. It is recorded in John 3:16: "For God so loved the world, that he gave his only begotten Son, that whosoever believeth in him should not perish, but have everlasting life." Now I hold on to that. God has made that covenant. I never asked Him to make it. He did not make it because of who we are. He did not wait for you or me to make a suggestion. He did it 1900 years ago. He said, "Here it is; take it or leave it." I take it, by the way. I rest upon that. David said that his covenant was "ordered in all things, and sure." Friend, you can depend upon God. David says, "This is all my salvation." Well, God's covenant with me is my salvation. It is what I desire, friend. It should be the desire of every believer's heart, "although he made it not to grow."

DAVID'S MIGHTY MEN

Next we are given a catalog of David's mighty men.

> **These be the names of the mighty men whom David had: The Tachmonite that sat in the seat, chief among the captains; the same was Adino the Eznite: he lift up his spear against eight hundred, whom he slew at one time [2 Sam. 23:8].**

These men, you will recall, came to David during the time that he was in exile. When David was being driven by Saul, he was an outcast, hunted like a partridge. He had to hide in the dens of the earth. It was during this time that those who were in distress came to him. They were persecuted and oppressed by Saul, and they fled to David. Others also came to him: those who had gotten into debt and could not pay, those who were discontented, and those who were bitter of soul. In this same way men come to Christ. They are in distress. According to their letters, many young rebels were once in distress. They write to me and tell me about their experiences with the Lord. They came to Christ with debts of sin, and He cancelled those debts. Are you discontented with life? If you are living a fulfilling life and doing all right, I guess I don't have any message for you at all. But if you are discontented down deep in your soul, and you want to be saved and have fellowship with God, come to Christ. He will remove your guilt and give you satisfaction in your life.

These men who came to David were outstanding men in many ways. They did many remarkable things. Let us look at a few of them.

And after him was Shammah the son of Agee the Hararite. And the Philistines were gathered together into a troop, where was a piece of ground full of lentiles: and the people fled from the Philistines.

But he stood in the midst of the ground, and defended it, and slew the Philistines: and the Lord wrought a great victory [2 Sam. 23:11–12].

Defending a patch of lentils may not seem very important, but Israel needed the food. It was the custom of the Philistines to wait until an Israelite's crop was ready to harvest, then they would come ravaging, plundering, and robbing. This year, as usual, everyone ran when they came—except one man, Shammah. He stopped, drew his sword, and defended it. One man against a troop of Philistines! "And the Lord wrought a great victory."

> And three of the thirty chief went down, and came to
> David in the harvest time unto the cave of Adullam: and
> the troop of the Philistines pitched in the valley of Re-
> phaim.
>
> And David was then in an hold, and the garrison of the
> Philistines was then in Beth-lehem.
>
> And David longed, and said, Oh that one would give me
> drink of the water of the well of Beth-lehem, which is by
> the gate! [2 Sam. 23:13–15].

David was brought up in Bethlehem, and he thought about the re-
freshing water from the well there. I know how David felt. I was raised
in a little town in Texas. My dad built our house and dug our well. The
water was "gyp" water. A few years ago I went back to that place. I
could hardly wait to get a drink of that water. I lay down on the ground
by the faucet by the well and lapped up that water. My, it was deli-
cious! I was raised on it. It took me back to my boyhood. Now David
longed for water from the well at Bethlehem. He never gave a command to anybody to go and get him water, but three of his mighty men
broke through the Philistine lines to get it for him. That is the way
they became mighty men.

I think of the command that the Lord Jesus gave in Matthew 28:19–
20 to go into all the world and preach the gospel. Then I think back
in the past to the men who broke through the enemy lines and took
the gospel to those who needed to hear. Think of the pioneer
missionaries—I don't like to mention just one man, but think of men
like the apostle Paul or Martin Luther. A great company of missionaries followed after them, and they have been breaking through the
enemy lines ever since and getting out the Word of God. These are
mighty men of David's greater Son, the Lord Jesus Christ.

Here is another of David's mighty men.

> And Benaiah the son of Jehoiada, the son of a valiant
> man, of Kabzeel, who had done many acts, he slew two

> **lionlike men of Moab: he went down also and slew a lion in the midst of a pit in time of snow:**
>
> **And he slew an Egyptian, a goodly man: and the Egyptian had a spear in his hand; but he went down to him with a staff, and plucked the spear out of the Egyptian's hand, and slew him with his own spear.**
>
> **These things did Benaiah the son of Jehoiada, and had the name among three mighty men [2 Sam. 23:20–22].**

I love this one. This fellow slew a lion. That is not an easy thing to do, and he did it when there was snow on the ground. I know a lot of people who won't even come to church when there is a little rain on the sidewalk. May I say to you, they could not have much fellowship with a man like Benaiah. He was out there when there was snow on the ground. He was a tremendous man.

> **Uriah the Hittite: thirty and seven in all [2 Sam. 23:39].**

Uriah the Hittite was one of David's mighty men. This is the man he sent to the front lines to be killed. This is the blot on the escutcheon of David.

CHAPTER 24

THEME: David's sin in taking a census

David commits another sin in taking a census. By now he should trust God instead of numbers. God again punishes David but permits him to choose his punishment. David casts himself upon the mercy of God. God sends a pestilence. David buys Araunah's threshingfloor on which to rear an altar to God. David's refusal to accept it as a gift reveals his deep dedication and devotion to God. This spot became the place where Solomon erected the temple. Although the Mosque of Omar stands there today, Israel will sometime in the future build again a temple to the Lord God of Israel on that spot.

THE CENSUS

Actually, there are many who would not label this a sin. I call this another sin in the life of David. In God's sight, David's numbering the people was just as bad as his other sins. When you are guilty of breaking one part of the Law, you are guilty of all. His actions evidenced a lack of trust in God.

> And again the anger of the LORD was kindled against Israel, and he moved David against them to say, Go, number Israel and Judah.
>
> For the king said to Joab the captain of the host, which was with him, Go now through all the tribes of Israel, from Dan even to Beer-sheba, and number ye the people, that I may know the number of the people [2 Sam. 24:1–2].

At the beginning God had instructed David to number the people. God wanted it done in order to encourage David and to strengthen him. God wanted him to know that there was a great army behind him.

Friend, faith is not a leap in the dark. It is not a gamble. Faith is not even a "hope so." Faith is a sure thing. God never asks you to believe something that is not true. Faith rests upon a rock, a sure foundation. The Lord Jesus Christ is the foundation. Faith, therefore, is not just leaping out into space.

However, there is a time in your life, my friend, when you need to live and move by faith and to recognize that you cannot live by your own effort or by numbers. Unfortunately, the church today has not learned to trust God. As a result, at the congregational meetings the spiritual victories are never mentioned. The things that are mentioned are how much we have in the treasury, how many we baptized this year, and how many members we took in. If the figures look pretty good, we consider that it is a great spiritual victory. Actually, it might have been the worst thing in the world that could have happened in that church.

David sins in numbering the people at this time. Why? He is now an old king. David knows that God has put a foundation beneath him, and he knows that he can overcome the enemy. He does not need to number the people at all. I sometimes think that the curse of the church today is to have a fellow in it who is always figuring up something, always putting it down in black and white, but knows nothing about the spiritual victory that should be taking place. That is what David does here.

And David's heart smote him after that he had numbered the people. And David said unto the LORD, I have sinned greatly in that I have done: and now, I beseech thee, O LORD, take away the iniquity of thy servant; for I have done very foolishly.

For when David was up in the morning, the word of the LORD came unto the prophet Gad, David's seer, saying,

> Go and say unto David, Thus saith the LORD, I offer thee
> three things; choose thee one of them, that I may do it
> unto thee.
>
> So Gad came to David, and told him, and said unto him,
> Shall seven years of famine come unto thee in thy land?
> or wilt thou flee three months before thine enemies,
> while they pursue thee? or that there be three days' pes-
> tilence in thy land? now advise, and see what answer I
> shall return to him that sent me [2 Sam. 24:10–13].

God gives David a choice of punishment. David's answer to the Lord
is remarkable. It reveals that he is a man who knows how to trust God.
I have said it before, and I will say it again: David failed, it is true; he
committed sin, but down beneath the faith that failed was a faith that
never failed. Basically David did trust God, as his answer to Gad reveals.

> And David said unto Gad, I am in a great strait: let us
> fall now into the hand of the LORD; for his mercies are
> great: and let me not fall into the hand of man [2 Sam.
> 24:14].

God gave David a choice of three punishments. He told David to
choose one of them. David did not choose any of them. Instead he told
the Lord that he did not want to fall into the hands of a man. That is
one of the things that I have always prayed in my ministry: "O God,
never put me in a position where I am subject to a man, or men."
Fortunately, as I look back on my ministry, God never put me in the
position where I had to lick shoe leather. I feel sorry today for some
men in the ministry who have to go around licking shoe leather in
order to continue. God have mercy on them! David did not want to be
subject to man. He was willing to fall into the hands of God because
he knew how to trust God. How wonderful it is when you see David
doing this. The Lord decided to send a pestilence upon Israel. David

knew he would be all right in the hands of God. This is the way you and I should feel when God punishes us.

My friend, those whom the Lord loves, He disciplines. From experience I can tell you that there is a tenderness in His discipline, there is a comfort in it all, and there is a blessing in it. He alone can wipe away the tears. He alone can bind up the brokenhearted. He alone can heal the wounds that are in the heart. The doctor can sew you up when you have been in an accident, but in great emotional accidents only the Lord Jesus can bind you up and put you together again. How we need Him today in our lives!

DAVID BUYS THE THRESHINGFLOOR
OF ARAUNAH

Now we come to the last part of this book. David wants to build a temple for the Lord.

> And Gad came that day to David, and said unto him, Go up, rear an altar unto the LORD in the threshingfloor of Araunah the Jebusite [2 Sam. 24:18].

Notice that Araunah was a Jebusite, not an Israelite.

> And David, according to the saying of Gad, went up as the LORD commanded.

> And Araunah looked, and saw the king and his servants coming on toward him: and Araunah went out, and bowed himself before the king on his face upon the ground.

> And Araunah said, Wherefore is my lord the king come to his servant? And David said, To buy the threshingfloor of thee, to build an altar unto the LORD, that the plague may be stayed from the people [2 Sam. 24:19–21].

David explains his reason for wanting the threshingfloor.

> **And Araunah said unto David, Let my lord the king
> take and offer up what seemeth good unto him: behold,
> here be oxen for burnt sacrifice, and threshing instru-
> ments and other instruments of the oxen for wood.**

> **All these things did Araunah, as a king, give unto the
> king. And Araunah said unto the king, The LORD thy
> God accept thee.**

> **And the king said unto Araunah, Nay; but I will surely
> buy it of thee at a price: neither will I offer burnt offer-
> ings unto the LORD my God of that which doth cost me
> nothing. So David bought the threshingfloor and the
> oxen for fifty shekels of silver [2 Sam. 24:22–24].**

It is a noble thing that David does. Oh, that God's people would learn
this lesson! Some folk feel that we should not mention finances in
God's work today. I recognize that there is an overemphasis on money,
but consider what David did. Araunah wanted to give David the
threshingfloor. David said, "You can't give it to me. I am going to pay
for it." Why? David continued, "Neither will I offer burnt offerings
unto the LORD my God of that which doth cost me nothing." God have
mercy on folk today who are taking a spiritual free ride. My friend,
pay your way, and God will honor and bless you. This action of
David's is heart-searching. Are we attempting to give to God that
which costs us nothing? God forgive us for being niggardly with Him.
May we give as David gave—David, the man after God's own heart.

BIBLIOGRAPHY
(Recommended for Further Study)

Crockett, William Day. *A Harmony of the Books of Samuel, Kings and Chronicles*. Grand Rapids, Michigan: Baker Book House, 1959.

Darby, J. N. *Synopsis of the Books of the Bible*. Addison, Illinois: Bible Truth Publishers, n.d.

David, John J. and Whitcomb, John C., Jr. *A History of Israel*. Grand Rapids, Michigan: Baker Book House, 1970. (Excellent.)

Epp, Theodore H. *David*. Lincoln, Nebraska: Back to the Bible Broadcast, 1965.

Gaebelein, Arno C. *The Annotated Bible*. Neptune, New Jersey: Loizeaux Brothers, 1917.

Gray, James M. *Synthetic Bible Studies*. Westwood, New Jersey: Fleming H. Revell Co., 1906.

Jensen, Irving L. *I and II Samuel*. Chicago, Illinois: Moody Press, 1968. (A self-study guide.)

Kelly, William. *Lectures on the Earlier Historical Books of the Old Testament*. Addison, Illinois: Bible Truth Publishers, 1874.

Knapp, Christopher. *The Kings of Israel and Judah*. Neptune, New Jersey: Loizeaux Brothers, 1908. (Very fine.)

Laney, J. Carl. *I & II Samuel*. Chicago, Illinois: Moody Press, 1982.

Meyer, F. B. *David: Shepherd, Psalmist, King*. Fort Washington, Pennsylvania: Christian Literature Crusade, n.d. (Devotional.)

Meyer, F. B. *Samuel the Prophet*. Fort Washington, Pennsylvania: Christian Literature Crusade, n.d. (Devotional.)

Sauer, Erich. *The Dawn of World Redemption*. Grand Rapids, Michigan: Wm. B. Eerdmans Publishing Co., 1951. (An excellent Old Testament survey.)

Scroggie, W. Graham. *The Unfolding Drama of Redemption.* Grand Rapids, Michigan: Zondervan Publishing House, 1970. (An excellent survey and outline of the Old Testament.)

Unger, Merrill F. *Unger's Commentary on the Old Testament.* Vol. 1. Chicago, Illinois: Moody Press, 1981. (A fine summary of each paragraph. Highly recommended.)

Wood, Leon J. *Israel's United Monarchy.* Grand Rapids, Michigan: Baker Book House, 1980. (Excellent.)

Wood, Leon J. *The Prophets of Israel.* Grand Rapids, Michigan: Baker Book House, 1979. (Excellent.)